ANTHROPOLOGY INSIDE OUT

We gratefully acknowledge the funding of the following bodies, and thank them for making this publication possible:

Aarhus University Research Foundation
Department of Anthropology, Aarhus University
Department of Anthropology, University of Copenhagen
Department of Culture and Learning, Aalborg University

First published in 2020 by
Sean Kingston Publishing
www.seankingston.co.uk
Canon Pyon

British Library Cataloguing in Publication Data
A catalogue record for this book is available from the British Library.
The moral rights of the editors and authors have been asserted.

Paperback ISBN 978-1-912385-21-8

Ebook DOI 10.26581/B.ANDE01

Anthropology inside out

Fieldworkers taking notes

Edited by

Astrid Oberborbeck Andersen,

Anne Line Dalsgård,

Mette Lind Kusk,

Maria Nielsen,

Cecilie Rubow

and Mikkel Rytter

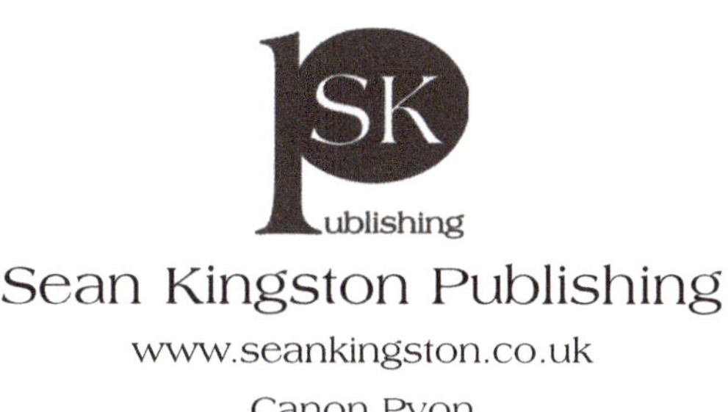

Contents

What is a field note?

It is written, drawn, recorded in some way or imprinted in shoes, instruments, leaves, papers, maps, other artefacts or in a body (we include bodies in this book)

— produces analysis, layers upon layers, some intended, others not, some risky

— does something to the fieldworkers, reminds them of themselves in the field, informs them

— may become sticky or a mess with an unknown surplus

— does something to a reader or another researcher, a secret service police man, a committed archivist, misunderstood perhaps

— is sometimes recalcitrant and unwritten after all (something is always missing)

— is wrapped up in folders, boxes, files, veins, and only a very few are displayed on walls, screens, and other surfaces like this one

— does something! We are interested in what notes do and their role in the production of anthropological knowledge.

[note from the editors]

1
Introductory notes

ANNE LINE DALSGÅRD, CECILIE RUBOW AND

MIKKEL RYTTER

This book is dedicated to those field notes that seldom attract much attention: on bewilderment, U-turns and instances of excess. It is also dedicated to those fieldworkers who wish to go beyond safe traditions and experiment with new field-note-taking practices.

We reach out to a mixed readership:

1. Students from various subject areas embarking on their first fieldwork: familiar with their curriculum, but uncertain about what to do themselves, and curious to know more about experimental practices teetering on the edge of the tradition.
2. More experienced fieldworkers, who could take this as an opportunity to give their own practices a second look, seeing if they hide riches to be shared, or incipient ideas about the art of taking notes in the extraordinary situations that fieldwork always gives rise to.

The chapters show how fieldworkers with anthropological training work with, and in some cases rework, established field-note practices. In classical anthropology concrete field notes are invisible to the reader: they are primarily a tool for use in the analytical process. Ethnographers work through their notes and leave them behind when displaying their findings. In this book we reverse the focus, and reflect on the vibrant backstage life of field notes.

We ask whether field notes are worth considering as entities in themselves, rather than merely being regarded as a means to an end. Working with this question through a number of cases, we are inclined to answer: 'yes, they are something in themselves, and they do a lot of things' (see our introductory note above). Having reversed our focus, we have learned to appreciate field notes as analytical works in themselves, including those that seem to lead nowhere. Not only is anthropology cultivated through these notes. In them, one witnesses the running of a productive, analytic motor that keeps the anthropological mind busy. By inviting others into the machine, this engagement can be shared and – this is our experience – can deepen our understanding of the stuff analysis is made of.

By turning these note-taking practices inside out, we intend (so to speak) to keep the ethnographic laboratories open for visitors.

The practical definition of field notes in this book is: the materials (in the widest sense) that fieldworkers collect, produce and absorb in the field; and the drafts, comments, outlines, sketches and so forth made before and after fieldwork, before, eventually, making a formal presentation or publication.

All the contributors to this volume are trained in the Scandinavian anthropological tradition. Briefly, this tradition is based on British social anthropology's belief in long-term fieldwork, in the realistic sense of 'being there', often combined with French theory, and American cultural critique.

The chapters have been inspired by three events held in 2015 and 2016, and in which the contributors participated: a workshop discussing field notes as a genre (or several genres) at the biannual MEGA seminar for Danish anthropology, August 2015; a PhD seminar entitled 'The art of fieldwork and ethnographic notebooks' with Michael Taussig, June 2016, at the Department of Anthropology, Aarhus University; and the exhibition entitled 'Let's talk about field notes' in the 'Ethnographic Exploratory', April 2016, at the Department of Anthropology, University of Copenhagen.

> From my own experience, I can say that, very often, a problem seemed settled, everything fixed and clear, till I began to write down a short preliminary sketch of my results.
>
> (Malinowski 1922:13)

Collective and shared field notes

The classical ethnographic field-note tradition is centred on: a) individual fieldworkers; b) who write field notes to themselves in a personal way due to the intimate character of ethnographic knowledge and ethical principles of confidentiality; c) which enables a convoluted writing process ending in an individual publication, typically a monograph and a number of articles.

These days, data management is becoming increasingly formalized in order to secure validation processes, the protection of ethnographic data, and ownership among many partners. This development seems to be in conflict with the anthropological research environment. De facto, field notes end up on anthropologists' shelves, personal archives or hard discs, which might be convenient in a short-term perspective, but is questionable in the long run. Can anthropologists safeguard such field notes adequately? What happens to their field notes after a project, or their career, ends? Who is responsible for security, or for sharing valuable records? Could open access be applied to field notes and other ethnographic materials – at least in some cases – so as to benefit both research participants and future researchers, including our students?

The first three chapters show how field-noting experiments and archival traditions close to anthropology indicate that collaboration and the sharing of notes is indeed possible.

Chapter 2 deliberately challenges the ethnographic norm of individual research. Instead of one person doing research in the field for 100 days, Fritsch, Hedegaard and Rubow report from an anthropological and sociological project in which around 100 people did fieldwork for one single day in a coordinated programme. They show how multiple fieldworkers can make readable and useful notes that feed into a collaborative analytical process unfolding across several cohorts of participants. The authors suggest that having students and researchers alike engaged in collective fieldwork fosters a helpful teaching environment for learning the basic crafts of ethnographic methods; note-taking being one of these crafts. While the chapter demonstrates the advantages of collectively writing and sharing notes, showing for instance how digital platforms can contribute to the wider ecology of field notes, it also points to possible pitfalls in both digital and analogue collective field-note practices.

In Chapter 3, the reader is introduced to a note-taking tradition surprisingly close to that of ethnography, where the sharing of notes is indispensable – albeit across the passage of time. At the Dansk Folkemindesamling (Danish Folklore Archives), since 1904, records have been produced for the archive, and for sharing with an unknown audience in a distant future of 30 or 70 years hence. Pedersen and Rømer, anthropologists employed at the folklore archives, trace generations of professional and amateur researchers through the layers of inscriptions, colourful underscores, dating etc. found in the records. These exhibit, across time, multiple theoretical underpinnings as well as traces of the personal habits of the contributors. Moreover, the authors discuss their use of old material, and the dilemmas involved in the production of new field notes for an unknown audience.

In Chapter 4, Ahl considers an exhibition held in 2016 at the Department of Anthropology at the University of Copenhagen, where field notes produced by students and senior researchers were exhibited side by side. Based on the exhibition, the chapter reflects on the field-note craft of anthropologists.

It brings hidden scripts out into the open in their unvarnished form, and emphasizes the dialogical role of writing field notes as one way of coming to terms with the taboo aspects of fieldwork practices. Discussing the significant role of notes in the process of becoming a 'real' anthropologist, and how field notes offer a glimpse into the making of both the ethnographer and the field, Ahl suggests they exemplify a proto-language, a language of becoming. The chapter invites readers to view a selection of the exhibition and explore what it reveals about ethnographic practices, arguing that field notes are not only a tool for learning, remembering and analysis, they are also texts and language in their own right.

> ...sit down and write full field notes as soon as possible after the day's (or night's) research is done.
>
> (Emerson, Fretz and Shaw 1995:40)

> Observations are not data unless they are recorded in some fashion for further analysis.
>
> (Dewalt and Dewalt 2002: 142)

Disturbing field notes

The first commandment in classical anthropology is that you, the fieldworker, should write notes every day for several hours, because the second commandment is that everything in the field should be regarded as potentially meaningful. This ideal of radical openness towards the world of the 'other' and the resulting fundamental contingency of ethnographic notes and knowledge production are in many ways defining for the discipline, and afford the power and potentiality of anthropological writings. However, with contingency there comes an ethos of uncertainty (did I get it right?), particularity (we know that we can never tell the full story) and liminality (fieldwork and notes are in many ways disturbing and will most likely transform the ethnographer and her or his perspectives on the world).

Field notes are inscriptions of local events and knowledge that can be potentially damaging and thus must be handled carefully – they are our attempts to capture the complexity of fieldwork experiences, and here the aesthetics of our interlocutors may be more valid than our own written word. Field notes are no longer the prerogative of ethnographers – our informants also make various kinds of notes and document our temporary presence in their life-worlds. And finally, field notes can be recalcitrant and uncanny, they can disturb the ethnographers – not only in the field where they are struggling to make sense of local worlds, but also after returning from the field, at the desktop in front of the computer, where they are supposed to produce a neat analysis. Rife with transgressions and disruptive experiences, field notes may continue to haunt us and inform our professional work and private lives in different ways. However, even slight feelings of alienation or a glimpse of the uncanny can be extremely productive – both during fieldwork and afterwards.

Chapters 5 to 8 examine four instances in which field notes are disturbing and tricky, insisting that they should be taken seriously and dealt with by the ethnographer – one way or the other.

> Social anthropology has one trick up its sleeve: the deliberate attempt to generate more data than the investigator is aware of at the time of collection.
> (Strathern 2004:5)

In Chapter 5, Frederiksen follows a group of self-proclaimed nihilists in Tbilisi, Georgia. In exchange for allowing him to hang out with them and become part of their lives, they demand from the beginning that he stops taking notes when they are together, because from their perspective any search for meaning is counterproductive. Frederiksen also struggles to write notes after their meetings, because everything seems unnoteworthy. This chapter outlines the way the nihilists cultivate the art of not making sense of their lives, and the way their ethnographer had to rework his own practices of note-taking accordingly. Frederiksen finds inspiration in the work of the Russian filmmaker Andrei Tarkovsky, who is celebrated among the Georgian nihilists. Tarkovsky's films are known for their non-linearity and 'sculpting in time', in particular the film *Mirror* influences Frederiksen's impressionistic style when writing the chapter.

In Chapter 6, we read that Nielsen has returned from her long-term fieldwork in Recife, Brazil, with some mango leaves full of dust, among other things. When you unpack a fieldworker's notebooks, printed documents and photographs, other quasi-scientific artefacts may accompany them. One finds numerous odd objects, seemingly lifeless at first sight, they are potentially effective triggers for valuable ethnographic memories: smells, fleeting feelings, pains. Carefully placed in a wooden frame behind glass, a small bunch of mango leaves take Nielsen back to the site of her fieldwork, an area covered in the disturbing dust that emanated from one of the construction sites for the World Cup in Brazil, 2014. Once signalling a promising future for an impoverished neighbourhood, and now settled and unseen, the dust becomes an entry point for the analysis of larger questions concerning the relationship between time, the local population and urban infrastructures. Nielsen poetically rediscovers her ethnographic world in a few grains of dust.

> I am a field note.
>
> (Jackson 1990)

> [T]he notebook becomes not just the guardian of experience but its continuous revision as well [...] no less than an outrigger of the soul.
>
> (Taussig 2011:25)

Imagine yourself immersed in a Russian cult, and beginning to find yourself attracted to the hard, simple life, the intense religious experiences and the possibility of establishing a romantic relationship with a local woman. In Chapter 7, Schütt explains how he struggled to retain his ethnographic 'self', as he became attracted and drawn towards the possibility of 'going native'. At stake was nothing less than his previous identity, world-view and sanity. Moreover, Schütt bears witness to the confusing experience of becoming a character in his key informant's film, which distorted the conventional (that is, asymmetrical) relationships of ethnographer-informant, researcher-respondent and self-other. The film became both a mirror of, and a reflection upon, fieldwork practices in general. Feelings of bewilderment, loss of control and betrayal often follow when notes are edited and used to construct characters in our polished ethnographic publications; but Schütt chose to 'stay with the trouble' and write his chapter from the liminal position. The genre of the chapter is 'confessional', and one may well question whether it is actually anthropological. However, we suggest that the chapter addresses an essential aspect of anthropological fieldwork. Conveying notes from his struggle and existential doubt, as they take form and unfold over an extended period of time, Schütt honestly showcases the way personal lives and fieldwork experiences are always entangled in complex ways.

After the Arab Spring in 2011, at a time when the intelligence service was (as it still is) monitoring political activists and foreign researchers, Thorsen questioned the implications of recording notes during her fieldwork in Cairo, Egypt. In Chapter 8, she describes how her fieldwork notes are potentially damaging and dangerous for her informants, and herself. In this way, the chapter emphasizes that notes are never innocent, but always have potential impact and effect in the world. While writing up her notes, she becomes absorbed in the suspicions and creeping paranoia that characterize the everyday lives of her informants. The chapter addresses the ethical and practical questions of confidentiality, as well as other ways of protecting informants in circumstances of political turmoil, uncertainty and instability, where notes are not only disturbing but potentially dangerous.

> All anthropologists use not only their 'factual' notes but also, surely, to varying degrees the memory that they have of the context, the implications, the reactions that lie behind the notes.
>
> (Mayer 1989: 207)

> Field notes may be no more than a trigger for bodily and hitherto subconscious memories. We cannot write down the knowledge at the time of experiencing it.
>
> (Okely 1992:15)

Other field-note forms performed

Field notes do not necessarily consist of words on paper or voices recorded on a phone or other device. They may be photos, drawings or artefacts from the field. They may have smell, weight, size, colour and other material qualities that drive the analyses and the dissemination of ethnography. In this section, writing may be part of the note-taking described, but it is the sensorial, intuitive and aesthetic aspects (of writing too) that are in focus: everything that is part of being a questioning body in the field, touched by a world one is getting to know. The authors discuss notes in forms that transgress the boundaries of what constitutes a standard academic text. They demonstrate that analysis does not necessarily mean leaving sensorial field experiences behind, as the presence of the field may still be there in a drawing, a collage of different visual materials, or a few lines of poetic language. Allowing sensorial experiences to inform and form our work also means allowing room for affect and ambiguity, and remaining open to readers' or viewers' further interpretations. These can be utilized in collaborative processes, with interlocutors from the field adding to (or confronting) the ethnographer's analyses. Attention to the sensorial qualities of life may also intensify the ethnographer's sensitivity and observations in the field, and once the ethnographer returns home this sensorial engagement may convey a sense of commitment towards that which was lived and experienced in the field.

> Why draw in notebooks? In my own case, if not in others, one reason, I suspect, is the despair if not terror of writing.
>
> (Taussig 2011:16)

> To accept sensuousness in scholarship is to eject the conceit of control in which mind and body, self and other, are considered separate.
>
> (Stoller 1997:xvii)

In Chapter 9, Kusk experiments with uses for the common (yet underdeveloped) technology of pencil drawings in notebooks. She draws events, characters and environments from her fieldwork – drawings saturated by personal style and aesthetic quality. The drawings are not only notes portraying particular situations, they also stand out as analyses in their own right. In a drawing, we witness the hand giving life to the impressions of a specific field encounter. Drawings stay close to the original experience of engagement, wonder and perhaps unease through the drawer's search for the right form. In this search, attention to the material details of particular physical surroundings is deepened, and by bypassing the analytical mind's expectations the drawing may elicit details that would otherwise pass unnoticed. Presenting a catalogue of personal drawings, Kusk shows the potential applications of graphic notes and their ability to convey the 'surplus' insight that written academic language may leave out in the effort to be precise.

In Chapter 10, Vium experiments with re-interpretations of photographs found in archives from Amazonia, Australia and Siberia. Vium visits the places the photographs were once taken, a hundred years ago or more, and, together with descendants of the people portrayed in the original pictures, re-interprets the scenes depicted. The re-interpretation opens a space for talk and reflection upon family, kin, homes, memory and traditions, but also more potent political issues such as colonialism, racism and exploitation. For the purpose of future re-interpretations, Vium plans to assemble old and new photographs in an archive, with all the items being given exact time and GPS coordinates. His work indicates the potential of visual note-taking, or 'note-making' as Vium himself puts it, while also emphasizing that this largely stems from the openness of photography to interpretation (and re-interpretation).

In Chapter 11, Dalsgård makes a point about the temporality of ethnographic research. She is stuck with a collection of Havaianas (Brazilian flip-flops) that she keeps in a cardboard box on her shelf, and she ponders how they got there and why she has not yet thrown them away. Considering the very concrete and practical materiality of the flip-flops and the space they take up, Dalsgård concludes that a material field note – which she eventually considers the flip-flops to be – is like a mark in a landscape we once inhabited and are drawn back to by way of remembering. A question mark, you might say, to which an answer is somehow awaited. While note-taking is often depicted as a rational and measured process, the case of these flip-flops flops exhibits a fumbling search for meaning. Given this background, Dalsgård concludes that note-taking includes a willingness to be acted upon. Through its material and affective qualities a note may capture the attention of the ethnographer and engage her imagination in productive, though perhaps torturous, ways.

Taussig, in Chapter 12, writes about the notebook as an indeterminate world, full of potential, and comparable to a scrapbook. He characterizes the ethnographic notebook as 'basic writing' with a 'paragraphic form' without order, argument and edge, yet full of potentials and possibilities, and ascribes it almost rebellious qualities. The chapter literally turns the relation between field note (here a painting) and final text upside down, making the text the appendix. Towards the end of the chapter, Taussig states that, considered as an end in itself, the notebook challenges the authority of academic texts, as much as thought itself is threatened by the institutionalization of knowledge, with its bureaucracy and drive towards professionalization. In other words, up against the institutionalization of knowledge, thought and the notebook are allies.

Anthropology inside out

From its inception, this edited volume was motivated by a shared curiosity among the authors. We wanted to explore, play and experiment with notes and note-taking practices in the widest sense. Throughout the book, we examine not only 'what a field note is', but also 'what a field note does' and 'what a field note could be'.

By focusing exclusively on field notes, it was our ambition to turn the production of anthropological knowledge inside out. In order to do this, we had to make field notes visible, accessible and transparent; we had to urge ourselves to be more open about how they are produced and what role they play in anthropological research, theory construction and the general production of knowledge. Having done this, we conclude that field notes are not only the means to certain professional ends (presentations, articles, monographs and the like), they can also be seen as analytical in their own way – a body of interpretive material that shapes and exceeds our thoughts. The analyses embedded in our field notes are open-ended and productive, but typically tacit rather than assertive, perhaps felt more than thought. As such, they are both more and less than the usual 'finished' or highly polished analyses that appear in our publications. This volume does not oppose more traditional approaches to note-taking and analysis; but in suggesting both a sensibility towards apparent aporia and excesses, and strategies for expanding the research methods we use in the field, we hope to give inspiration to new experiments where fieldwork, field notes and analysis are more open, inclusive and collaborative. Thus, the chapters in this volume can be read as a catalogue of the possibilities of new note-taking practices in anthropological research.

References

Dewalt, K. and Dewalt, B. 2002. *Participant Observation: A Guide for Fieldworkers.* Lanham, MD: Rowman & Littlefield.

Emerson, R., Fretz, R. and Shaw, L. 1995 *Writing Ethnographic Fieldnotes.* Chicago: Chicago University Press.

Jackson, J. 1990. '"I Am a Fieldnote": Fieldnotes as a Symbol of Professional Identity.' In R. Sanjek (ed.), *Fieldnotes: The Makings of Anthropology.* Ithaca: Cornell University Press.

Malinowski, B. 1984 [1922]. *Argonauts of the Western Pacific.* London: Kegan Paul.

Mayer, A.C. 1989. 'Anthropological memories.' *Man* (NS) 24(2):203–18.

Okely, J. 1992. 'Anthropology and autobiography: participatory experience and embodied knowledge.' In J. Okely and H.Callaway (eds.), *Autobiography and Anthropology*. London: Routledge.

Stoller, P. 1997. *Sensuous Scholarship.* Philadelphia: University of Pennsylvania Press.

Strathern, M. 2004. *Commons and Borderlands: Working Papers on Interdisciplinarity, Accountability, and the Flow of Knowledge.* Wantage, Oxon.: Sean Kingston Publishing.

Taussig, M. 2011. *I Swear I Saw This: Drawings in Fieldwork Notebooks, Namely My Own.* Chicago: Chicago University Press.

2

An ecology of notes in a utopian fieldwork

Ester Fritsch, Marianne Hedegaard and Cecilie Rubow

The photographs overleaf (Figure 2.1) show collective ethnographic materials that have been organized as three compendia, amounting to approximately 300 pages in total. They are written in Danish and English, authored by more than a hundred people, and offer an entrance to what we call an 'ecology' of notes. They manifest one outcome of a series of ultra-short, large-scale fieldwork sessions conducted in 2014 and 2015 in a collaborative project, 'Utopia', involving a research group consisting of professors and students from anthropology and sociology departments in Copenhagen. Or rather, to be more precise, they constitute one version of a larger body of notes proliferating in several directions, into handwritten jotted notes, photographs, digital soundtracks, blogs, initial memos, drafts and published texts like this one.

In the first season of Utopia, the research group asked whether it is possible to invert the blueprint for ethnographic fieldwork, in which a single researcher stays in the field for (say) a hundred days? What would the opposite look like? What if (say) one hundred fieldworkers went into the field for a single day? This is what we now term 'ultra-short large-scale fieldwork', in which a swarm of researchers undertake a large semi-coordinated ethnographic intervention, and (ideally) by the end of the day share and store their notes.

In this chapter, we unfold how we have tried to make an ecology of field notes through a collective fieldwork design embracing numerous people, places and materials. Seen as an ecology, field notes are not only empirical material to be turned into formal description and analysis, but a living archive with many entry points. The ecology of the notes is brought to life in a distributed

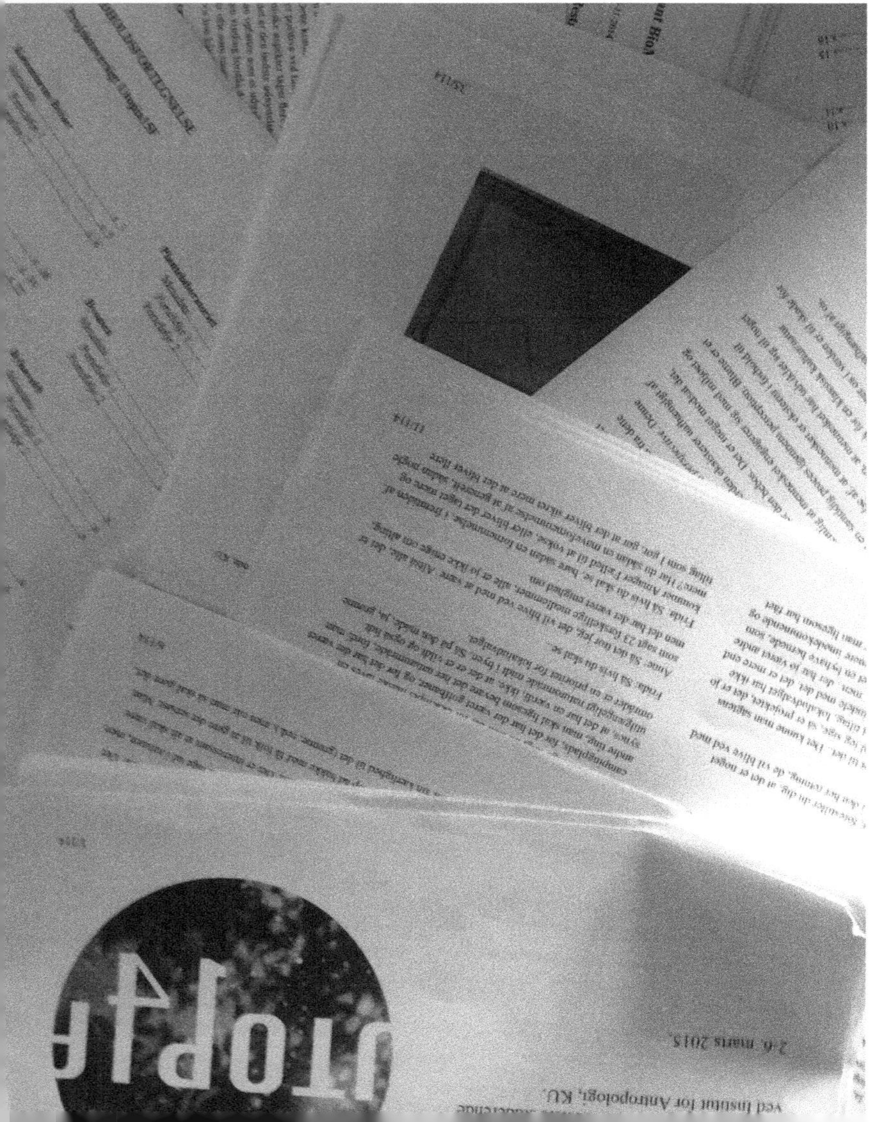

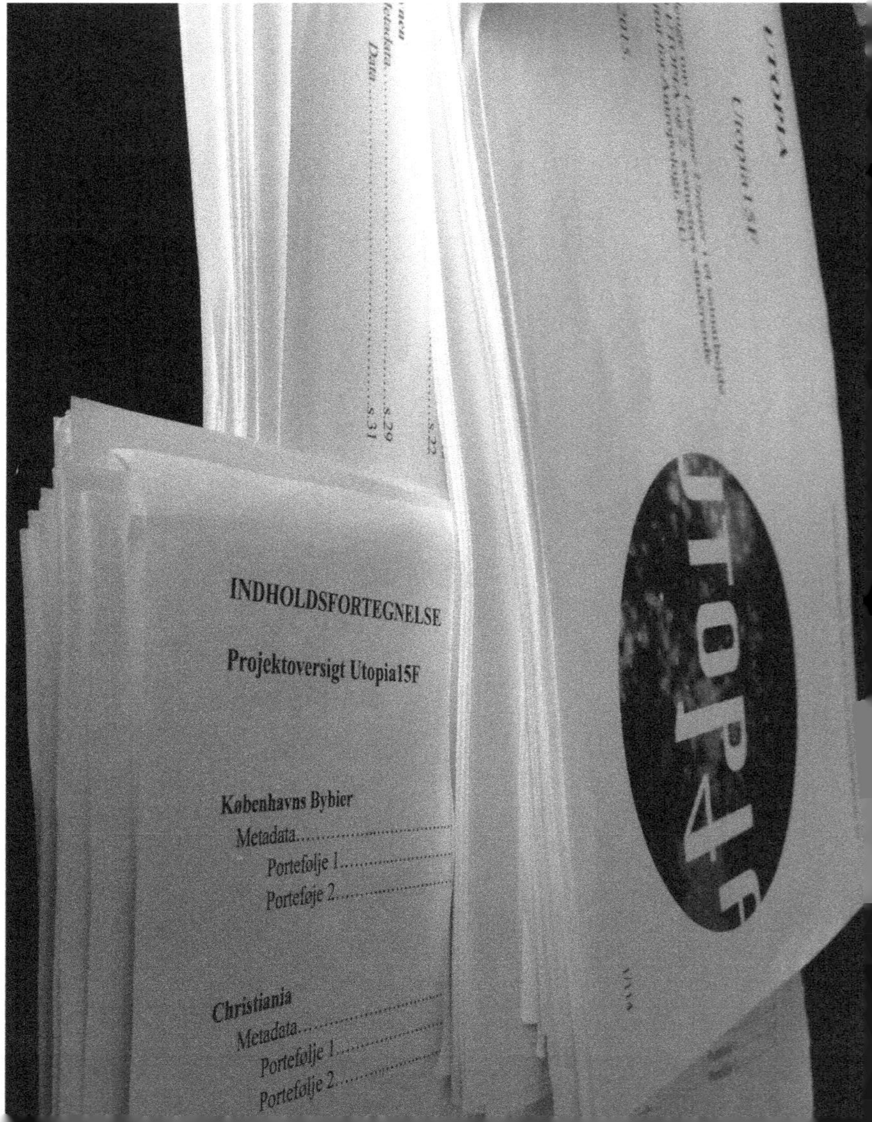

UTOPIA

Utopia15F

.....s.22

Metadata.....s.29

Data.....s.31

INDHOLDSFORTEGNELSE

Projektoversigt Utopia15F

Københavns Bybier

Metadata.....

Portefølje 1.....

Portefølje 2.....

Christiania

Metadata.....

Portefølje 1.....

Portefølje 2.....

ved Institut for Antropologi, KU.

2-6. marts 2015.

Frida: Så hvis du skal se.

Anne: Så det tror jeg, det vil blive ved med at være. Altså alle, det er som sagt 23 forskellige medlemmer, alle er jo ikke enige om alting, men det har det været enighed om.

Frida: Så hvis du skal se, bare sådan en fornemmelse, i fremtiden af, kommer Amager Fælled til at vokse, eller bliver der taget mere og mere? Har du sådan en mavefornemmelse af at generelt, sådan nogle tiltag som I gør, gør at der bliver sikret mere at der bliver flere

11/114

ethnographic collective of students, cameras, citizens and computers (among other entities) moving along trails in the larger environment of the city of Copenhagen. Below, we describe the practical set-up of Utopia, the cultivation of a (not yet finalized) project design, and show how experiments with collective and public notes turn field notes inside out by making them accessible, readable and recyclable for other interested actors. In the same vein, we show how ultra-short large-scale fieldwork can serve as a critical mirror for individual fieldwork and point to ecological ways of teaching and doing research. Thus, we shed light on the value of sharing and recycling field notes while students are learning the craft of writing notes. Since classical field notes are often tied to the individual fieldworker, with a degree of mystery and secrecy, we point to how inviting students to read original note material from fellow students and teachers is valuable in the process of learning how to write field notes.

Ultra-short large-scale fieldwork and utopian methods

On the 5th May 2014 an ultra-short large-scale fieldwork was carried out in Copenhagen by students and associate professors from the anthropology and sociology departments at the University of Copenhagen. This was the initiation of Utopia and our engagement with collective note-making practices. Following the initial fieldwork in spring 2014, two similar ultra-short large-scale fieldwork sessions were carried out in autumn 2014 and spring 2015, involving new members in the research teams. Every time new members embarked on Utopia, field notes were recycled from previous phases. From the beginning, a central aim of the project has been to experiment with teaching-based research that brings professors and students together in the process. The participants in Utopia and authors of the notes are primarily first-year anthropology students (around 80) and an organizing body composed of three consecutive groups of graduate students plus two associate professors from the sociology and anthropology departments (14 persons altogether).

The project not only aspires to employ 'utopian' ethnographic research methods, it also takes 'utopian practices' in urban Copenhagen, the capital of Denmark, as the subject of its investigations. Well aware that working with a hundred people in the field simultaneously goes beyond the norms of ethnographic fieldwork tradition, we have intentionally sought out a design of 'excess', 'play' and 'estrangement', which according to Lucy Sargisson (2012) comprise the main features of a utopian method. Working with an open-ended experimental design has allowed us to operationalize what we see as a foundational quality of anthropology: the search for 'the possible' and a power to 'envision other worlds' (Ingold and Gatt 2013:147). In Utopia we play with

Figure 2.1 (opposite) An analogue archive of Utopia's collective notes.

The Danish Folklore Archives were founded in 1904, but the basis of the collection had already been established in the second half of the nineteenth century, when Svend Grundtvig (Figure 3.1) issued two calls, a specific one for 'Danish heroic ballads' in 1843, and later, in 1854, a broader call for 'all old Danish memories' (Koudal 2004:18–19). Grundtvig regarded himself as one of the builders of the Danish nation, and by collecting and preserving folklore from the rural population, he believed that he would be able to preserve for posterity a part of its autochthonous basis. Over the next forty years he received records from approximately six hundred people around the country, a total of at least ten-thousand pages, with original transcriptions of folklore. The most prominent contributor to Grundtvig's collection was the schoolteacher Evald Tang Kristensen, who can be considered the first fieldworker in Denmark (Christiansen 2013). Over a period of sixty years, Kristensen visited the rural population in western and northern Jutland and recorded their stories, songs, legends and other kinds of narratives. During his journeys, he wrote more than 24,000 pages of field notes, and based on his materials he published 79 books, including seven volumes of Danish legends (Kristensen 1892–1901).

When the Danish Folklore Archives were established, the effort to collect and research folklore was expanded nationally. Obviously, the folklore collectors who founded the archives had different interests than most fieldworkers today. First of all, they sought to collect memories of the past, not descriptions of life as it was currently lived. This means that they were interested in the memories themselves, not in the people, their own perceptions of what they said, or the situations in which the memories were shared (Hansen 2013:3). As Jonas Frykman phrased it, the folklore collectors were interested in 'the culture in man' rather than 'man in culture' (Frykman 1979:235). Secondly, they wanted to systematize the material in order to be able to detect the spreading of certain traditions. These interests affected the ways in which they wrote their records and the kinds of metadata they added. To ease the organization of the material, the archivists created a one-page template that collectors could use to record their notes. (Figure 3.2).

The template included separate lines for metadata such as the shire, parish and place name tied to the material, as well as the year the record was made, the name of the collector and personal details about the informant, such as name, age, occupation, place of birth and current residence. For material that was not collected using the template, such as the material Grundtvig received and Kristensen's notes, metadata would be added in pencil by the archivists. The records were subsequently archived according to genre (e.g. legends,

Figure 3.2 (opposite) Template for records to the Danish Folklore Archives.

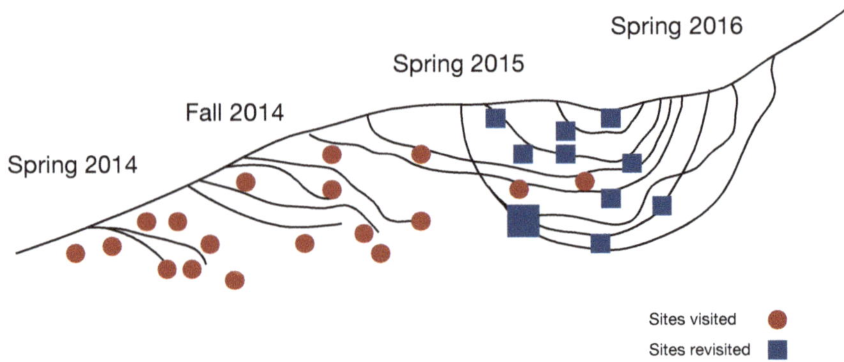

Figure 2.2 Overview. The stream of field sites. Some have been visited several times.

this perspective through a method of 'mirroring' (Foucault 1984) the tradition of individual ethnographic fieldwork that we, as students and researchers, share in our day-to-day teaching and research practice. Essentially, we try to do the opposite of what we have been accustomed to doing.

In four seasons of Utopia we have tried to make the ethnographic material both collective and public. Though playful and experimental at the onset, we also anticipated that Utopia required some boundaries and formal guidelines in order to calibrate our collective action. In the following section we highlight the peculiar mix of openness and closure in the project design, and discuss possibilities and difficulties in designing collective, recyclable notes as public archives of ethnographic materials.

Shades of green: examining utopian practices and field notes ecologically

Utopia started out with a broad, shared interest in urban utopian projects. This sphere of interest has remained through all the seasons of fieldwork, but in autumn 2014 it was narrowed down to green utopian practices. Thus, when we now look at the field sites visited, we have a list of around 35 sites, comprising construction sites, schools, laboratories, parks, urban gardens, streets, town-planning offices, exhibitions, restaurants and coffee shops, web pages and various social enterprises. Some have been visited once, other places several times, and one case has been the locus of observational and note-taking experiments by several cohorts of organizing groups. This particular site is the Ladegårds Å, and will be referred to many times in this chapter. Ladegårds Å is a stream (*en å*, in Danish) in central Copenhagen, that is at present covered, running beneath a densely trafficked road, but which is also the target and inspiration for numerous citizen groups and urban planners hoping to create a green urban space by opening up the *å*.

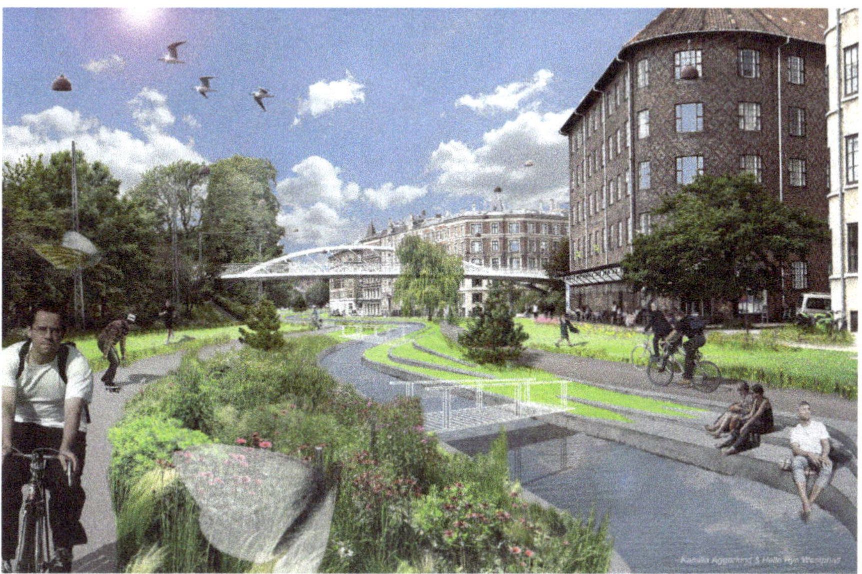

Figure 2.3 The future of Ladegårds Å? Source: visualization from ladegaarsaaen.dk.

Politiken, a major Danish newspaper, has twice celebrated the idea of opening the stream and rebuilding the road as a green space, as the most visionary urban planning project of recent times. The design combines three main features: i) exposing Ladegårds Å; ii) directing cars into a tunnel, that iii) may also act as a reservoir and discharge of rainwater in case of extreme rain, which is anticipated to become more frequent due to climate change. For several years numerous actors have committed themselves to promote what has continuously been perceived as a really good idea that was, however, not (yet) possible to realize and, we suggest, was (perhaps) an expression of utopian thinking.

Conventionally speaking, Ladegårds Å is a 'green' project, signalling a more nature-oriented city space with less polluted air, more green park-like areas and a running stream. Many of the cases in Utopia are green in similar ways, although 'green' comes in many shades. Some are explicitly devoted to, or affiliated with, organic farming and gardening, biodiversity and sustainability (again in different versions).

The organizing groups have also experimented with adopting green practices, sometimes quite literally, by only serving green coloured food at workshops (with very non-organic items also included in order to challenge our expectations about greenness). Sometimes organic food was prioritized by choosing local products, and sometimes 'being green' consisted in identifying field sites within reach of bicycles. This is one sense in which we were aiming to create a green, ecological project. Another, was the design of Utopia to nurture a teaching-based research practice that itself aimed at producing an ecology of knowledge (cf. Star 1995:14) by valuing continuity (over discontinuity and hierarchy), pluralism (over elitism), dynamic project practices (over frozen theory) and relativity (over absolutism). Elsewhere, we have written extensively about the use of ecological perspectives in doing research as a teaching practice, stressing the sharing of resources (among them, notes), and the continuous feedback mechanism between many actors in the evolution of the project, both of which contract with conventional lecturing and learning objectives (Blok *et al.* 2017). A third sense of greenness is present in our experimentation with what we call an ecology of notes in the genesis of the project design, which has included recycling processes in the collection, storing and analyzing of the ethnographic materials. The questions we turn to now are: what characterizes this ecology, how does it take shape and, eventually, does it reflect some lacuna in classical field-note practices?

From a single fieldworker to a collective of notes

Utopia's inverted form of fieldwork sets new requirements for the collection, storing and use of qualitative empirical material. Because Utopia attempted to foster a collective of students at different stages of their education alongside professors and to 'recycle' both interlocutors and field notes, techniques had to be developed to harness the many wild-growing projects under a broadly defined frame. These included, for instance, limiting the number of collective research questions and the shared bodies of theory that were engaged with. To this end, the first generation of the organizing group developed a minimal fieldworkers' guide (a small, illustrated eight-page leaflet) and a collaborative oral introduction in a lecture hall where instructions were given and questions from the participants discussed. The leaflet and the oral presentation introduced the common topic of 'green utopias in urban Copenhagen' and suggested free choice of method. References were made to a few inspirational texts (notably Lucy Sargisson on 'utopia' and Michel Foucault on 'heterotopias'), but apart from these we relied on the participants' own preoccupations and research interests. Most importantly, we, the organizing group, gave instructions on certain requirements concerning the format of the field notes that the participants would bring back at the end of the day, for example, suggesting a maximum number of words and length of video clippings. Over the years, we have tried out various arrangements concerning the timing and form of note-taking. On some occasions, when we have involved students from qualitative-method courses, the note-writing process has been extended to two days. On other occasions, the introduction, group preparation, participant observation, several stages of note taking and the submission of field material have all been squeezed into a single day.

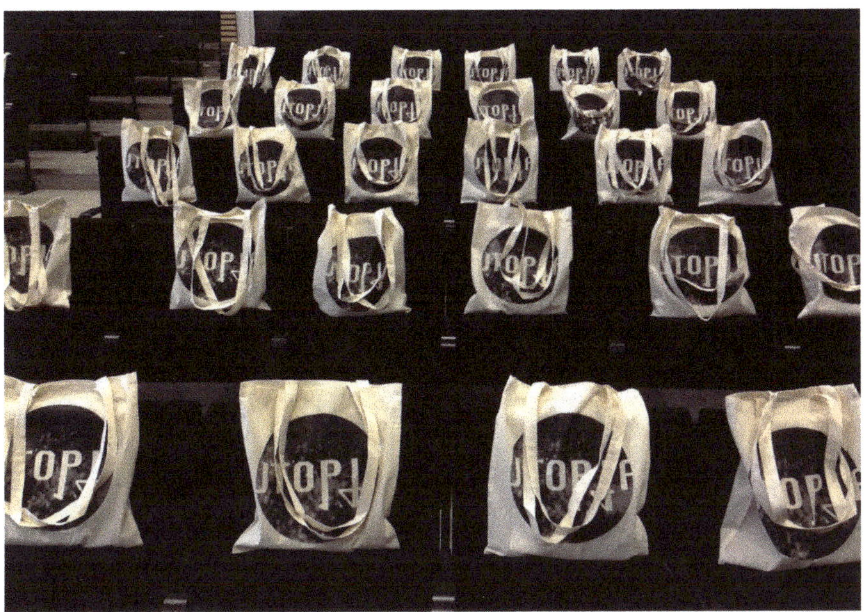

Figure 2.4 Fieldworker bags, May 2014.

Knowing that empirical material would be written up and shared, participants were invited to look out for field locations with open access, and to engage with interlocutors who would accept non-anonymity. Typically, groups of fieldworkers prepared research questions and guidelines for observations and interviews in the morning, and spent some hours at the field site in the afternoon. For practical reasons, a few participants did fieldwork individually, but typically 3–6 members went to the same site as a group. On one occasion, the organizing group had funding for a 'fieldworker bag' containing a notebook, a pencil, a sandwich, a bottle of water and a piece of chocolate. Thereby, we intended to provide the participants with all they needed for a day in the field. Perhaps we should note too, that we expected all the participants to be equipped with a smartphone and a bicycle – standard for Danish students and staff in central Copenhagen. Thus furnished in the morning, each group chose its own destination in the urban environment of the university campus.

Making notes accessible for others to read

So, what is a collective note in Utopia? What does it look like and how does it come about? In our search for alternatives to existing ethnographic practices, we have looked for inspiration in experimental design processes. Design resembles research in its pursuit for something unknown, an uncertainty, that drives the creative process (Ingold and Gatt 2013:146). Proposing an

Metadata Utopia

To be submitted with the fieldnotes

Project

Members of the group

Place(s) (the precise address)

Time (start time and end time of the encounter)

Participants (names or pseudonyms - and issues concerning anonymity)

Methods (research design)

Context (characterize the social situation)

Empirical material (kind and size)

First Interpretation

Theoretical inspiration

Other comments

Figure 2.5 Metadata sheet (original in Danish).

Metadata Utopia 15 Spring

To be submitted with the field notes

Project
Bybi (City Bee). Group 2

Members of the group
Lotte Schack, Laura Østergaard, Marie Munkner, Frida Gammelgaard

---

Place(s) (the precise address)
Sundholm's Activity Center, Copenhagen S
Two telephone interviews

Time (start time and end time of the encounter)
2.30–5pm

Participants (names or pseudonyms – and issues concerning anonymity)
An anonymous woman employed in The Local Council of Amager
Rasmus Ejrnæs, biologist, Aarhus University
Morten Valentin Lundsbak, Amager Brewery

Methods (research design)
We conducted three interviews and wrote descriptive field notes based on observation

---

Context (characterize the social situation)
We meet the city bees as they have gone into hibernation, and our informants while 'on duty'.

Empirical material (kind and size)
About 15 pages of notes
We have included all the data we have compiled
- Transcribed interviews (13 pages)
- Photos
- Descriptive notes (1 page)
- Analysis

First interpretation
Rasmus Ejrnæs relates critically to the city bees. We have become aware of how the companies see the bee as a social project, as a means in the production, and as PR

Possible theoretical inspiration
Tim Ingold about ecology
Design anthropology

Other comments

Figure 2.6 Example of a metadata sheet from a group in Utopia, in the third season, revisiting Bybi (lit. City Bee), a social enterprise producing urban honey (translated into English by the authors).

experimental 'ethnography of the possible', Joachim Halse (2013) suggests that ethnographic methods can be augmented through design events, which can serve as living laboratories for bringing something new into being through a playful, experimental mode of action. Nevertheless, with reference to Sneath *et al.* (2009), Halse also invites us to 'ethnographically qualify the imaginary' by 'moving into the concrete' (Halse 2013:182). Inspired by this, Utopia has facilitated an ecological lab where concrete doing was prioritized over preparatory planning, and face-to-face dialogical practices over individual reporting. In this process a body of interwoven notes was created.

In order to organize the experimental collecting and archiving of notes we designed a 'metadata information sheet', which became the structural backbone of the different versions of the collective archive. The metadata information sheet (see Figure 2.5) now wraps up the material from each group within a single front page that offers a minimum level of orientation for navigation of the notes by readers. The sheet shows the names of the members of the fieldwork group, the date and time of the fieldwork, addresses of visited sites, a short description of the situations and events observed, names of the interlocutors, the intended methods and the adjustments made. Finally, there is space for informal analytical reflections and referencing potential theoretical inspirations.

The intention with the metadata sheet was twofold: on the one hand, it was designed to secure basic information about time, place, people involved and the research questions. On the other, it invited the researchers to make explicit both expectations and spontaneous and informal interpretations. Here we tried to press for an excess, as it were, of first impressions, immediate lines of thought and, if possible, analyses of the material.

Each 'wrap' of notes in Utopia thus consists of rewritten versions of the rough notes of three to six individuals, organized in different groups, enfolded within the larger archive and often enfolding other, earlier, wraps and lines of thought. Thus, in every single entry, field notes are transformed from 'my' notes (and 'your' notes) into 'our' notes; and this, in many cases, we suspect, changed the character of the notes from the classical closed and personalized maze-like structure of the notebooks in individual fieldwork to an open network of notes. In the third season of Utopia, we even tried to orchestrate a recycling of notes and interlocutors. In one instance, a transcribed interview with a key person in an urban-development project from the second season was handed over to two participants, who then conducted a follow-up interview, adding new questions and discussions to the conversation. In another instance, notes were circulated between fieldworker groups, and the field sites were visited by new groups. One can see the sense in which multiple dialogues have taken place between the notes, the participating ethnographers and interlocutors in various places in Copenhagen. This excess of entries and fresh starts makes it possible, to a certain extent, we think, to digest others' notes, and thereby foster an open ecology of notes.

Shared notes on a stream

Running as a continuous stream of inspiration throughout the four seasons of utopian investigations was, as mentioned, the Ladegårds Å project. To exemplify what an ecology of notes might look like, the following section presents field notes written by eight members of Utopia, who approached the Ladegårds Å project in various ways. The notes were written in the second season of Utopia, with the purpose of contributing to an understanding of the life of Åboulevarden in its current form as a densely trafficked boulevard, and in its projected shape as a utopian car-free meadow (see Figure 2.3 for one example). The examples we present are extracts from the metadata sheets in which the fieldworkers explain their notes and their context to fellow fieldworkers.

This field note (Figure 2.7, overleaf) is a 'map' of the online life of Ladegårds Å. It came into being with the assistance of digital methods and shows how websites referring to Ladegårds Å are linked in a larger network. The software package Navicrawler was used to visualize how web pages are connected through links, thus indicated shared interests across sites. Gephi was another kind of software used to visualize networks of web pages, as in Figure 2.7. In the quote from the metadata sheet, Fieldworker A, reflected on the process of creating the map:

> I meet the websites in quite diverse 'contexts'; each of them is very different from the other – official, unofficial, updated and outdated, closely engaged with 'Uncover the stream' or only peripherally relevant [...] This map should be considered as one amongst many tracing the movements that led me through the websites.

Fieldworker B works more phenomenologically, by walking down Åboulevarden. Here she writes about her impressions of 'greenness':

> At first I see lush green nature down by the lakes. [Ladegård Å ends in these lakes in Central Copenhagen.] Further up the boulevard it fades to tiny green squares of trees tidily coordinated along the concrete road. Straight lines wherever I look – with the rare exception of weeds creeping up between the tiles, unintended and more 'alive'...

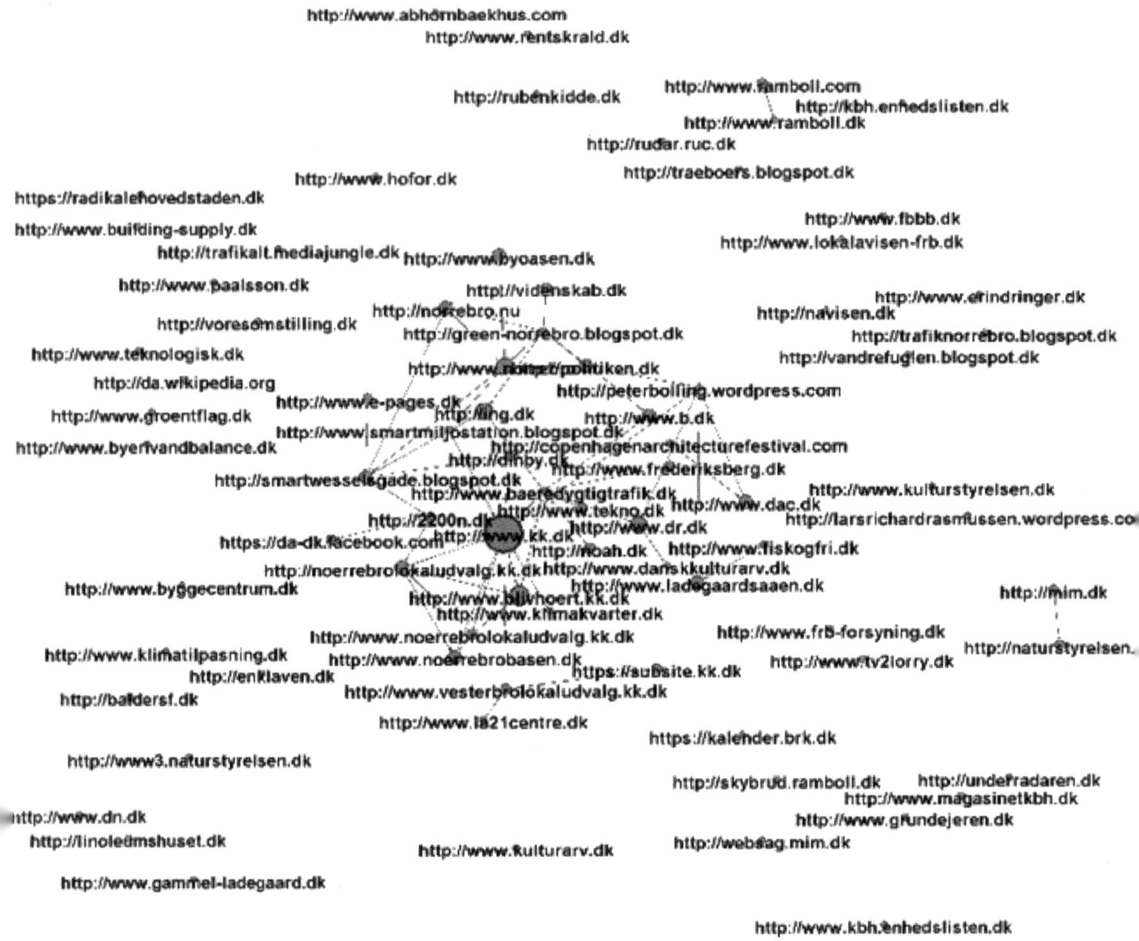

http://www.abhornbaekhus.com
http://www.rentskrald.dk
http://rubenkidde.dk
http://www.ramboll.com
http://kbh.enhedslisten.dk
http://www.ramboll.dk
http://rudar.ruc.dk
http://www.hofor.dk
http://traeboers.blogspot.dk
https://radikalehovedstaden.dk
http://www.fbbb.dk
http://www.building-supply.dk
http://www.lokalavisen-frb.dk
http://trafikalt.mediajungle.dk
http://www.byoasen.dk
http://www.paalsson.dk
http://videnskab.dk
http://www.erindringer.dk
http://noerrebro.nu
http://navisen.dk
http://voresomstilling.dk
http://green-norrebro.blogspot.dk
http://trafiknorrebro.blogspot.dk
http://www.teknologisk.dk
http://vandrefuglen.blogspot.dk
http://www.politiken.dk
http://da.wikipedia.org
http://peterbolling.wordpress.com
http://www.e-pages.dk
http://www.groentflag.dk
http://ing.dk
http://www.b.dk
http://www.smartmiljostation.blogspot.dk
http://www.byerivandbalance.dk
http://copenhagenarchitecturefestival.com
http://dinby.dk
http://www.frederiksberg.dk
http://smartwesselsgade.blogspot.dk
http://www.kulturstyrelsen.dk
http://www.baeredygtigtrafik.dk
http://www.dac.dk
http://www.tekno.dk
http://larsrichardrasmussen.wordpress.co
http://2200n.dk
http://www.dr.dk
https://da-dk.facebook.com
http://www.kk.dk
http://moah.dk
http://www.fiskogfri.dk
http://noerrebrolokaludvalg.kk.dk
http://www.danskkulturarv.dk
http://www.byggecentrum.dk
http://www.ladegaardsaaen.dk
http://mim.dk
http://www.blivhoert.kk.dk
http://www.klimakvarter.dk
http://www.noerrebrolokaludvalg.kk.dk
http://www.frb-forsyning.dk
http://www.klimatilpasning.dk
http://naturstyrelsen.
http://www.noerrebrobasen.dk
http://www.tv2lorry.dk
https://subsite.kk.dk
http://enklaven.dk
http://www.vesterbrolokaludvalg.kk.dk
http://baldersf.dk
http://www.la21centre.dk
https://kalender.brk.dk
http://www3.naturstyrelsen.dk
http://skybrud.ramboll.dk
http://underradaren.dk
http://www.magasinetkbh.dk
http://www.dn.dk
http://www.grundejeren.dk
http://linoleumshuset.dk
http://www.kulturarv.dk
http://webtag.mim.dk
http://www.gammel-ladegaard.dk
http://www.kbh.enhedslisten.dk

Figure 2.7 (above) *Map illustrating the life of Ladegårds Å online: 'A collection of websites (and thus, indirectly, an assemblage of different software, servers, webmasters, bloggers and so on' – Fieldworker A.*

Figure 2.8 (opposite) *Photographs of Åboulevarden, edited (cropping and colour adjustment) with the purpose of highlighting contrasts along the boulevard. Part of a series.*

Another fieldworker, C, observes social interaction and the people walking up and down the boulevard. Here is an extract from her field notes:

> Waves of excited children flood the path along Sortedams Dosseringen [one of the lakes]. It is the last day of school before the holiday, reserved for physical activity. The fresh autumn air is turning the cheeks red. Children's voices, laughter and the sound of shoes on the gravel.

An Extract from Fieldworker D's notes on the soundscape of Åboulevarden highlights the rhythms of heavy traffic:

> There is a halt in the noise, when the cars stop at the red light, leaving room for other sounds of the city. A solitary whistle from a bird. Cyclists crossing the road (squeaking tires and the rattling of bike chains). Then: green light and the roar of accelerating cars whizzing along.

Fieldworker E describes Åboulevarden through a series of photographs:

> Took 40–50 photos, of which I selected 6 shots. They convey the story that I sensed on the boulevard and brought home with me; the way the boulevard is an insistent expression of car-life in the city.

Fieldworker F approaches Åboulevarden through a conversation with two members of the Facebook support group 'Uncover the Stream' (which has over 10,000 members). In the metadata, she writes:

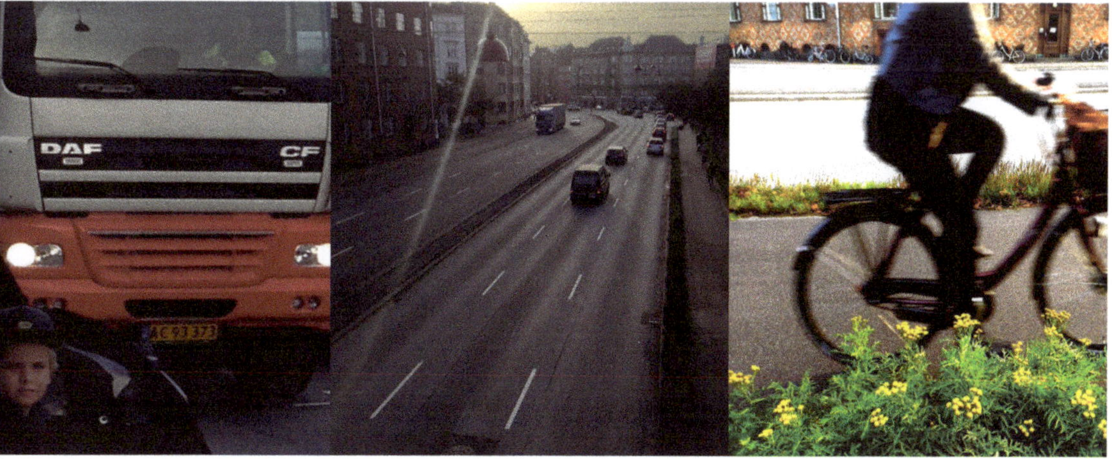

> Jacob and Marie have a shared dream of transforming Åboulevarden – a place they really detest – into a 'functional' green haven in the city. For them, the boulevard means only negative things: noise, pollution, traffic and stress.

Fieldworker G took a digital tour around the Facebook group 'Uncover the Stream', reading all the posts and comments, and used screenshots to convey the visions – and the visionary spirit – brought forward in the discussion between the members of the group (see Figure 2.9).

In the metadata Fieldworker G explains:

> The number of posts has decreased since the site was created in 2012, but the number of comments, likes and shares are continuously high and growing. In the comments, group members discuss the (utopian) future of Åboulevarden. They focus on: 1) freedom, peace, quality of life; 2) nostalgia; 3) what makes a good city; and 4) pollution and traffic.

Fieldworker H meets up with two architects working with 'Uncover the Stream' and describes the meeting to his fellow fieldworkers in this field note:

> I arrange the meeting beforehand and meet up with the architects in their cosy office, a basement space filled with drawings and collages. A radio is on. We speak about the contrast between the utopian visions of the architect and the practicalities of people's everyday life. 'We need utopias', one of them remarks.

These eight extracts from the notes show the manifold ways a swarm of fieldworkers may engage with a shared field site in a very short span of time: by means of digital methods, seeing and sensing the scenery, observing social interaction, taking photos, and interviewing activists and architects. In this particular experiment we distributed participant observation and authorship into eight different modes of engagement (one person 'is' ears, another works digitally etc.), creating a body of data that is synchronic and distributed. Each fieldworker dwelt in his or her specialized field of observation, knowing that others would work the boulevard in supplementary ways. In this sense, the larger body of notes had the potential to acquire a density, less from any individual depth than from a shallow, networked width. The field note as a trigger for the fieldworker's memory is thus superseded by a broad, horizontally shaped body of data with many entry points.

Ladegårdsåen Facebook thread

Of course – it is a project that has to be realized. 2 billion [Danish kroner, DKK] is a lot of money, but the value of the project far exceeds the financial costs. I would looove to see the long trafficked road replaced by green areas, water and people enjoying the peaceful area. The value for those living nearby is priceless. Here you really have a 'Kinder Egg' that solves problems for all in not only a good, but a fantastic manner. Let's get started! Is there anything we can do???
26 April 2013: 09:35
6 Likes

A big congratulation – hope that this can be a part of making the ideas come true.
26 April 2013: 9:40

Fully deserved! it is just the best initiative!!! I completely agree with [anonymous person] and chime in: is there anything we can do?
26 April 2013: 9:41
2 Likes

This is big – hope it's not an illusion;-)
26 April 2013: 9:45
1 Like

(...)

It was wonderful with a 'car free' city this Saturday – and completely fantastic to see how people occupied Åboulevarden and Ågade along the route and used the free road to hang out, roll, and bike. I really think this gave a taste of just how much joy Copenhageners would get out of a blue/green stretch of land if the road was digged away and the stream opened again. I hope this has opened the eyes of more politicians!

(...)

You can probably see the project from several perspectives!? My primary focus is less pollution from cars, as few vehicles as possible in the city and after a reopening of Ladegårdsåen – 'city embellishment' and thereby increasing the quality of life!!!

Figure 2.9 An example of the conversations, translated from Danish, in the Facebook support group 'Uncover the stream'.

A living body of data

The material was stored on a public digital platform and in a Google Drive folder, and was eventually compiled into the three compendia mentioned above, comprising about 300 double pages of text, photographs and other material. In the first two seasons of Utopia the notes from each field site were uploaded by the field-groups on the digital platform, which in this way worked as an open-access digital archive. The idea was to create an archive accessible to all who visited the web page, and to maintain it for reading and comments, allowing an online dialogue. However, we faced some ethical challenges related to ongoing debates about digital fieldwork (Murthy 2013), specifically with regard to the coordination of many participants' handling of anonymity and consent from informants. Therefore, we decided to introduce an embargo on newly uploaded material in order to protect such data from outsiders until it had been read, and accepted, by the organizing team.

Another problem dawned when we, in between fieldwork, tried to make sense of the material, and began searching for recurrent themes in the notes. The blog-like structure of the digital platform proved to be too disparate, as it hosts so many other types of materials. Therefore, we decided to create a supplementary version of the digital archive in a more typical pdf format, enabling us more easily to locate the themes at stake across the field sites. In this manner, different designs for collective notes and archives have been created by the succeeding generations of fieldworkers. A continuous effort has been made to make space for the particularity of each field, while maintaining the collective spirit that has been central to our endeavour. We anticipate that we will, sometime in the future, develop or find better software, at once flexible and more effective for storing, ordering and analyzing heterogeneous materials.

Less on the technical side, though more critically, we have faced the question of the quality of field notes that are not anyone's in particular, and are thus lacking the confidentiality of ordinary field notes. Are there indispensable qualities to be found in the individual and personal note-taking practices? If so, how could we test this? Or is it more to the point to emphasize that new qualities emerge in Utopia when compared with classical fieldwork's intense and unique intertwinement of the fieldworker, the field and the notes? Referring to her set of interviews with anthropologists, Jean Jackson raises the even more troubling question of whether fieldworkers themselves are field notes (Jackson 1990:10), and by implication whether 'being there' is indispensable. 'If I look at them [the field notes], all this emotion is coming out', says one of Jackson's interlocutors in an interview. Another anthropologist says: 'because the design and values are in my head it's dead data without me' (ibid.).

Nevertheless, Jackson also asks whether others' field notes could be valuable (ibid.:9); and we would add, perhaps the actual idea of sharing your initial observations and notes with others, before they are written up, might be of value. Geoffrey Walford has interviewed a number of ethnographers about their field-note practices, one of whom lamented that he 'lost a fair bit of notes just by not writing it up' (Walford 2009:124). We might sharpen the point by adding that losing material is a part of every fieldwork; you never catch everything! In Utopia we have, nevertheless, noticed how the requirement that fellow researchers should have access to and be able to read and understand our field notes has motivated us to rely less on our personal memories. Since the sharing of field notes has been a fundamental part of the experiment, so has immediate note-taking and rewriting among participants – potentially reducing lost fieldwork material. Consequently, aware of what we might lose in sharing notes and in detaching them from the original fieldworker –

perhaps balancing on the edge of creating dead data without emotions – we have also been curious to explore what might be gained in sharing field notes.

While field notes are possibly very valuable triggers of memories, emotions and thoughts for the single fieldworker who wrote them down, they are often by the same token secret and obscure to everyone else. As pointed out by Nicolas H. Wolfinger, researchers' tacit knowledge and expectations often play a major role in determining which observations are worthy of annotation. Ethnographers take notes and make sense of the field site based on their background knowledge (Wolfinger 2002:85, 88). Reflecting on the role of the individual fieldworker in relation to his or her field notes, Nigel Rapport says, in a similar vein, that: '[w]riting field notes means operating within a variety of conventional frameworks of sense-making, juggling these in situational usage and personalizing them to particular individual purpose' (Rapport 1991:13). One of the aims of an ecology of notes is to be able to understand and share notes, gain new perspectives on the material and to learn from each other through the process. When the notes in Utopia go from being single- to multi-authored we see a more distributed sensibility and authority, which is different from the individual fieldworker's close relationship to her or his notebooks, and which is implicated by a specific background knowledge and specific research agenda. The notes now contain several perspectives of different authors, in a way closer to that of an ongoing conversation than a personal reflection. This is not to say that collective field notes manage to avoid being biased by the frame of the project, institutional interests, agreements in the group and so forth. The methodological reflections on limitations and bias do not get any simpler when groups of participants develop different types of analysis.

The question of the quality of field notes is in all cases a tricky one. How can one determine the quality of notes within classical fieldwork? Do we have any criteria? What do we teach students of anthropology; and how do we assess our own note practices? We might well reach the conclusion that it is impossible to find a generalized answer. There may be a rule of thumb, but there is no framework for external enquiry. Even the 'final analysis' proves nothing. The notes, and their quality, depend on the research design and question, the field and the interlocutors, the development of the analysis, the genre in which we write and so forth. Thus, our working hypothesis is that collective notes are no different in terms of ethnographic quality, which is to acknowledge the complex, contextual and diverse nature of this matter. In our reading, so far, collective notes seem to display both ordinary qualities (e.g. precise description as well as telling and imaginative writing) and common flaws (e.g. missing links, superficial awareness, repetitions).

While presenting a range of qualities characterizing the collective notes in Utopia, we also note some (potential) pitfalls in the project's excessive mirroring of classical field-note practices. These may become even more apparent if aspects of the Utopia experiment are taken out of its context to be incorporated into other collective research projects that are designed differently. One challenge concerns the way notes can be forced too quickly into coherent tales so as to be sharable and understandable by others. The specific qualities of field notes partially derive from their fragmentary briefness when their author seeks to enter new worlds and languages. It can take time before bunches of notes find their new connections, and this demands patience from both the note writer and other project participants. Another challenge that may be encountered relates to ownership and intellectual property, as notes are originally authored and tie into field relations built over time, and this brings with it ethical responsibilities. Hence, this experiment can be extended to other contexts, but the move would call for careful modification, attention and up-front discussions.

As a teaching-based research project, one quality in Utopia stands out as exceptional. Anthropologist Robert Whittemore notes that: 'While we profess how much our work depends on fieldnotes, you wouldn't know it by the way we teach our discipline!' (Whittemore 2005:25). For students and staff the sharing of notes uncovered individual practices and ways of writing and making visuals that have proved inspiring in the learning process. The production of ethnography is often double-edged, explorative and anxiety-provoking, constantly dragging the individual fieldworker in opposite directions. Sometimes in fruitful ways; other times in ways that are downright unproductive (Bundgaard and Rubow 2016; Pollard 2009). Utopia, by juxtaposing many examples of note-taking, has opened up many questions concerning genre, authorship and analysis, and has prompted many types of feedback, with the effect that fieldworkers have learned how to try out, manage and present ways of taking and using field notes in a playful and productive learning environment. The combination of teaching and research has offered a looking glass into a serious playground of individual practices, and has nurtured new ways of sharing the craft of note-making.

Our utopia: analyzing collective notes

With the large body of notes connected to utopian practices in urban Copenhagen assembled in the three compendia and in the digital folders, in the spring of 2016, the third generation chose to develop collective analyses. Inspired by utopian method, design anthropology and classical ways of organizing analysis of qualitative data (Emerson, Fretz and Shaw 1995; Hoek 2014; O'Reilly 2005), a design was developed in order to approach the material. This involved a number of reading strategies, ways of categorization and brainstorming, re-interpretations of the intentions and outcomes of the former seasons, new supplementary visits to the fields and a (re)reading of the entire corpus. Additional material was incorporated (primarily regarding Ladegårds Å), and we searched for new analytical inspiration in social scientific literature and genres as divergent as poetry, science-fiction and other forms of storytelling, with a preference for utopian content. In addition, individual and collective writing methods were tested. At one point, five members simultaneously drafted a feature article, written in the style of utopian futurity, in a single online document submitted to, and subsequently published in, a web-based magazine (Utopia 2016).

It goes beyond the scope of this chapter to dwell on the design and content of this particular analysis involving imaginary Latourian earthlings (Latour 2010) in the field of Ladegårds Å. Instead, we will stress that the sheer realization of collective analysis, in this context taking place between eight people around a table, through access to the archives and informal types of oral and printed analysis, was yet another process of turning note-taking inside out. How can you organize your (and others') material in the process of analysis and writing up? How can you develop an analysis based on notes from other researchers and in dialogue with a larger scholarly environment? We asked: how would you do it on an individual basis? And, how can we do it collectively?

Presently, we are not ready to assess whether the design of Utopia is a sustainable and repeatable template for teaching-based research. Many other versions could turn out to be more productive for both research and training. However, we do see some potential usefulness in the lessons learned from the collective note-taking practices, particularly in a research ethics perspective. The classical anthropological fieldwork tradition has harboured generations of fieldworkers whose work has mainly come to the fore through its academic and public dissemination. Yet apparently, for the now booming number of retiring members of a relatively young and still expanding discipline, there are no measures in place for archiving fieldworkers' collections of notes, drafts and artefacts, at least not in the Danish research environment. However, national initiatives are currently enjoined to put together frameworks for data management, including that of the qualitative research traditions. Moreover, rumours and reports are distributed worldwide in informal and formal anthropological networks about lost collections of fieldwork materials and the arbitrary handling of personal archives. Due to the individual fieldwork tradition, presumably, many collections are not even in a shape where they are useful for others, being wholly idiosyncratic in content and order and subject to unclarified criteria for access due to personal agreements of anonymity.

Judged within the classical tradition of fieldwork, the personalization of fieldwork material may stand out as tenable and well-grounded. Though currently, in projects grounded in anthropology, it seems as if this position is generally more a question of routine and convenience than one of deliberate consideration in the research design.

In Utopia we have, by means of a utopian conceptualization of an ecological research process, tried out the opposite way of thinking. The utopian methods of excess, play and estrangement have encouraged a teaching and research process in which we have intentionally distanced ourselves from classical fieldwork design for the sake of experimentation. By fostering an ecology of notes, framed as being public (accessible and readable), recyclable (alive with many feedback mechanisms) and nested (by collectives of researchers with a distributed authority), we have deliberately mirrored the classical fieldwork tradition. At the conclusion of this process, we may now hypothesize the following:

1. Taking into consideration the richness of classical ethnographic bodies of notes and other ethnographic material, it seems untenable that the politics of closure is the norm.
2. Fieldworkers' material can be recycled to students and scholars within and outside academia throughout the research process if the ecology of the notes is thought through methodically.
3. Many further experiments with turning anthropological note-taking inside out could be inspirations for sustainable ways of teaching and research that would give life to new ecologies of notes.

From the vantage point of Utopia, where we have been continuously absorbed in the generation and oversight of a morphing body of notes, we anticipate an era of new collective modes of note-taking in which the combination of classical fieldwork practices and open-source mechanisms in all stages of the research process turns out to be not only affordable, but also intellectually potent in teaching and research.

References

Blok, A., Bøgkjær, T., Due, T.A., Fritsch, E., Hansen, C.J., Hedegaard, M., Jensen, L.N., Pedersen, M.M.S. and Rubow, C. 2017. 'Undervisningsbaseret forskning som økologisk viden: et (utopisk) forsøg på kollektivt feltarbejde i stor skala', *Tidsskriftet Antropologi* 76:37–54.

Bundgaard, H. and Rubow, C. 2016. 'From rite of passage to a mentored educational activity: fieldwork for Master's students of anthropology', *Learning and Teaching: The International Journal of Higher Education in the Social Sciences* 9(3):22–41.

Emerson, R.M., Fretz, R.I. and Shaw, L.L. 1995. *Writing Ethnographic Fieldnotes.* Chicago: The University of Chicago Press.

Foucault, M. 1984. 'Of other spaces: utopias and heterotopias', *Architecture/Movement Contunité* 5:46–9.

Halse, J. 2013. 'Ethnographies of the possible'. In W. Gunn, T. Otto and R.C. Smith (eds.), *Design Anthropology: Theory and Practice.* London: Bloomsbury.

Hoek, L. 2014. 'Sorting things out: organizing and interpreting your data'. In N. Konopinski (ed.), *Doing Anthropological Research: A Practical Guide.* London: Routledge.

Ingold, T. and Gatt, C. 2013. 'From description to correspondence: anthropology in real time'. In W. Gunn, T. Otto and R.C. Smith (eds.), *Design Anthropology: Theory and Practice.* London: Bloomsbury.

Jackson, J. 1990. '"I am a fieldnote": fieldnotes as a symbol of professional identity'. In R. Sanjek (ed.), *Fieldnotes: The Making of Anthropology.* Ithaca: Cornell University Press.

Latour, B. 2010. 'A plea for earthly sciences'. In J. Burnett, S. Jeffers and G. Thomas (eds.), *New Social Connections: Sociology's Subjects and Objects.* London: Palgrave Macmillan.

Murthy, D. 2013. 'Ethnographic research 2.0: the potentialities of emergent digital technologies for qualitative organizational research', *Journal of Organizational Ethnography* 2(1):23–36.

O'Reilly, K. 2005. *Ethnographic Methods.* London: Routledge.

Pollard, A. 2009. 'Field of screams: difficulty and ethnographic fieldwork', *Anthropology Matters* 11(2):1–24.

Rapport, N. 1991. 'Writing Fieldnotes: the conventionalities of note-taking and taking note in the field', *Anthropology Today* 7(1):10–13.

Sargisson, L. 2012. *Fool's Gold: Utopianism in the Twenty-First Century.* Hampshire: Palgrave MacMillan.

Star, S.L. (ed.) 1995. 'Introduction'. In S.L. Star (ed.), *Ecologies of Knowledge: Work and Politics in Science and Technology.* Albany, NY: State University of New York Press.

Sneath, D., Holbraad, M. and Pedersen, M.A. 2009. 'Technologies of the imagination: an introduction', *Ethnos* 74(1):5–30.

Utopia 2016. 'At drømme København [Dreaming Copenhagen]': Turbulens.dk.

Walford, G. 2009. 'The practice of writing ethnographic fieldnotes', *Ethnography and Education* 4(2):117–30.

Whittemore, R.D. 2005. 'Fieldnotes, student writing and ethnographic sensibility. Academic affairs', *Anthropology News*: 25–6.

Wolfinger, N.H. 2002. 'On writing fieldnotes: collection strategies and background expectancies', *Qualitative Research* 2(1):85–95.

3

Field notes from a field of notes

Anthropology and the afterlife of notes in archives

MARIANNE HOLM PEDERSEN AND

LARS CHRISTIAN KOFOED RØMER

At the Danish Folklore Archives in the Royal Danish Library, anthropologists are regularly employed as researchers. The interviews, observations and notes they produce during fieldwork are archived there together with project proposals and published material. The main purpose of the Danish Folklore Archives is to document, research and communicate everyday lived culture in Denmark, and their research is thus part of the continuing work of collecting new material for the archive. However, the ethnographic field notes they produce are inscribed in a longer folkloristic tradition of recording what is presently termed 'intangible culture'. This means that the field notes are included in a larger collection of more than two-million pages of written material such as manuscript notes, autobiographical records and other kinds of recorded data, generally referred to as 'records'. Although field notes are produced during research, the field note itself becomes a product that is valued as a contribution to the archive collections. Furthermore, whereas ethnographic field notes typically remain private to the ethnographer, notes produced for the archives are intended, sooner or later, to be made public. Field notes may in the first place be used by the researcher in his or her work, but further analysis is also left open to future readers. Contrary to note-sharing in collaborative projects, in which researchers already know each other and hence are also aware of the preconceptions of the research, notes produced for the archive are shared with unknown readers who may approach the material from different historical or discursive perspectives.

Within the anthropological tradition, field notes are often praised for their 'thickness' and their ability to bring their writer back to a particular situation. Moreover, the kind of knowing found in ethnographic notes is often more fragmented, personal and open to interpretation than what ends up in published texts. Anthropologist Michael Taussig has suggested that field notes 'with at least one foot in the art of sensuous immediacy [are] so valuable as an alternate form of knowing to what eventually gets into print' (Taussig 2011:49). If this is true, how does it affect the field notes if the writer is aware that there will also be other readers? How are notes used when the reader cannot draw on the unwritten, contextual knowledge? When field notes become a primary product, the open-endedness of their interpretation challenges the relationship between text and context, notes and published text, and ultimately the distribution of authority between writer and reader. It also feeds into what it means to take notes in the first place.

In this chapter, we will investigate the production and use of field notes and records within the archival tradition by presenting two examples from our own work at the Danish Folklore Archives. We begin by discussing Marianne Holm Pedersen's production of field notes in a recent research project in order to investigate what it does to field notes when you know that others will be reading them. We will then look at what kind of knowledge Lars Christian Kofoed Rømer gains from reading the records of others in his use of archival material. The examples show that notes are not only produced at a specific time, but that they also live through time and change their meaning and nature along the way. By comparing the production of new notes and the analysis of old ones, we hope to shed light on the value of the particular form of 'knowing' embedded in field notes, and the tension between this knowing and published texts (cf. Taussig 2011). We also want to underline the importance of every note-taker being aware of the kinds of knowledge they produce with their notes. In Denmark, research funders are increasingly demanding data-management plans, as is already standard in many other countries. While the specific cases here concern notes in archives, the question of metadata and sharing notes with others should be relevant for all researchers. Before we know it, cultural changes may impact the field, and the ethnographer will no longer be able to keep all his or her notes private.

A field of notes: the Danish Folklore Archives

A discussion of the use and production of field notes is only a small part of a much broader debate about the general construction of archives. Studies have highlighted how not only the structure of the archive, but also library and archival technology, determine 'what can be archived and therefore what can be studied' (Manoff 2004:12; see also Derrida 1995). Likewise, the building of archives cannot be separated from the professional and political interests of the archive's founders and subsequent archivists (Schwartz and Cook 2002).

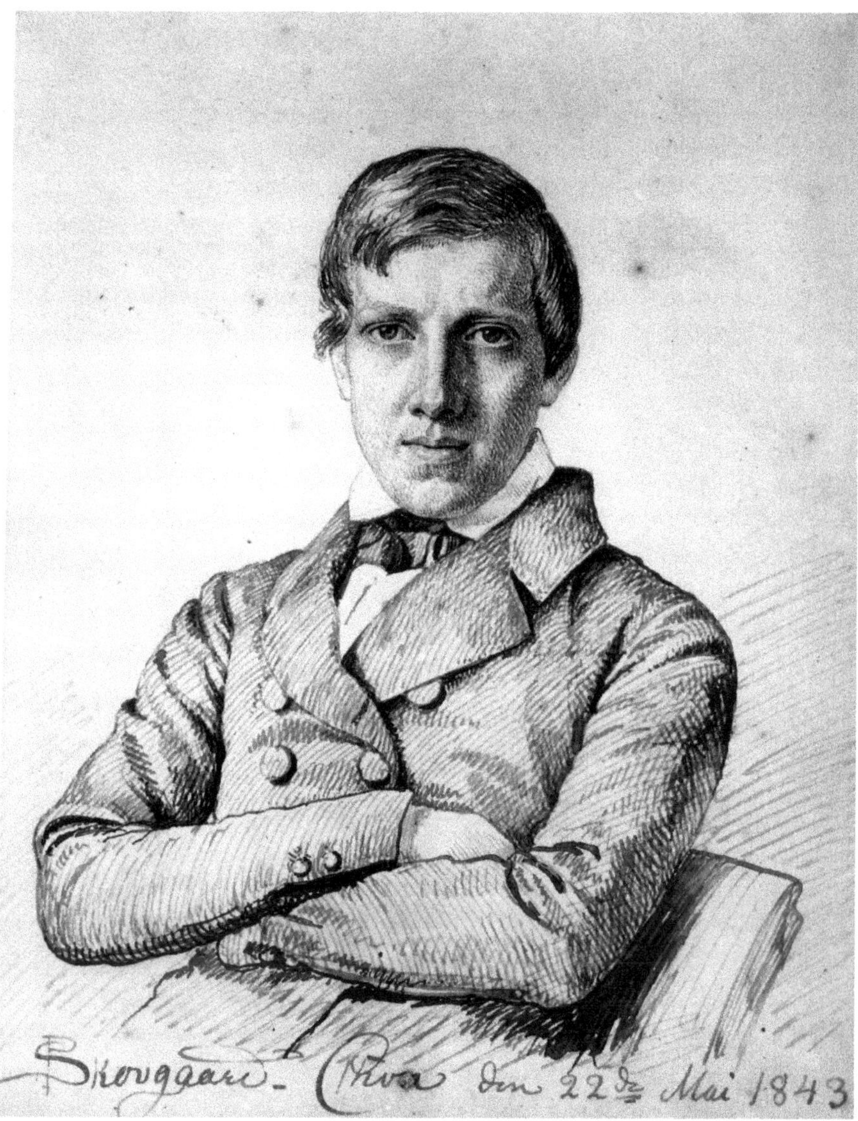

Figure 3.1 Svend Grundtvig, drawn in 1843 by P.C. Skovgaard (DFS image number 02417).

If we take a look at the history of the Danish Folklore Archives, it is clear that different policies, interests and approaches have shaped what kinds of written material were collected and produced for the archives at different times, and what kinds of context were supposed to accompany them. This latter would include what, in archival language, would today be called metadata, that is data that describe or classify other data, and which provide the basic information required to find the content.

	efter mundtlig meddelelse af:
herred	navn ....
sogn	stand og alder ....
optegnet 19 .... af	boende i ....
boende i	meddelerens fødested el. andre oplysninger } ....

32723

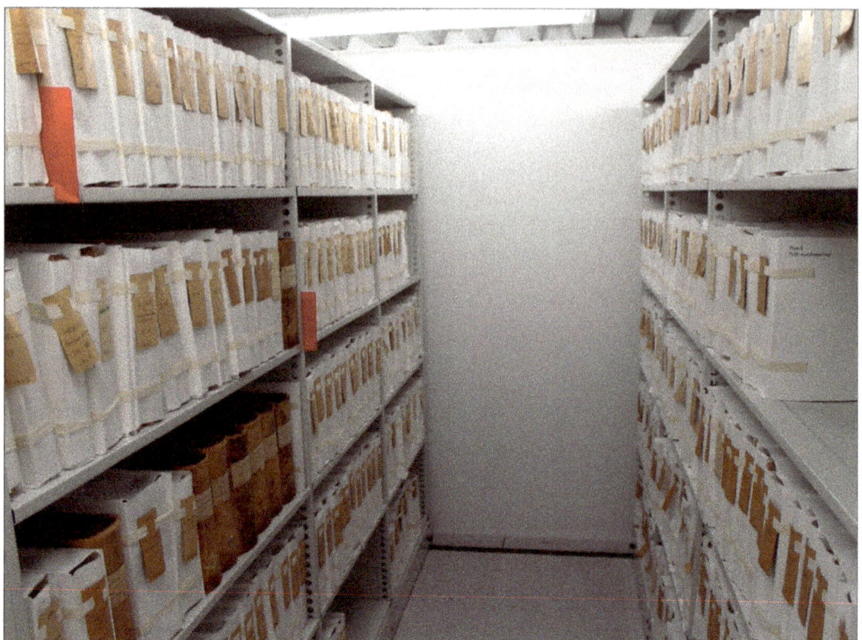

Figure 3.3 The Danish Folklore Archives.

ballads, fairy tales) and topography. If a submitted record contained several notes from different genres or referred to different places, it would either be copied or separated into different pieces (literally cut apart) and placed in different sections of the archive (Figure 3.3). This way of organizing the archive was maintained until the 1960s, when a new research paradigm slowly took over (Koudal 2004).

From the 1960s onwards, the archive's focus was broadened to include contemporary culture among all parts of the Danish population, and there was a change in perspective from seeing data as 'things in themselves' (see Christiansen 2004) to studying people, situations and processes of change (Hansen 2013). Due to a greater focus on context, sets of notes were no longer separated and were no longer recorded on a template. Today they are often in digital form. Since the 2000s, research and documentation has been coordinated through various thematic programmes on, for example, 'historical worlds', 'immigration and cultural encounters' and 'faith and magic in everyday life'. One of the purposes of making such programmes was to increase the amount of data on a particular topic, and also to use studies to contextualize each other. During this period, anthropologists joined the cross-disciplinary team of researchers, and material for the archive was also collected through ethnographic fieldwork. Nevertheless, there have been limited methodological discussions of what field notes are and how they should be written with a view to their being archived. While there are guidelines for the kinds of metadata that need to be added when material is archived, there are no methodological guidelines as to how to produce material for the archive. It also seems that many smaller anthropological research projects carried out by visiting researchers in the archives have mostly deposited recorded interviews and pictures, and only a limited number of field notes.

In sum, the historical development of research paradigms and understandings of records in the archives have changed the kinds of information that researchers want to record for the future. Moreover, a look at the old notes raises the question of what knowledge future readers may take from our current notes. In the following, we explore these questions by taking a look a Marianne's current note-taking.

Producing field notes for the archive

In 2010–11, Marianne carried out a research project on the religious practices of Muslim families in a Danish provincial town. Among other things, she interviewed parents, young people and children of Muslim background about how parents attempt to pass their religion on to their children and how the children appropriate it. During her fieldwork, Marianne produced different kinds of texts that will all be stored in the Danish Folklore Archives: a project proposal, interview guides, transcribed interviews, descriptions of the interview situations, field notes from visits to the school, the families and other events, and essays written by the children. When deposited in the archive, the project as a whole will be given a reference mark that refers to the year of its accession and a serial number (e.g. 2016/037), and it will be registered in the Royal Danish Library's database. As part of the process of registration, an archivist will add metadata. These include the title, scope and a list of the field notes and other kinds of material, the researcher's name ('collector'/*optegner*), the names of the main participants (key informants/ *meddelere*), the time of collection, a topography number, a geographical name and the most important keywords. Not all of these metadata will be visible in the public database, but together they are meant to provide some necessary contextual information about the notes' origin.

However, during her fieldwork Marianne also wrote notes that will not be given to the archive: diary-like notes, rough notes with ideas and questions, and analytical notes that represent attempts to make sense of the material. The fact that these 'process notes' are not kept in the archive means that, while a future reader will be able to engage with the data that Marianne produced, she or he will not necessarily be able to track the different turning points that made Marianne follow some links and not others. Retrospectively, the distinction between different kinds of notes seems not only to concern content, but also the literary quality, as rough notes are rarely intelligible to others. Knowing that others may eventually read her notes affected Marianne's writing. Descriptions of interview situations, for example, are written out in full sentences (always a verb and a noun), and the origin of a meeting is explained more carefully than Marianne would have needed to do for herself. The notes are also not as blunt in their expression as they could have been, for instance, in the description of people's physical characteristics or in the ways they refer to what people say about each other. By comparison, the process notes may consist of just questions, keywords or sentences that would be incomprehensible to others, such as 'remember to ask Luke about yesterday'. In a sense, then, rather than being her own completely 'raw' notes, the sorts of notes Marianne has produced for the archive are already one step on their way to becoming the sort of accounts others might read in a finished chapter or article.

In addition, Marianne also has a third category of notes, those that currently form part of the data, but which she is not particularly comfortable about sharing with others. Here is an example:

> The interview went well. Nevertheless, as usual there are things that I don't enquire into enough. For example, as we are speaking about her life as a 40-year-old she says that she will speak with her potential daughters about the veil in a different way than her parents did. 'Of course we spoke about it', she says, 'but I felt… yes.' While she is saying this, she looks down, then up at me, and away again. It's in the air that the last word missing is 'pressured', but I don't get her to explicate it. Why not? On the one hand because her entire body language shows (and here she is sitting a little closed with her body together and the legs tight, turned away from me) that she feels uncomfortable about saying it. On the other hand, maybe also because it is uncomfortable for me to be confronted with what I would otherwise often contradict when others are speaking. Here is a young woman who is totally independent and able to manoeuvre, and yet she feels that she was… (pressured?) to wear the veil. Next time I'll ask her if she ever considered taking it off.
>
> (Slagelse 24 June 2011, author's translation)

This excerpt is from an interview with Muna, a 21-year-old woman of Palestinian background, in which she reflects on how she imagines her life will be at the age of 40. During her reflections, she touched upon a topic that seemed difficult for her and apparently also for Marianne, who did not stop her and ask her to explain more, but let her continue with her story. Marianne's subsequent reflections provide important information about the interview situation, but they also shed light on the retrospective reflections of the ethnographer about her methodology, the kind of reflections we do not always show to others. Marianne's discomfort with sharing these particular notes primarily concerns a desire to protect her informants. Muna did not want her parents to know her story. Although Marianne's notes will be provided with a clause that keeps them inaccessible for thirty years, in theory there is a possibility that Muna's family or other informants will eventually read them. Hence, not just in this family, but also in other cases, notes may potentially affect relationships in the future. The need to 'protect' also concerns the fact that the religious practices of Muslim immigrants in Denmark are a highly politicized topic. Although the situation may have changed in thirty years, it may also remain the same; and hence Marianne is worried that her notes could be misinterpreted by a person who does not have the relevant anthropological knowledge or general insights into the topics she is writing about. This last worry correlates with Marianne's awareness that her notes are the ultimate window into her method and abilities as ethnographer. Thus, Marianne's concern with sharing notes also relates to a subtle desire to protect her own reputation as an ethnographer. Because of their intimate nature, field notes are closely linked with personal practice and the anthropologist's self-understanding as a researcher (Jackson 2016:50–2). Moreover, they are not just full of the things we accomplished, but also the questions we did not ask or the relations that did not work; in other words, all the frustrations that are also part of fieldwork (ibid.:48, 56). Yet, Marianne's concern also builds on a sense of insecurity over whether the sensibilities and prior knowledge that made her make certain choices in the field will be clear to a future reader. For instance, it may well be that Marianne did not pursue Muna's statement because she sensed that this would not be productive in the current situation. Methodological reflections regarding the choices made during fieldwork are often later steps in the ethnographic work process, written and published long after the field notes were produced. The lack of meta-reflections (or their eclectic appearance) within the notes leaves Marianne's methods and findings open to criticism in a different way than if a reader simply criticizes the arguments of a finished article. It might be an option for Marianne to simply include a note on these considerations when the interview is handed in to the archive, but on a practical level this would be impossible in a large project with many field notes. All in all, these concerns made Marianne consider whether she should edit all her notes before archiving them.

This description raises a number of questions regarding the production of notes for the archive. What kind of contextual information is necessary to understand the field notes of others? What kinds of information and knowledge can be discerned in them? And when is a field note finished – may it still be edited long after it was initially made? Taken together, these questions seem ultimately to concern the shifting movement of authority from the writer to the reader that happens when field notes are no longer in the ethnographer's hands (or desk drawers). A privileged understanding of context is often emphasized as one of the main benefits of 'having been there' through fieldwork. When handing over the notes to the archive, the ethnographic writer also grants the reader the right to place the notes in what she or he perceives to be the proper context (whether theoretically, empirically or methodologically).

In order to pursue the above questions further, we now look at how Lars uses the archival records of others in his research project, and the light this may shed on the issues just raised. As we will show, the relations between text/context and writer/reader are not new issues of concern.

The notes of others: 'Hoglebjergnisserne'

Lars's PhD project focuses on perceptions and experiences of the local landscape on the Danish island of Bornholm in the Baltic Sea. As a supplement to classical anthropological fieldwork, Lars uses legends from Bornholm in order to gain a better understanding of the way past generations experienced and narrated their local surroundings, and also to get a feel for the way these legends are currently being referred to. In order to do so, however, he has had to begin by digging into a range of historical metadata to decode what can be seen as a vast field of notes. The material from Bornholm includes several thousand pages covering different genres, such as legends, ballads, fairy tales and general folklore. Even the number of local legends within this material can be counted in the thousands. These cover a range of different subgenres, such as revenants, haunted places, omens, place legends, legendary rocks and, in particular, a large number relate to encounters with *underjordiske* (a local and subterranean kind of pixie).

One of these legends is entitled 'Hoglebjergnisserne'. Together with fifteen other legends from Bornholm and two from Zealand, it was sent to Svend Grundtvig by the 47-year-old schoolteacher Christian Weiss (Figure 3.4). As in many other legends from Bornholm, references to *underjordiske* are frequent and detail how they could be both friends – helping with daily chores on the farms, returning favours and helping protect the island from invading foreign troops; and foes – when from time to time they would try to steal both wives and children, as well as punish disturbance by humans of their homes in the many burial mounds and barrows found there. By way of illustration, in the first eighteen lines of this legend written on a blue sheet of paper, we learn how:

Figure 3.4 (opposite) Christian Weiss photographed by Fritz Ridiger (DFS image number 01556).

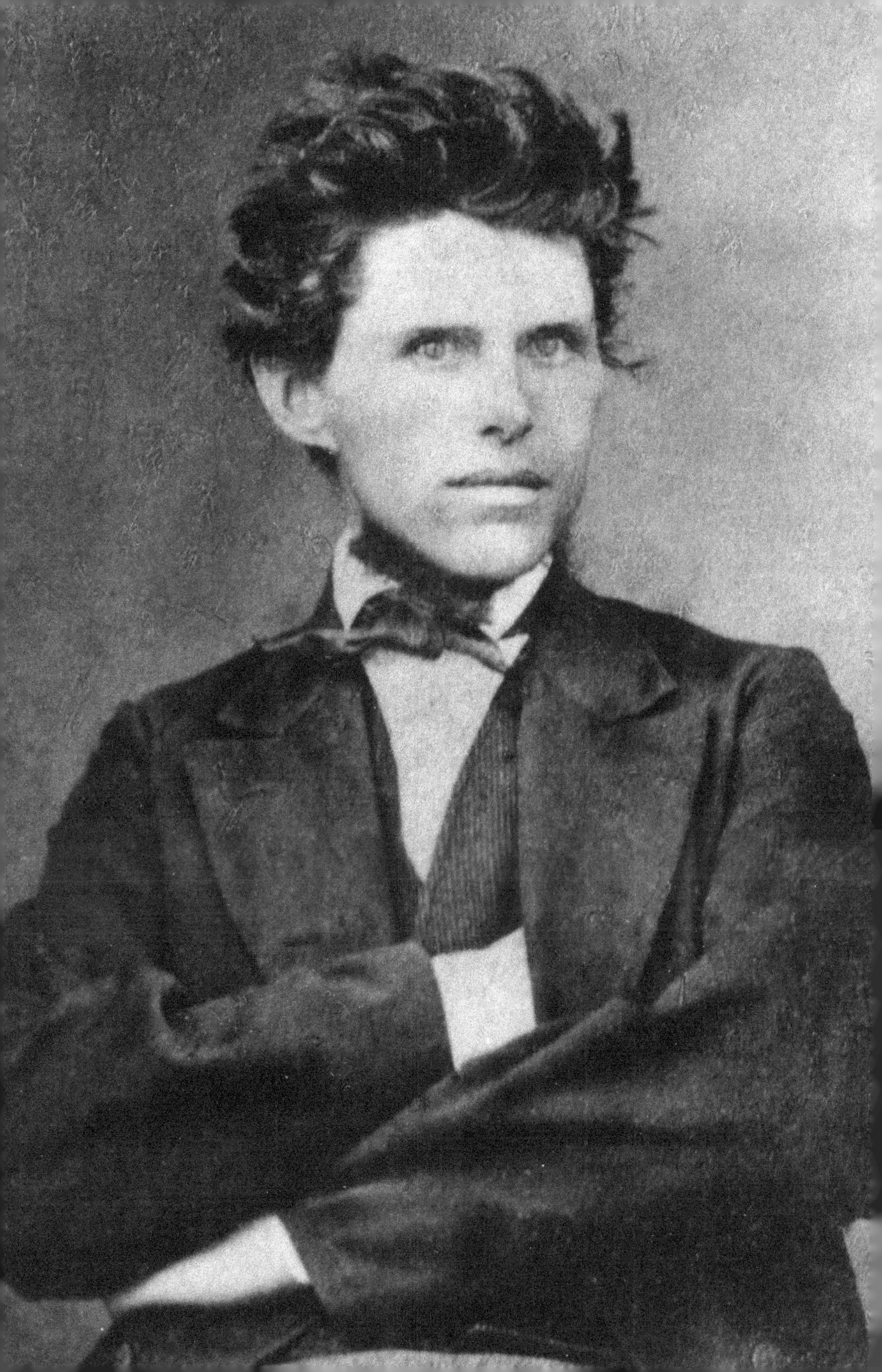

> One evening after sundown some boys [on Bornholm adult farmhands were called boys or *drenge*; actual boys were called *horra*] rode out to look for some untethered horses that were to be used the next day. When the boys came to the top of Hoglebjergbakkerne they encountered an unknown man, who asked them what they were doing. 'We are out looking for little devils', they said cheerfully. At once it appeared to them that the entire hill was ablaze. Terrified, they were unable to get off the hill until the next morning, and after that they took great care with regard to these bad hills.
>
> (Weiss 1881: DFS XVI/16:408, authors' translation)

When found in the archive today, Weiss' record contained not only his own writing, but also the notes of several other individuals (Figure 3.5). Together, they make up a range of metadata that contextualize the legend in different ways. At the top centre of the page we find '4. Hoglebjergnisserne' in Weiss's handwriting, indicating that this is the fourth of his legends, which he has entitled 'Hoglebjergnisserne'. In the top left corner, 'DS I 555' is written with a lead pencil. As Lars quickly learned when reading through the material, this is an abbreviation for the 555th legend in the first volume of *Danish Legends* published by Evald Tang Kristensen in 1891. To the right of the title, 'Top 661', also in lead pencil, refers to the topographical number of the parish where the legend takes place, the parish of Klemensker in the central-north part of Bornholm. Further to the right, '☐ 28 1', probably from the same pen, means that the legend has been copied to the first of the three capsules registered as 1906/28, where it can be found under its topographical number. Most likely, all three notes were made by the archivist Hans Ellekilde sometime after he began working at the archive in 1917. Finally, at the top right corner, '408' is the number of the leaf within the nineteenth of Grundtvig's alphabetically organized capsules of the material he received from his many interlocutors, and which is usually referred to as DFS XIX and 1883/XIX. This is written in blue pencil and may thus be from a different person.

This staccato list of abbreviations or codes and the details in the legend both point to the different settings in which the legend can be placed, and the types of metadata the archivists were interested in. For instance, the legend can be approached within the context of Weiss's work as a collector of folk memories, which has its own ambiguities. Thus, one of Weiss's other rather peculiar legends, entitled 'Something which has to be believed', describes the discussions between a schoolteacher and some participants at a funeral about the nature of supernatural beliefs on Bornholm, in particular the participants' conviction that a young woman had been punished by the *underjordiske* because her father had taken soil from the hill where they lived. This discussion is in itself very informative about how the local farmers understand

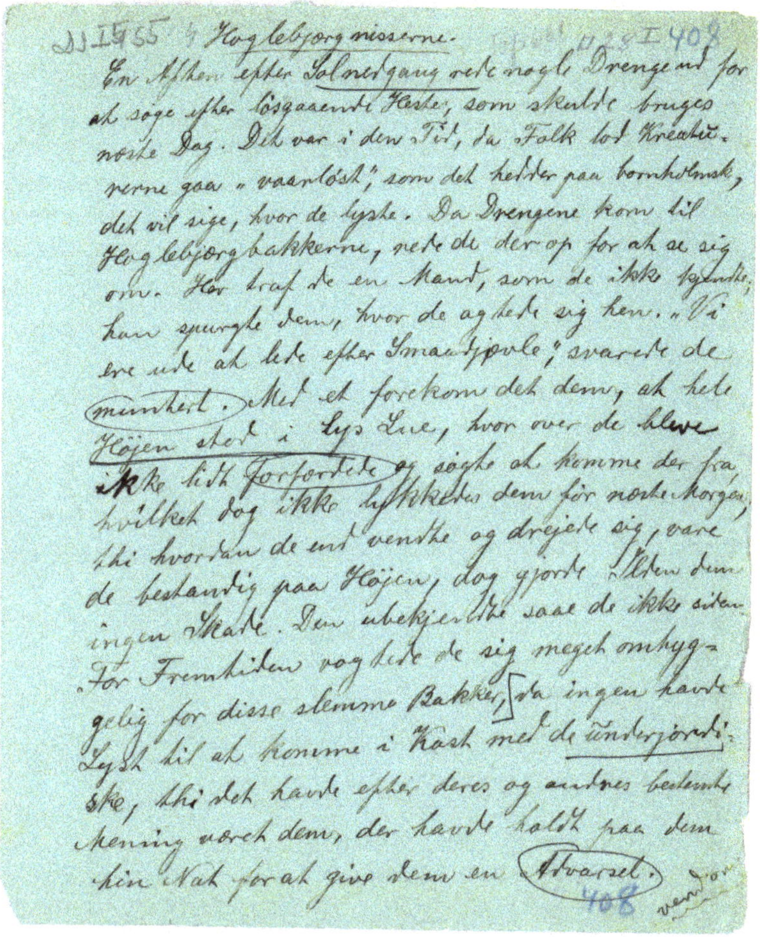

Figure 3.5 Christian Weiss's 'Hoglebjergnisserne' (DFS XVI:408).

the relationships between superstition, belief and facts, but within the theme of this chapter what is most interesting is how Weiss has deleted and changed some sentences concerning who the narrator is. Ellekilde also pointed this out in the version he published (Ellekilde and Grundtvig 1944:194-202), and it raises the suspicion that the sceptical schoolteacher may in fact be Weiss himself.

This may seem a minor issue, but Weiss's possible unease about appearing as part of the story, rather than merely recording it second-hand, points to the tension and sometimes distinction between what you note down for yourself and what you present to others that Marianne also describes (above). Pursuing this line of analysis may thus deepen the contextual understanding of how these legends ended up on paper. It also points to some of the general methodological uncertainties concerning the workings of earlier endeavours to collect folklore. Whose stories are we actually reading?

In this way, even though Weiss is but one member of Grundtvig's extensive network of informers, and his work is but a minor part of the large corpus of material Grundtvig collated, this example can illustrate how at least some of it was created and subsequently published. Most of Grundtvig's material remained unpublished at the time of his death. Evald Tang Kristensen, however, used this to his advantage, as up to twenty per cent of the content in his first volume of *Danish Legends* is actually not his own but Grundtvig's. Upon closer examination, the previously mentioned reference to Kristensen's volume reveals that, whereas Kristensen is usually praised (and praises himself) for publishing his material in the actual words of his informants, in this case he has omitted the last nine and a half lines of 'Hoglebjergnisserne'. Whereas Kristensen (1892) punctuates the sentence 'and after that they took great care with regard to these bad hills' with a full stop, Weiss has a comma and continues:

> As nobody wanted to come to grips with the *underjordiske*, for this was in their and others' solid convictions what had held them on that night, so as to give them a warning. This was now over sixty years ago, and no one has heard suchlike since that time, whether it stems from people staying away when the gnomes were having fun, or whether these are not as bold as in the old days.
>
> (DFS 1883/16:408, authors' translation)

In other cases, Kristensen quite clearly states that, while he has sometimes left the most sexually and religiously offensive folk songs out of his publications (or put them in an appendix) in order not to disgust his scholarly and bourgeois readers, he generally believes this to be a bad habit – stories should be printed as they were told, and in any case his records have been kept for others to study (Kofod 1984:123–34). However, foul and offensive words do not seem to be the reason for leaving out a part of 'Hoglebjergnisserne', and in fact the editing of this record is far from an isolated case, at least when it comes to Kristensen's use of Grundtvig's material. In other published legends, Kristensen often leaves out the names of places or persons, information of preceding events or the aftermaths of the legends (as in this case), as well as generally omitting debates, doubts and discussions found within the legends. While Marianne had ethical concerns over issues of anonymity and how to present another person's story, Kristensen and the early collectors of folklore were interested in the 'pure story' rather than the ways in which it may be experienced, interpreted or debated by its tellers. Omitting the last nine and a half lines of 'Hoglebjergnisserne' is a concrete example of this. If there was an ethical consideration, it was not about how the storyteller was presented, but whether the published material would sit well with the reader. Yet one of Kristensen's concerns, like Marianne's and perhaps also Weiss's, also seems to relate to how he may be perceived as a publisher. Without good credentials and critical acclaim, the audience might be reduced in number and future funding thus jeopardized. This example highlights the strained relationship between the archival records and the published text, something that is also very relevant to the depositing of ethnographic field notes in archives.

Comparing notes

Although the notes in Lars's project are very different from Marianne's, they shed light on the changing understanding of records and notes over time. Until the 1960s, the notes in the archive seemed very much like works in progress. On numerous pages, new information, comments or corrections have thus been added over the years. This is somewhat similar to how, upon rereading their notes, anthropologists may recall other details relating to the particular situation, which may then be added somewhere on the page. Today, once the notes have been archived, they become a 'completed' work in their own right. Lars thus had to make a copy of Weiss's legend in order to be allowed to add his own notes in the margins, and add circles and lines to the text. The idea that notes are less 'authentic' if they become altered is also one of the reasons why Marianne hesitates to edit her notes.

Just as certain information about the earlier production of notes is necessary for others to best use the notes today, one may ask what information is necessary in order to best use current notes in the future. Within anthropology, there is strong concern with ethics and anonymization that often leads to the deliberate alteration of names, places and particular details in publications. In contrast, the Danish Folklore Archives does not anonymize material, though not all the information may be accessible to everyone. The only way to limit access to notes is to put a temporary embargo on the material, the length of which (30, 50 or 75 years) is determined from case to case according to general archival practice. Eventually, when the clause is lifted, the field notes will be publically accessible and, as such, open to other interpretations. Thus, there is a tension between how much information should be removed to protect informants and how much information can be removed or left out of field notes if they are to serve as useful archival material (see Caplan 2010).

The case of 'Hoglebjergnisserne' provides an example of how metadata may become useful. Compared to fairy tales, which often take place once upon a time in a land far away, most local legends actually contain references

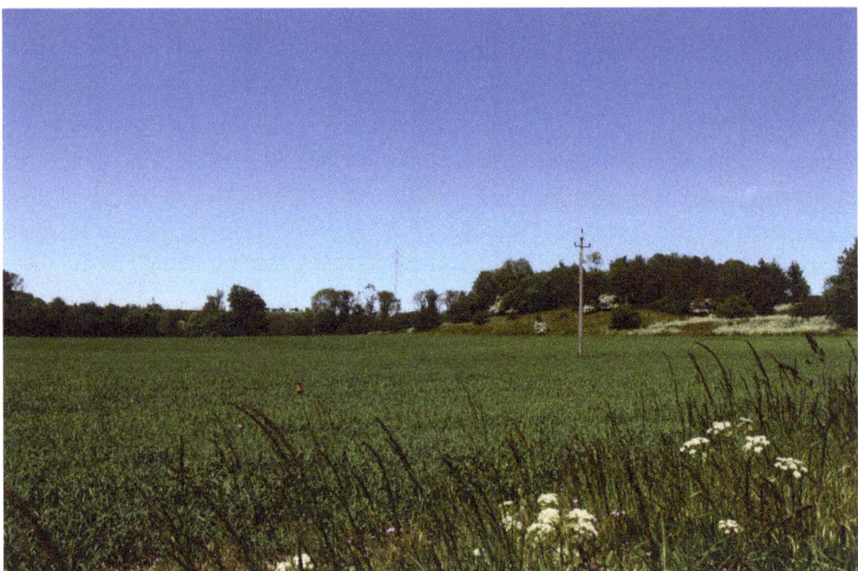

Figure 3.6 Hoglebjerg in 2015.

to actual places and/or real people. The legend discussed here thus takes place at 'Hoglebjergbakkerne' and, as mentioned above, the added note 'top661' refers to the local parish of Klemensker. This information makes it quite straightforward to revisit the place of the legend. Accordingly, Hoglebjergbakkerne (Figures 3.6 and 3.7) is a clearly defined hill with a diameter of about a hundred metres and a summit that is seventy-one metres above sea level. East of the hill, the landscape continues to rise, and there are several other hilltops. However, a few kilometres further west the landscape falls significantly to a plane at about twenty metres high above sea level, before reaching the Baltic Ocean. Currently the centre of the hill is covered by a line of trees, which to some extent limit the view from the top, making it less suitable as a lookout post. While older maps show that this was not always the case, a new map from the Danish Agency of Culture shows that in 2008 a test excavation, marked by the purple dot, revealed traces of neolithic, Bronze Age and early medieval settlements, as well as a later Iron Age grave. As Lars has later learned, by talking to local archaeologists, it was actually Kristensen's version of the legend that, combined with the topographical characteristics of the area, resulted in the test excavation. Thus, on the website of the Danish Agency of Culture we read that the discovery of the grave explains 'why Hoglebjerg is inhabited by *underjordiske*. It rarely fails to be the case that there is a direct connection between Iron Age burials and *underjordiske* strongholds. We did not have any previous knowledge of graves on Hoglebjerg.' (Kulturstyrelsen 2008, our translation).

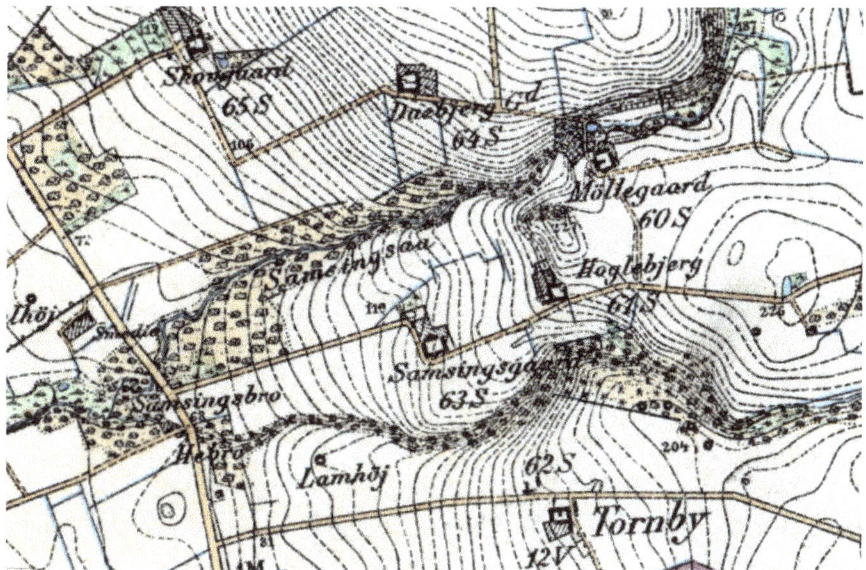

Figure 3.7 Topographical map of Hoglebjerg showing trees only on the northern part of the hill. Contains data from Styrelsen for Dataforsyning og Effektivisering; Høje Målebordsblade (1842–99).

This particular case implies that, if ethnographic field notes are to be valid as archival material, they should not be anonymized or altered to any great extent. While there may be other situations in which anonymization is necessary, none of the above depositions would have been possible without the inclusion of place names. Moreover, it seems impossible to anonymize a whole corpus of notes, not only due to its size and the many cross-references within it, but because of the way notes are produced on a daily basis in the midst of fieldwork. Anonymizing while writing requires a stringent method of translation, or it would otherwise make the notes barely intelligible to their writer. Subsequent anonymizing would require a large and time-consuming editing process. All in all, questions of anonymity and protection remain issues that are only partly solved through temporary embargoes, and there may simply be personal experiences or reflections that the anthropologist feels obliged to leave out. There may also be instances when people will refuse to participate in a project if they know that their statements will be archived. At the same time, it is important to emphasize that a lack of anonymity in field notes is not automatically negative. Marianne has previously interviewed ethnic Danish families about their parenting practices, and they were generally delighted that their stories would enter the archives. Likewise, many visitors actually come to the archives to find material that their grandparents or others before them have contributed.

The old material shows that the value of the actual notes in the archive, together with their metadata, lies in their ability to reopen the story for the reader with regard to the life, diversity and uncertainties that are most often left out in publications. Unlike the published article, in which we have already framed our analysis, the field note is supposed to be open to different interpretations. Field notes read by others no longer serve as mnemonic devices that trigger memories in the way that they do for their writers, but they may reveal other stories. As Lars' rereading of Weiss's material shows, working with the notes of others may make it possible to shed light on the methods of their production and, in some cases, point out inconsistencies between practice and purpose that may challenge the public perception of the producer of the story, both as a fieldworker and as an author of academic texts. This is also exemplified in a recent work by Palle Ove Christiansen (2013), who made extensive use of Kristensen's field records in combination with his personal letters when they became accessible 75 years after Kristensen's death. Christiansen's analysis shows that Tang Kristensen was perhaps driven more by personal experiences of loss and tragedy than concerns about nation-building or serving his fatherland – the kinds of motivations so often ascribed to the early endeavours of folklore studies. This shows how a rereading of notes may sometimes shed greater light on the research process than on the data collected.

Regarding the content of notes, there is a tension between the original idea of the archive, with the kind of notes that Lars studied (descriptions of concrete stories, places etc., and the occasional personal story), and the more processual, relational approach used today, where the context is essential and where it is a known fact that no field note will ever be more than a partial account. This presents a challenge concerning how to transmit reflections and processes on how notes are created today. One suggestion might be to supplement the more factual metadata (regarding names, places etc.) with notes on process and some reflections regarding how the material is perhaps more storied, experiential and open-ended in nature than a long collection of strict positivistic facts. This kind of metatext would not shed light on the content of the note, but rather emphasize the different kinds of embodied and sensuous knowledge that are also written into field notes, and which shape the ways knowledge and notes are produced. However, the question is whether adding more text will necessarily also add more information for future readers, or whether it will just be a new kind of note that they will interpret in the same way as other notes – or both. Like Weiss's records, our notes today will serve as historical sources that will be interpreted in a context based on the kinds of questions that future readers will ask. Historical sources are neither good nor bad in themselves. Rather, the quality of the source depends on how much the notes can be made to assert in relation to the questions raised by the reader (Olden-Jørgensen 2001:50). Hence, notes on notes may seem irrelevant in relation to a future researcher. Yet, they may still provide some background to the more unskilled reader, for instance, the relatives of those who are being interviewed today.

Final notes

Archival records seem to live a life of their own, 'given birth' to by a writer, put into hibernation in the archive, and then brought to life by new readers in a new context. In this chapter, we have focused on the different kinds of records and notes from early collectors of folklore and contemporary ethnographers. There is great potential in using the material of others, but in relation to both existing and newly produced archival material, there are uncertainties when it comes to determining what it is important to record. From a historical perspective, we can see that the issues of what is problematic and the ways the materials should be 'cleansed' change over time. In the old material, context and doubt should be removed in order to produce singular data that can be archived according to genre and topography. Today, we want as much context as possible and worry about ethics and anonymity. It is not unlikely that future readers will be interested in completely different criteria to those we are now concerned with. It is probably not possible to anticipate the kinds of questions future readers will raise or the kinds of information they will want to include in their notes.

If notes are saved, it seems important that it is worth the trouble to disturb their hibernation. For this to be the case, the revised note should contain something not found in the published text. If it does not, why bother? There will probably always be a surplus of stories, but what we are aiming for is both a surplus of metadata and an insight into the uncertainties, problems and reflections encountered during fieldwork. What makes field notes interesting reading is their ability to take the reader, whether their writer or someone else, to new places and bring out new stories. In Lars's case, waking Weiss's notes out of their hibernation opened up a range of alternative storylines, several of which, although they remain to be pursued, were not presented in Kristensen's published version. Whether Weiss or Kristensen would have appreciated Lars's analysis is uncertain, but there seems to be no other solution than for contemporary note writers to accept that, in archiving their notes, they are handing over the authority to contextualize and interpret them to future readers.

In this regard, it may not make much sense to adjust our notes and note-taking to some unknown future. It would seem problematic if, already during the note-writing process, the ethnographer took notes that were less potent or less blunt out of nervousness over the intentions and abilities of a future reader or the future life of the notes. If Marianne chooses to edit her notes, she will be rereading and rewriting them not for the sake of analysis, but with an unknown future and an unknown reader in mind, potentially leading to a Malinowskian separation between the private diary and public field notes. The somewhat fearful anxieties concerning future readers should not lead us to leave out the key elements of our field notes or to minimize the uncertainties they contain, as by and large this is what makes them valuable in the first place.

Thus, the best way to prepare notes for an unknown future is to make them as clear as possible according to current standards. Every ethnographer, not just those working in archives, should reflect on what metadata they include and how notes become useful over time. In practice, all anthropologists are creators of archives. On the one hand, at a time when institutions such as archives and libraries discard books or limit the amount of donated material they accept in order to save money, one may ask what room this leaves for the kinds of material notes represent. Will it be possible for notes to hibernate in archives awaiting future researchers to draw on their potentiality? On the other hand, universities and libraries are working together to explore the potentials of new technology in terms of how to preserve data in the long term. Likewise, there are initiatives to make data more ecological and to establish the ability to share notes (see Chapter 2). All in all, this means that in the near future anthropological notes, and not just research in the natural sciences, may need to be accessible to other people than the original ethnographer. In addition to the challenges we have mentioned concerning the protection of informants, the relationship between notes and text and the distribution of authority between writer and reader, the sharing of notes will probably also require a change in culture among ethnographers. Following the quote from Taussig that we referred to in the introduction, one answer might be for anthropologists to adopt the archival point of view and to regard field notes and notebooks as ends in themselves. Ends that should be cherished, read and shared because of their unavoidable inconsistencies and open-endedness, as they embody a kind of knowledge that is perhaps sometimes just as important and representative of what unfolds in the worlds anthropologists study as the analytical conclusions found in academic publications. If this were to become the dominant understanding of the notes, both in the archival setting and in anthropology in general, the anxiety about sharing one's notes and the worry about their shortcomings should diminish and perhaps, down the line, new ways of publishing ethnography could open up.

References

Caplan, P. 2010. 'Something for posterity or hostage to fortune? Archiving anthropological field material', *Anthropology Today* 26(4):13–17.

Christiansen, P.O. 2013. *Tang Kristensen og tidlig feltforskning i Danmark: National etnografi og folklore 1850–1920*. Copenhagen: Det Kongelige Danske Videnskabernes Selskab.

——— 2004. 'En kulturinstitutions plads i samfundet: om Dansk Folkemindesamlings forhold til arkivmaterialet, formidlingen, forskningen og sin egen samtid gennem 100 år', *Fortid og Nutid* 4:21–41.

Derrida, J. 1995. *Archive Fever: A Freudian Impression*. Chicago: The University of Chicago Press.

Ellekilde, H. and Grundtvig, S. 1944. *Danske Folkesagn 1839–83*. (ed. H. Ellekilde). Copenhagen: Munksgård.

Frykman, J. 1979. 'Ideologikritik av arkivsystemen', *Norveg* 22:231–42.

Hansen, L.H. 2013. 'Indsamling iværksat af Dansk Folkemindesamling – i fortid, nutid og fremtid', *Magasin fra Det Kongelige Bibliotek* 26(3):18–26.

Jackson, J.E. 2016. 'Changes in fieldnotes practice of the past thirty years in U.S. anthropology'. In R. Sanjek and S.W. Tratner (eds.), *eFieldnotes: The Makings of Anthropology in the Digital World*. Philadelphia: University of Pennsylvania Press.

Kofod, E.M. 1984. *Evald Tang Kristensens syn på folkeminderne*. Copenhagen: The Danish Folklore Archives.

Koudal, J.H. 2004. *Folkeminder og dagliglivets kultur. Indføring i Dansk Folkemindesamlings arkiv*. Copenhagen: C.A. Reitzel.

Kristensen, E.T. 1892–1901. *Danske Sagn, som de har lydt i Folkemunde. Udelukkende efter utrykte Kilder samlede og til dels optegnede af Evald Tang Kristensen* (ed. E.T. Kristensen). Aarhus og Silkeborg.

Kulturstyrelsen. 2008. Hoglebjerg. Fund og Fortidsminder: www.kulturarv.dk/fundogfortidsminder/Lokalitet/200480 (accessed 28 January 2016).

Manoff, M. 2004. 'Theories of the archive from across the disciplines', *Libraries and the Academy* 4(1):9–25.

Olden-Jørgensen, S. 2001. *Til Kilderne! Introduktion til Historisk Kildekritik*. Copenhagen: Gads Forlag.

Schwartz, J. and Cook, T. 2002. 'Archives, records and power: the making of modern memory', *Archival Science* 2:1–19.

Taussig, M. 2011. *I Swear I Saw This: Drawings in Fieldwork Notebooks, Namely My Own*. Chicago: The University of Chicago Press.

4

The 'proto-language' of anthropological practice

An exhibition of original field notes

SOFIE ISAGER AHL

Many anthropologists consider field notes to be a core element of ethnographic research. We are even taught by some that 'if you didn't write it down in your fieldnotes, then it didn't happen' (Dewalt and Dewalt 2002:141). Field notes play a crucial role in connecting ethnographers with their subjects, and we often spend an enormous amount of time writing them. For these and other reasons, the notes may take on a unique importance. Robert Sanjek even writes of their 'sacredness' (Sanjek 1990). Still, as Robert Whittemore (2005) notes, we can't tell by the way we teach our discipline that we attach this amount of value and authority to our field-note writing. Very little is taught about field notes; very few experiences are passed on.

In the Department of Anthropology at the University of Copenhagen, a small group of researchers and students conceived the idea of hosting an exhibition of original field notes, accompanied by a workshop in order to further our understanding of anthropological field-note practices and share our experiences. This chapter is based on the notes and questions I collected during the process of curating and participating in the exhibition, '*Skal vi ikke snakke om feltnoter?*' '(Let's talk about field notes'), which took place in April 2016, and was attended by approximately 30 people from anthropology and similar disciplines.

The primary aim of the exhibition was to demystify this somewhat hidden practice of anthropology and to use the collection of field notes as a starting point for a discussion about what they are, or can be, and how we might get better at writing them. We were interested in uncovering how fieldworkers actually write notes and whether it would be possible for us to identify specific genres of writing, and maybe even create a new and more precise language for our own ways of writing and using notes.

For the French author, Leslie Kaplan, writing is a dialogical form always involved with the *Other* (Kaplan 2003). I believe the same can be said of field notes; they are many-voiced texts, filled as they are with different intentions and perspectives: our interlocutor's accounts of events or practices are scribbled down side by side with the anthropologist's own observations, her sensory impressions or thoughts on everyday utterances, practices or conflicts. According to Kaplan, writing has a dialogical nature because there is always an element of 'not knowing' in writing; there is always some kind of mystery involved in writing because we can never fully know how any given word, sentence, perspective or text comes about, or is read and understood. In her book, *Les Outils* (2003), Kaplan writes about the meeting between the text and the writer or reader, and how writing can become a tool to think with. To use the tool of writing, according to Kaplan, means to enable yourself to read a piece of writing – including your own – as if it were written by somebody else; opening up to the mystery of the text in order to see and explore it so that in turn it can move you or the text forward (Kaplan 2003).

We think with the tools we are given throughout our life and education. Field notes are one such anthropological tool, but like any other tool we need to learn how to use it, otherwise it can just get in the way. The anthropologist has a certain insight into how the perspectives and observations in her field notes came about – she might remember the places described, the people quoted; she might even have been aware of their intentions. A book read before the fieldwork might prompt one to notice a certain aspect of a practice – and the anthropologist might have had this in mind when writing the field note, or might recall it when rereading notes. But there is always also a mystery as to why and how we write something down; and there's a mystery to how a certain event, utterance or perspective is either amplified or dissolves over time in our minds, and how different perspectives recur or disappear, moving like waves, through our notes. And there's a mystery to the relationship between our memory and our notes: thoughts or observations from our field may haunt us, but when we find them in our notes the concrete wording might surprise us – how few words we actually wrote on the matter or the context in which we wrote it.

Basically, the dialogical form of writing does not end the moment we close our notebooks after our fieldwork – it continues when we read, re-read, remember or share our notes. Exhibiting field notes gave us the possibility to discuss how we use this tool; it gave us the opportunity to read each other's field notes and to engage in the dialogical form of the texts. It allowed us to follow the creation of these texts; how they seemingly move from some deep conversation to dialogues, to notes on the sound or smell of a place, to some tentative conclusion or confusion. This chapter explores how a linguistic awareness of our noting practices came about when we began to rethink our own notes in the course of witnessing the noting practices of others.

The craft of anthropology

During the colder months of 2016 we asked students and researchers alike to look through attics, drawers, folders and iPhones in the hope of finding old or new field notes that they would agree to share for scientific and educational purposes. Each was asked to scan the original note, if it was physical, or simply send us a pdf in the case of digital notes. And all fieldworkers were to note when and where the note was written, and why they had chosen this particular note to send. We got sixteen notes in total, which is not too impressive when you think about the amounts of field notes that must be in the drawers and folders of anthropologists and students at University of Copenhagen alone, where 500 students, 40 academic staff, and 30 PhD students make up the Department of Anthropology. We exhibited each of the field notes next to the comment sent by the writer, and alongside five very different statements on field notes from the anthropological literature, with which we aimed to highlight the diverse opinions on the role of field notes in anthropology. These included Kathleen and Billie Dewalt's (2002) statement, that if you didn't write it down, it didn't happen; sceptical quotes from Michael Agar (1980) on how overrated field notes are; Robert Whittemore's (2005) poetic perspective that writing field notes is a way of living in the present; and the more practical guidelines by Elizabeth Chiseri-Strater and Bonnie Stone Sunstein (1997) that sum up what should be included in all field notes and how one can structure them.

When collecting the notes, the amount of resistance we met in the process came as somewhat of a surprise. Although half jokingly, some people declined to participate in the exhibition due to 'wanting to get a job afterwards'. Others declined with expressions of fear that their field notes weren't written in 'the way they were supposed to be' or by dismissing them altogether as just notes on random pieces of paper written down too quickly for anybody else to understand. Participants also expressed some of the same feelings during the workshop. One stated that showing one's field notes was unnerving because of the fear that you might be exposed as not having sufficient anthropological craft. This comment seems to hit the core of several of the participants' reactions to the exhibition – especially the students' but also some of the more experienced researchers. Jean Jackson recounts similar experiences in an interview study of anthropologists' relation to their field notes: 'The topic of field notes sooner or later brings up strong feelings of guilt and inadequacy in most of my interviewees.' (Jackson 1990:27). Our small study showed that field notes apparently still have this tendency to bring up all sorts of feelings about one's professional and personal worth. The comments of the participants confirmed the need to open up a discussion on our field-note practices in a more explorative setting, one that could perhaps allow the slight taboo on our notes to be lifted. Exhibiting field notes outside their normal context seemed to have this effect, because it allowed a different framework for conversations on the subject. It was in this way that possible bases for understanding the feelings of fear and inadequacy became apparent. At the exhibition workshop a very experienced fieldworker, looking back at an early example of her own field notes, reflected that she could tell she had attempted to write in a way that would legitimize her as a researcher. In other words, there is a certain performativity to writing field notes that can help us confirm our identity as anthropologists, even when the writing is not directed to an audience. Fieldwork, and with it the symbolic and physical evidence of us 'having been there', our notes, are to be considered aspects of a particular rite of passage as an anthropologist. As Nigel Rapport (1991) points out, writing field notes ties us to an anthropological self in academia, and at the same time allows us to immerse ourselves in the local surroundings and the 'fieldwriting self' we are becoming there (Rapport 1991:11). The recording of anything and everything serves to increases our local belonging, as these notes help us remember the new codes and knowledge needed in order to deepen our understanding of the people and places we study – while at the same time confirming our identity as professional anthropologists.

At the workshop we discussed how our notes serve many and different functions – in the field and at home. Some rightly argued that the most import function of our notes is in the field, when we're learning about the people with whom we study. But if we allow ourselves to think of field notes as a piece of writing in Kaplan's terms – as a dialogical form – we could also ask whether this fear of then showing our field notes is connected to our own ability (or lack thereof) to 'read' our own writings. Does the fear of not having anthropological craft stem from having forgotten that at the time of the notes composition we did not know in full what we were writing – and that this partial ignorance is part of any writing process? Or is the fear rather that others may read something in our notes that we did not see ourselves? Or, on the contrary, do we fear that there is no mystery to be explored in our field notes – that they were just plain 'nothings' (cf. Dickinson 2013)? Either way, it seemed that in trying to decipher a field note together, we opened a gap in time that could only be bridged by imagination. Maybe this was what we needed to accept? That the context of any given note is neither ensured and stable, nor fully controlled by its writer.

Field-note pieces

Out of the sixteen notes at the exhibition, I have chosen seven that I found especially interesting for the purpose of this chapter. They represent the different types of notes we received: some are clearly written up after the fact to show a particular experience or a specific conversation in the field, others are brief and raw, copied directly from the notebook, and one of them is written by an interlocutor rather than the fieldworker himself. The chosen notes are also some of those that resonated most with me when I read them in the exhibition. I thus follow the selection criteria that the fieldworkers often recounted themselves, when picking out a note to exhibit: gut feeling. Most of the people who participated in the exhibition, when asked to contribute, instantly recalled one or more notes that they thought might be useful. In the following pages the translations of the selected notes are shown next to the original, along with the author's text on why they chose it. Part of our experiment with the exhibition was to see where the notes could take us without the contextual work that anthropologists are known for. Can they convey something of importance about the people or places that we have visited, when they leave out much of the information that we normally find indispensable? Are they opportunities for us to get our subject matter to a wider audience of non-anthropologists, because our thoughts and experiences are not encrypted by our normal scientific language and references? Can they be worm-holes for people other than ourselves to understand the places and people we have visited – or are they just black holes devoid of meaning for the uninitiated? In the following pages, you can be the judge.

Magic Technology managing the
energies

45 hectares
80 cows
70 people changed places because
12
You only know the quality of meat, when you
yourself have grown
60 kinds – politically

Being spiritual means goging
meaning to everything

Imaginative – magic cats in me

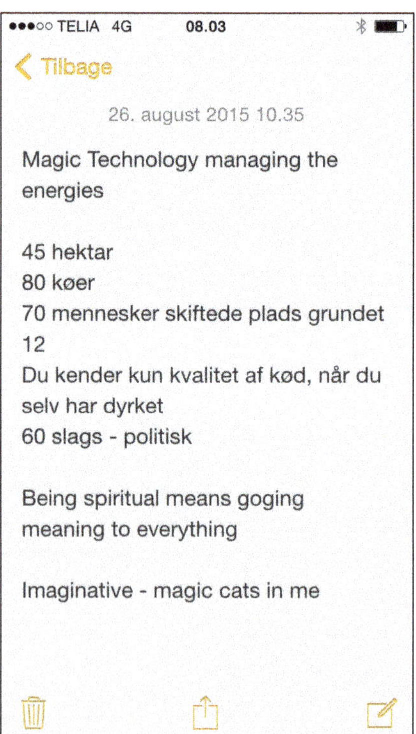

The note actually dates back to a visit to Damanhur after the fieldwork – and as is evident, I desperately needed to get a handle on some figures (people, animals, plants, hectares) and definitions (magic, spirituality, imagination) that had been lost in an optimistic attempt to understand the hundreds of philosophical questions Damanhurians grapple with. The fieldwork was five months long and took place in Damanhur, an eco-village in northern Italy, where I was interested in how the Damanhurians grow vegetables and exchange them with people in the surrounding areas. In Damanhurian agricultural practices, the relationship between humans and plants were presented as a cornerstone in the vegetable's becoming and life energy. They were notably proud of their experiments in the field, which involved singing plants via a technology that detects tensions between leaves and roots and transforms this into music – a bridge between man [*sic*] and the plant, as the Damanhurians say – as well as assistance from other creatures in the universe. Vegetables grown in Damanhur were more than organic, they stressed. But when they sold their fruits and vegetables they downplayed the vegetables' special becoming and life energy and simply presented them as organic and grown in one of the Italian villages, where Damanhur is located, rather than in Damanhur itself.

Ester Fritsch

Memo 10.7.1997

I came rushing across Thy, to the right then left left. Maja came out. Not that tall, pretty old and with her hair parted, amber around the neck and a blue shirt, white trousers. We saw the farm, the road, the garden, all the newly planted trees and the greenhouse with blown out glass windows. In a year our time here will probably be over. A grandchild moves in. A wall with photographs, farm and family, then and now. Coloured rosy cheeks, faded and brand new. Buns, cake and coffee. Talking about the project. At first she had thought no, but then her kids had said: 'If you can help, then why not?' And since then we talked on the phone twice. Yes, guess it would be okay. And why her? It's not something that is easy to talk about. I asked if I could take out the tape recorder, but couldn't we wait, yes, we could. And I changed time. Saw pictures and booklets from the local history association, the book from the film, *A Real Farm Life*, that Maja is in as well. Talked about this and that, mostly about old days, community in the country, family. An hour and a half later: 'Yes, it was okay now.' Then we talked three hours more. Then coffee, buns, cake. Good to calm down. It is still calm.

Excerpt of interview with Maja 6.7.1997

Maja: There are probably some who think I am a weird person, that I'm here slaving away and doing all this, but I feel the best when I'm outside and doing work instead of sitting in here brooding over all the stuff I could be sad about. I'd rather get out and have something succeed out there and enjoy nature, because it is so magnificent. The sunset says all kinds of things. In my opinion, that's where we are as close to heaven as we can come, yes, I think it's beautiful, magnificent. Back then we often drove out to the sea and saw the sunset, but I'm cut off from that today, if it started from there with the sunset, no, I don't think so, we did that on many summer nights, and to see the sun going down there and then that line across the water, oh, it's beautiful, it is. Now I can see it going down up there, and it's weird because when Jørgen [Maja's deceased husband] was a young boy, it was his biggest wish to get up on Møllebakken, because that was where the sun went down, and that he wanted to experience, how it was like up there, where it set and see it, yes yes. He couldn't imagine anything more at that time, but he did make it to Møllebakken, he made it further too. It was his firm belief that something happened up there, where it set. I have to go to the road, otherwise I can't see it properly through the trees. I have to get down there and then I often go for a walk, and I seldom meet anybody and that suits me fine. A calm comes over the mind, that's how I would say it, it is a calm that comes over the mind. 'There is a castle in Vesterled', but there are many other songs that one can connect to the season and the sun.

Memo 10.7.1997

Jeg kom farende hen over Thy, til højre til venstre til venstre. Maja kom ud. Ikke ret høj, ret gammel og med sideskilning, rav om halsen og en blå skjorte, hvide bukser. Vi så gården, vejen og haven, alle de nyplantede træer og drivhuset med udblæste glasruder. Om et år er tiden dér nok forbi. Et barnebarn flytter ind. En væg med fotografier, gård og familie, tilbage og nu. Malede lyserøde kinder, falmede og splinternye. Boller, kage og kaffe. Fortælle om projektet. Først havde hun tænkt nej, men så havde hendes børn sagt: "Hvis du kan hjælpe, hvorfor så ikke?" Og siden talte vi to gange i telefonen. Jo, det var så i orden. Men havde også spurgt sig for i området, og nej, der var ikke andre. Og det var ikke godt. Og hvorfor hende? Det er ikke noget, der er nemt at tale om. Jeg spurgte, om jeg måtte tage båndoptageren frem, men kunne vi ikke vente, jo, det kunne vi. Og jeg skiftede tid. Så billeder og hæfter fra den lokalhistoriske forening, bogen fra filmen, "Et rigtigt bondeliv", hvor Maja også er med. Snakkede om løst og fast, mest gamle dage, fællesskabet på landet, familien. Halvanden time senere: "Jo, nu var det i orden." Så talte vi tre timer mere. Og så kaffe, boller, kage. Godt at falde ned. Der er stadig ro.

Uddrag af interview med Maja 6.7.1997

Maja: Der er nok nogen, der synes, jeg er et mærkeligt menneske, at jeg går her og pukler og laver en hel masse, men jeg er bedst tilpas, når jeg ude og lave et stykke arbejde i stedet for at sætte mig her inde og ruge over alt det, jeg kunne være ked af. Så hellere komme ud og få noget til at lykkes derude og nyde naturen, for den er så storslået. Solnedgangen siger alverdens ting. Der synes jeg, vi er så nær himlen, som vi kan komme, ja, jeg synes, det er smukt, det er storslået. Førhen kørte vi jo tit ud til havet og så solnedgangen, men det er jeg afskåret fra i dag, om det også er derfra, det startede med solnedgangen, nej, det tror jeg som ikke, det gjorde vi mange sommeraftener, og så se solen gå ned der og så en stribe hen over vandet, åh, det er smukt, det er det. Nu kan jeg så se, at den går ned deroppe, og det er mærkeligt, for da Jørgen [Majas afdøde mand] var en bette dreng, der var hans højeste ønske at komme op til Møllebakken, for der gik solen ned, og det ville han altså gerne opleve, hvordan det var deroppe, der hvor den gik ned og se det, ja, ja. Hans fantasi rakte ikke længere på den tid, men han kom op til Møllebakken, han kom også længere. Det var hans helt faste overbevisning, at der skete noget deroppe, hvor den gik ned. Jeg skal ned til vejen, for ellers kan jeg ikke se den ordentligt igennem træerne. Jeg skal derned, og så går jeg tit en tur, og jeg møder som regel ingen, og det passer mig udmærket. En ro falder over sindet, sådan vil jeg nærmest sige det, det er en ro, der falder over sindet. "Der står et slot i Vesterled", men der er også mange andre forskellige sange, man kan sætte i forbindelse med årstiden og med solen.

Notes from the PhD project 'The religious interest'. Most of the interview revolves around Maja's experience with the church through a long life, but as is perhaps clear in the note, Maja lived in the countryside and was strongly oriented in the surrounding landscape in her daily life. Today, almost 20 years later, I am developing a research project on experiences of transcendence in nature and that is why I chose this particular excerpt.

Cecilie Rubow

… When I finally get back to Leonard and the others at the playground Leonard asks me if he can take this shovel (blue), that is lying on the ground. It was Emil's, but he left it. I say that I think he can, 'we can talk with Emil if he comes back for his shovel.' Leonard: 'We can say, that he can have this one (a yellow shovel). It is because I love blue.' I ask what he is playing, he continues with the colours he loves: 'I love blue and green.' Me: 'I love red and green.' Leonard: 'I love blue and green and red. And black.' I repeat with black and he says: 'Do you love black as well?' with a big smile.

Leonard walks away from me and leaves both his boat and shovel with me. I go over to Sigurd and Cassius, who are playing with two trucks on the ground by the tree slide. They fill the trucks with dirt 'to make a dirt slide.' Then Sigurd puts the truck on the slide and some dirt falls onto the slide as it glides down. They say that I can join in. I say that I don't have any truck but can use the boat. Sigurd says I can use his truck (<3). We dig for some time, then Leonard returns and says: '"He" won't give me my bicycle back and "he" says that he will open my eye with a key.' I ask who, he repeats everything with 'he.' I say I understand, but that I would like to know who said it. 'Maks.' I can feel myself getting angry. I say we can go and talk to Maks, he says that I can do it while he waits for me. I ask him to hold my shovel and go looking for Maks. I run around the playground and right then I'm so angry I think I could hit him, but I can't find him, so I go back to Leonard. He says that he knows where to find him and walks with me. We find Maks in the 'goal tent' with somebody, he's sitting on Leonard's bicycle. Me: 'Maks, is that Leonard's bicycle?' 'Yes, and he said I could borrow it.' 'No, he didn't. Give it back right now.' 'He said I could borrow it, right Leonard?' Leonard: 'No.' Maks stands up to give it back, while I say 'and stop saying that you can get people's eyes open with a key, nobody wants to hear that. And it's not even true, you can't do that. You cannot get an eye open with a key.' He answers calmly: 'Yes, I can, with this key.'

I walk away with the bicycle in my hand and Leonard by my side. Leonard wants to park the bicycle, where the other bicycles are parked. We go over there and 'then we can go back to Sigurd and Cassius through the wood.' We go into the wood 'and you lead.' I do, and then I let him lead for a bit and afterwards I lead again.

Arken, 14th of November 2012

… Når jeg endelig kommer tilbage til Leonard og de andre på legepladsen spørger Leonard mig, om han må tage denne skovl (blå), der ligger på jorden. Den var Emils, men han gik fra den. Jeg siger, at jeg tror han må "vi kan snakke med Emil hvis han kommer efter sin skovl". Leonard: "så kan vi sige, at han må få denne her (en gul skovl). Det er fordi jeg elsker blå". Jeg spørger, hvad det er han leger, han fortsætter med de farver han elsker: "Jeg elsker blå og grøn". Mig: "Jeg elsker rød og grøn". Leonard: "Jeg elsker blå og grøn og rød. Og sort." Jeg gentager det også med sort og han siger "Elsker du også sort?" med et smil på munden.

Leonard går fra mig og forlader sin båd og sin skovl med mig. Jeg går hen til Sigurd og Cassius, som leger med to lastbiler på jorden ved den træ-rutschebane. De fylder lasbilerne med jord "for at lave en jordrutschebane". Så sætter Sigurd lastbilen på rutschebanen og nogen jord falder på banen mens den glider ned. De siger jeg må være med. Jeg siger, at jeg ikke har nogen lastbil men jeg kan bruge båden. Sigurd siger jeg gerne må bruge hans lastbil (<3). Vi graver i nogen tid, så kommer Leonard tilbage og siger: "'han' vil ikke give mig min cykel tilbage og 'han' siger han vil få mit øje op med en nøgle." Jeg spørger hvem, han gentager de hele med 'han'. Jeg siger, at jeg godt kan forstå det, men jeg vil gerne vide hvem sagde det til ham. "Maks." Jeg kan mærke jeg bliver sur. Jeg siger, at vi kan gå og snakke med Maks, han svarer at jeg skal gøre det mens han bliver og venter på mig. Jeg beder ham holde min skovl og går efter Maks. Jeg løber rundt på legepladsen og lige der er jeg så vred jeg tror, at jeg ville kunne slå ham, men jeg kan ikke finde ham, så går jeg hen til Leonard igen. Han siger, at han godt kan finde ham og går med mig.

Vi finder Maks i 'målteltet' med nogen, hvor han sidder på Leonards cykel. Mig: "Maks, er det Leonards cykel?" "ja, og han sagde jeg måtte låne den" "nej, det gjorde han ikke. Giv den tilbage nu." "han sagde jeg måtte låne den, ikke Leonard?" Leonard: "nej". Maks rejser sig for at give den tilbage, mens han gør det siger jeg "og lad være med at sige at du kan tage folks øjne op med en nøgle, det gider ingen at høre på. Og det er ikke engang rigtig, det kan du ikke. Du kan ikke få et øje op med en nøgle" Han svarer helt rolig: "Jo, det kan jeg godt med den her nøgle."

Jeg går derfra med cyklen i hånd og Leonard ved mig. Leonard vil parkere cyklen der, hvor de andre cykler holder. Vi går derhen og "så kan vi komme tilbage til Sigurd og Cassius gennem skoven". Vi går ind i skoven "og du fører". Jeg gør det, så giver jeg ham lov til at føre lidt, og bagefter fører jeg igen.

Arken, 14.november 2012.

I chose this piece of ethnography because it was one of those moments in which feelings, friendship and personal involvement took over. It is also a piece of a typical day in the field, with our movement around the playground, our conversations and our flowing, started, interrupted and never finished activities. The part with the boys making a dirt-slide was used in my thesis (with a follow-up that is not here), but all the rest was left out.

The fieldwork took place in a kindergarten in Valby and focused on play.

Flora Botelho

8.7. [1981] visited Felina. Iao Maria is sitting on the floor sewing with ekede Anita. The Iao still has 'kele'. A white cloth wrapped around the neck, and 'mocam' around the over arms, and the hair, that is growing out, covering. An iao with kelé always has to sit low. Preferably on the floor. One is not allowed to go behind her back, should always pass in front. And she is naturally not allowed to have sexual relations. 'Si ela se sujar, os mocam vão até o oso!' says Anita later, when the iao has left. If she breaks any of the rules, especially the one about not having sex, the straw bracelet will penetrate all the way to the bone! She can't walk by the graveyard, eat with a fork, only the fingers. Anita talks more about the thing with 'pureaza'. If a filha-de-santa isn't clean, i.e., if she has had sex before a party, or she is on her period, she can't receive santo. In that case it is not the orixa who comes, but an 'escravo'. It is actually dangerous, if you are receiving, to go to a candomblé if you are unclean, instead of shutting out the slaves when you drum for Exu, you let them in, if there's somebody attending who is unclean. The ekedé can't touch any of clothes of the santo, or have anything to do with the santo if you are on your period. Just as one cannot help with limpezas etc. But at the same time Anita says that by taking a normal shower one can clean oneself after intercourse. Also spiritually that is.

But first Anita tells two long stories.

About her mother, or rather, how she, Anita began in candomble. Her mother was filha-de-santo, and when she died, Anita had to make 'a axexe'. 'Axexe quer dizer bater no pote, tocquar com abano'. She had no money to go through the entire ritual that is supposed to go on for 7 days, according to Anita. (She doesn't know anything about the thing Luisa talked about several times, if it is a mãe.) But she did it the best she could. Lit some candles, gathered her mother's santo's things and carried them out to the foot of a dendé tree. You can also immerse them in the water. That is in Anita's country, that is Angola. Luisa said that they never put anything in the water that has belonged to the dead, because they see the water as holy, in the gege country. The things that had belonged to the ekede at Luisa's were carried out to a place near the railroad bridge, where her country usually places the things. (And he wanted 2000 to carry it out, the bald guy.)

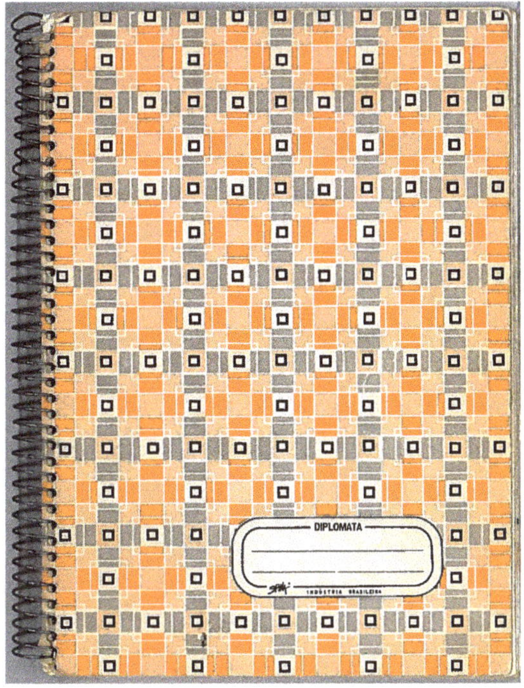
DIPLOMATA
INDÚSTRIA BRASILEIRA

3

[illegible] hele ritualet som [illegible] i 7 dage, iflg. Anita. (Hun kendte ikke noget til det Luiza sagde om flere gange, [illegible]). Hun [illegible] gjorde det så godt hun kunne. Tændte [illegible] lys, samlede sin mors santos [illegible] og bar dem ud ved foden af et dendê-træ. Hun kan også sænke dem i vandet. [illegible] i Anitas nation, som er Angola. Luiza fortalte, at de aldrig lægger noget i vandet, noget der har tilhørt afdøde, fordi de anser vandet for helligt, i jeje-nationen. Tingene der havde tilhørt [illegible] hos Luiza blev båret ud til et sted [illegible] i nærheden af [illegible], hvor hendes nation plejer at lægge tingene. (Og han skulle have 2000 for at bære det ud, han den skaldede mand).

Anita var bekymret fordi hun ikke kunne gennemføre ritualet korrekt. Men "graças a Deus, ela não me incomodaram. Os espíritos ~~[illegible]~~ sentiam, sabe? Eles chegam de noite e quem entrar ande [illegible],

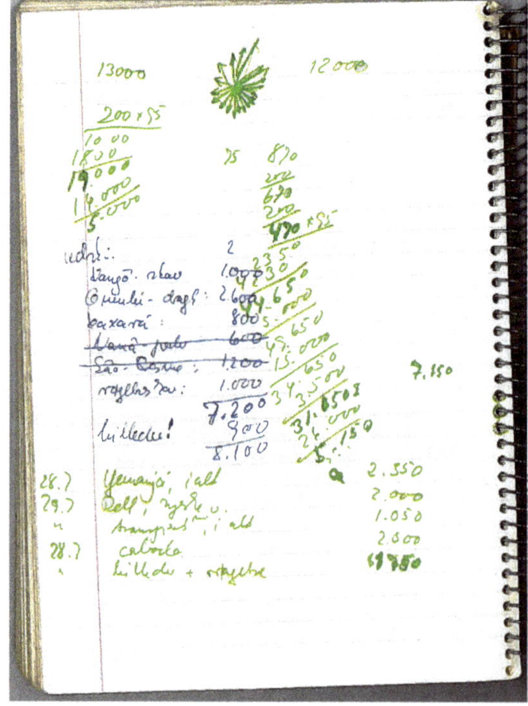

When these notes were written, I had been doing fieldwork in the small town of Cachoeira in Brazil for half a year. In 1981, the laptop was only just invented. I bought my first one in 1989 for 25,000 DKK. It was the most expensive thing I had ever bought. You could get a car for the same money. In 1981 I was on a budget and could not afford a typewriter. I got that later, and my field notes from the late 80s are written on a small red Hermes, which I later gave to my closest friend and informant, Cacau. At age 63, he is today doing his PhD and is very active on Facebook. At that time, he did not know what anthropology was. I told him and gave him Clifford Geertz's *The Interpretation of Cultures*. Since then he has been hooked, and has mapped the entire candomblé landscape in Cachoeiras hinterland.

Field notes from my first long fieldwork in 1981 are written in a notebook of the kind children use in school, and that you could buy everywhere. I had brought black-and-red Chinese writing books from home, but I had used them all.

You can see in the notes that I have written to someone other than myself. But I cannot say who I imagined would read them. I think it was a kind of conscientiousness towards being a researcher. I was extremely aware that I was doing research work and had received a grant – 107,000 DKK, for a year's fieldwork – from the Research Council. And I had of course read Evans-Pritchard and other classics. I think you can see that I have tried to imitate a style that I believed was ethnography. They had no thorough method courses at that time, and when I graduated as mag. scient. there was no guide. My 23 handwritten notebooks are characterized by the fact that I have tried to do what could legitimize me as a researcher. But they also bear the imprint of the fact that I always was in doubt about what that means.

The notes also show how much may be rewritten when working in another language and in a field that is full of alien concepts. *Iao, filha-de-santo, ekede, exu, Kele, axexe* – all these native terms that must be translated and explained before the text becomes meaningful.

Inger Sjørslev

If you have another
baby The mother
did have one more
no. 8 Darwin,
seven years gap.

Birthing, caring,
working mother

Her daughter tells
her she's like a
caribou. She tells
her daughter
to have just 1–2
children.

She repeats what
she has said
before, that

marriage is sacred
here

That kids complete
the marriage and that
earlier, childlessness
could lead to a
peaceful divorce.

Many children
is your wealth.

She says to her own
children, they don't
have to get
married, it's up to
them. Not like her
own parents, who
told her to

get married.

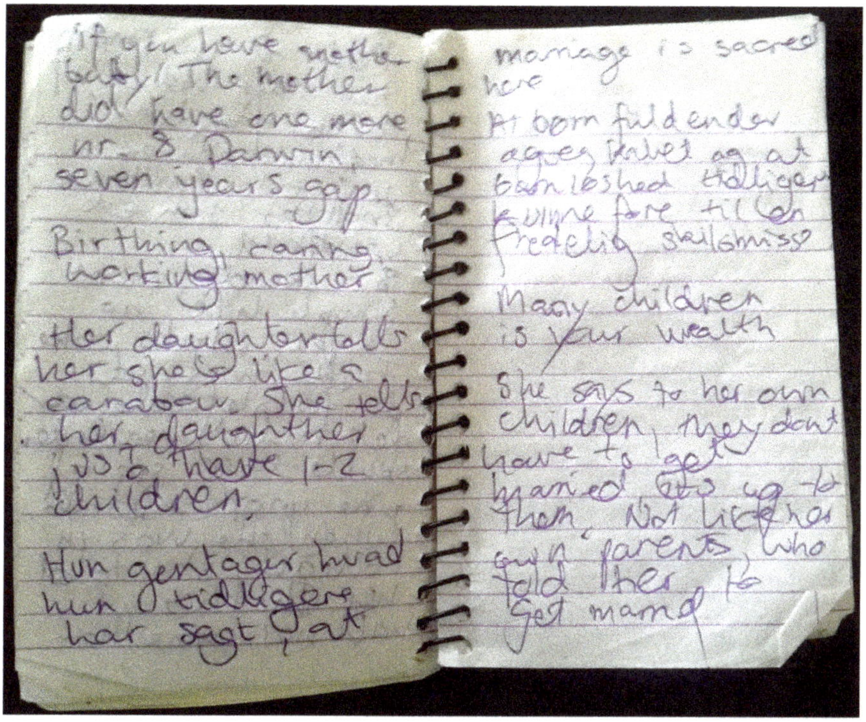

The field note is written in Sagada in the Philippines. I chose it because it is very typical of my notes, often trying to reproduce informal conversations I had in the field, this is quickly written down after a brief everyday conversation with one of my informants.

Marianne Frederiksen

L (12)

LEE

LEE (Tswoun khaub)

LEE

Taj Ntxom
Ntoum

1 2 3 4

LEEBANDED

PHADEE (deceased man)

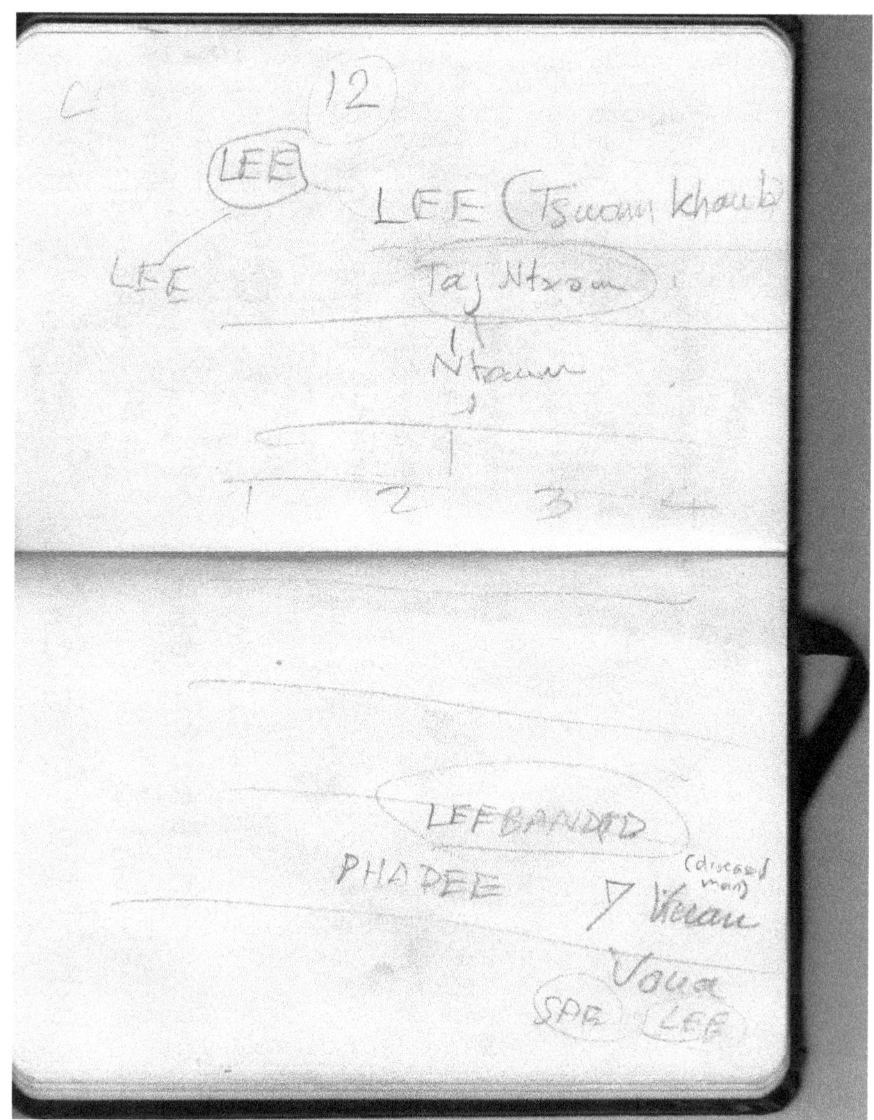

This was written at a funeral in the village of Ban Huai Nam Khao in Petchabun, Thailand, the 7th of March 2016.

I think it's fun because it's a field note written by the informant and not the fieldworker. My informant spontaneously grabbed my notebook and began to draw his family tree in order to explain about his family, relatives and ancestors. (And for me it's filled with ethno-kitsch in the form of clans, classificatory kinship and ancestors-religion.)

Christopher Richard Hansen

Satisfying with the Potato
Bed The soil: compost, fertilizer
Brandfork or tractor

Blow nose in cloth
System around cleaning
Coughing in the rain
Housing Bureau
(Rising prices/ ½ can't
buy house)

chANGE!
Feels good to do something
physical about it with your
hands.

Feels weird to drink out
of a plastic-bottle

Farm walk (what's going on)

Waste to move something
down - compost

Sunflowers towards the
school
(2 beds for kids)

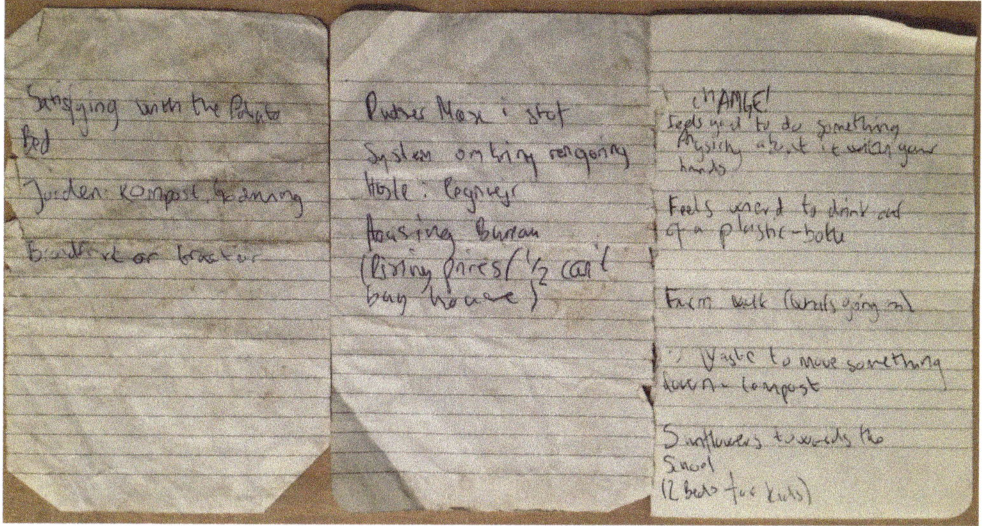

The notes were taken during fieldwork on urban agricultural in Portland, Oregon in the spring of 2015. To me, the notes represent not only the text they contain. They also elicit reflection on where and when they were written, since all three contain traces of the soil that I had on my hands while I took them. Furthermore, they are marked by a short stay in the pocket of a pair of worn-out Carhartt pants. These field notes thus recall a mood and setting as well as information about what happened exactly this day on the farm.

Maia Ebsen

The 'proto-language' of field notes

When reading the notes above I'm left with a strange feeling of suspense. I am there with the fieldworker, who may not know the complete significance of her observations. One catches the fieldworker experiencing something for the first time and I, as a reader, experience it for the first time along with them. I don't know exactly where to focus or what to expect as a reader, because the fieldworker doesn't either. This allows something unexpected to happen – it opens a space for me, the reader. The small drama of the playground above seems intensified when it stands alone without the calming presence of a knowing anthropologist who tells us how to interpret the drama and gives us a proper context for understanding it. We are right there with little Leonard in the playground, who lost his bike to a bully. For this brief moment of his life, we are feeling the confused anger of his situation – nothing more than that, a raw, simple feeling of right and wrong. And in another note we can almost feel the harsh west wind on the heath in Thy, when Rubow writes that she came rushing across the land, to the right, then left, left. The wind seems to be there in the rhythm of her notes – right, then left, left. The field notes all lack the intellectual overview that we are accustomed to in anthropological writings. When they are at their best, there's a direct and curiously enticing feeling of vulnerability and presence, at times like reading a random page in a novel – or in the case of Fritsch's, Ebsen's and Frederiksen's field notes, a curious form of modern poetry.

For most anthropologists, field notes are pieces in a large research puzzle. But by allowing these pieces of writing to stand alone we see that they can simultaneously be 'nothing yet' and engaged in multiple, potentially concurrent readings of otherness. This multi-temporality and multi-voiced quality endows them with an ambiguity closer to dream images. Or as Rapport puts it: 'Field notes' other-worldliness appears out of place within the literary genre of waking reality.' (Rapport 1991:13). Field notes are not normally read by anyone other than their writer before they are made 'whole' and given a place in a 'coherent' text as Rapport writes (Rapport 1991:13). But they alone have this quality that could best be described as a sort of proto-language: not yet cultural description; not yet anthropological writing. They are not full thoughts; they do not give coherent pictures. They are in the process of becoming. For Ludwig Wittgenstein, for instance, notes were an essential part of working and thinking. He archived his notes in boxes, named the boxes, and later constructed his manuscripts by dictating from these unstructured boxes of notes. His writing and thinking was bounded by loose notes. With reference to this note-taking practice, Rapport reflects:

> Field notes are a magical concept, magical in the dual conventionality of their composition and usage. What they deserve is an analysis 'with blurred edges,' in Wittgenstein's wording, producing a general picture whose lineaments are indistinct and do not prescribe one precise way of viewing or another.
>
> (Rapport 1991:13)

We may then ask, what would such an analysis with blurred edges look like? I believe there is an untapped analytical potential in paying attention to the proto-language of our own field-note practice. Could we not, by observing how we write in the field, get better at analysing our own field notes as texts, as language, as tools, and from there draw our subsequent analytical conclusions? Surely, as Rapport writes, if we refrain from transfixing the field note, it is possible to preserve the ambiguity of its author's position and the multi-voiced and multi-temporal qualities inherent it (Rapport 1991:13). Perhaps an analysis with blurred edges is one in which we take our own intuitive sense of language more seriously and let the proto-language of our notes inspire our thinking. Is there a potential in exploring the gaps in meaning when an iPhone autocorrects our words (when 'magic acts in me' becomes 'magic cats in me') or to actively use dreams or an interlocutor's note-taking in our analysis?

I suggest that we could draw on literary studies of language in order to enhance our awareness of this linguistic potential of our notes, looking, for instance, to Mikhail Bakhtin, who writes:

> The word in language is half someone else's. It becomes 'one's own' only when the speaker populates it with his own intention, his own accent, when he appropriates the word, adapting it to his own semantic and expressive intention. Prior to this moment of appropriation, the word does not exist in a neutral and impersonal language, […] but rather it exists in other people's mouths, in other people's contexts, serving other people's intentions: it is from there that one must take the word, and make it one's own.
>
> (Bakhtin 1981:293–4)

The field notes from the exhibition were caught in this in-between space that Bakhtin describes: still in part serving other people's intentions, other people's contexts. The notes were literally filled with other people's words when the fieldworker referred to what she had been told or when interlocutors were quoted. This is evident in Ebsen's notes, when she writes: 'Feels good to do something physical about it with your hands.' She wrote the phrase in English though most of the note is in Danish, and the wording thus indicates that she's quoting someone speaking English, but we can't be sure where the phrase is coming from, in what context it is written or whose intention it's serving. The same was true of Frederiksen's note, when she writes: 'Many children is your wealth.' I expect that this too is a quote from an interlocutor, as she writes in her comment that the notes try to reproduce an informal conversation she had with an interlocutor, but we don't know who it was and the phrase was – like Ebsen's – not framed with quotation marks. In the context of each note, the associated remarks seem conclusive, though they probably aren't the fieldworkers' own conclusions. This is especially true of Hansen's field note, which was written by an interlocutor who had sketched out his family tree – the note was literally out of the fieldworker's hands and was entirely serving an interlocutor's context and intention. The act of analyzing our notes constructs and reorients this language, to align it entirely with the anthropologist's own intentions and chosen context. But even though the intentions and contexts of the words in the notes seemed dispersed, Bakhtin can help us understand how our notes are not 'nothings', because the words are relics of complex interactions and negotiations of intentions. He writes: 'Within the arena of almost every utterance an intense interaction and struggle between one's own and another's word is being waged, a process in which they oppose or dialogically interanimate each other.' (Bakhtin 1981:354–5).

The utterances of the exhibited field notes are more complex and dynamic than they appear. Bakhtin's perspective on language allows us to understand them as a force constantly interacting with, shaping and reacting to both that which precedes and that which is still forming. He sees writing as an ongoing dialogue – many-voiced, playful, detailed, tentative, fleeting and always becoming. And so are the field notes: unfinished, relative, with many voices competing and intermingling; they shape the texture of the ideas being formed, but never fix them. In that way, they might even be wiser than we are.

We need tools to think with. We don't always know how our own writings and notes can become such a tool for us, but reading other people's writings might help us in this endeavour. Like speaking, writing is characterized by the fact that the one writing never has the full overview of what she has actually written. Surely, Freud has taught us this. There's more to our own writing than we know. But where Freud told us that a slip of tongue or pen reveals an unconsciously subdued wish or internal train of thought, this shared reading of field notes did not reveal an inner secret, but rather a professional secret, which, like the body of an ostrich hiding its head in the ground, has perhaps always been visible if we just dared to look. This public secret is that there is always more to a note than one can consciously grasp. Perhaps that is reason enough that we should dare to take our notes seriously – not only as a way to legitimize ourselves as anthropologists, not only as a tool for enhancing our learning and remembering in the field, but also as texts, as language in its own right.

The blind spots and perceived, but not consciously registered, observations of our notes may speak when others cast their light upon them. These others may include the fieldworker's future self or may be a colleague who looks at the note as a text, that is, as words intentionally put on paper by someone, but who and why? Or it may be an outside reader. So perhaps we should allow more space in our articles and publications for field notes. Either as raw notes in their own right – allowing space for the reader to imagine and interpret. Or, when the material and context allows it, share the path from fieldwork event to written text: how an event has been re-written again and again, slowly but surely aligning the intentions of the text with our anthropological analysis and authority. Or could we imagine fieldwork in which we involved people in the notes that they had inspired, and then incorporated this dialogue in the analytical process presented in the final text, so that the fieldworker wasn't the only 'text-worker'? Perhaps a more open and inclusive analysis – one with blurred edges as Rapport says – might not only be what our field notes deserve, but would also help us qualify and understand the dialogical aspects of anthropological knowledge formation and critique.

References

Agar, M.H. 1980. *The Professional Stranger*. Orlando: Academic Press, Inc.

Bakhtin, M. 1981. *The Dialogic Imagination* (trans. C. Emerson and M. Holquist). Austin: University of Texas Press.

Chiseri-Strater, E. and Sunstein, B.S. 1997. *FieldWorking: Reading and Writing Research*. Upper Saddle River, NJ: Blair Press.

Dewalt, K.M. and Dewalt, B.R. 2002. *Participant Observation: A Guide for Fieldworkers*. Oxford: AltaMira Press.

Dickinson, E. 2013. *The Gorgeous Nothings* (eds. J. Bervin and M. Werner). New York: New Directions.

Jackson, J.E. 1990. '"I am a fieldnote": fieldnotes as a symbol of professional identity'. In R. Sanjek (ed.), *Fieldnotes: The Makings of Anthropology*, pp. 3–33. Ithaca, NY: Cornell University Press.

Kaplan, L. 2003. *Les Outils*. Paris: P.O.L.

Rapport, N. 1991. 'Writing fieldnotes: the conventionalities of note-taking and taking note in the field', *Anthropology Today* 7(1):10–13.

Sanjek, R. 1990. 'Fire, loss, and the sorcerer's apprentice'. In R. Sanjek (ed.) *Fieldnotes: The Makings of Anthropology*, pp. 34–44. Ithaca, NY: Cornell University Press.

Whittemore, R.D. 2005. 'Fieldnotes, student writing and ethnographic sensibility', *Anthropology News* 46(3):25–6.

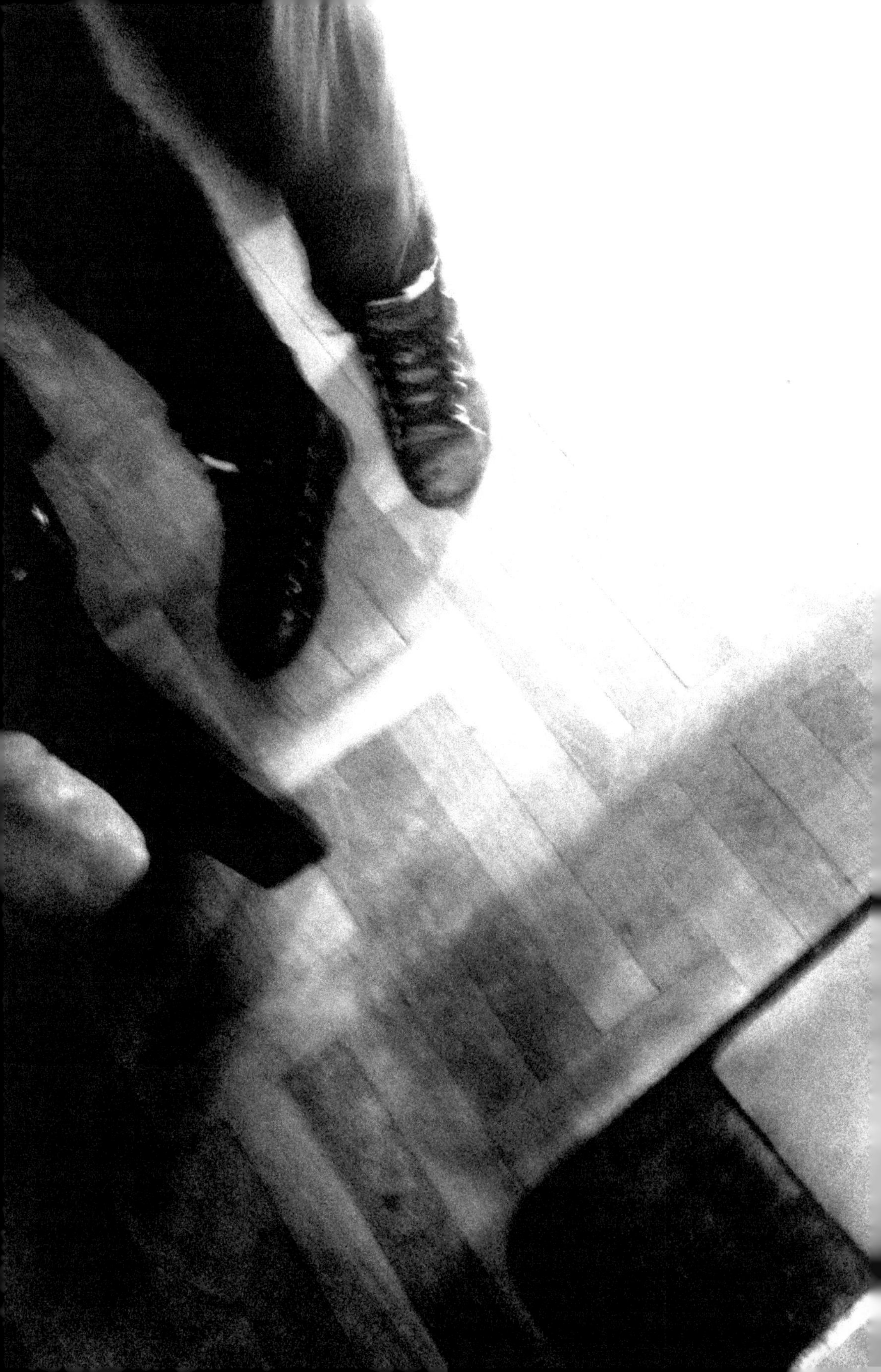

5

The wind in the mirror

Some notes on the unnoteworthy

Martin Demant Frederiksen

The weekend went by as usual, although I almost got killed on Friday. Vano and I texted each other back and forth during the day and agreed to meet up in front of his workplace in Vake [Tbilisi's business district] at 4 pm as has become custom. I walk from my apartment instead of taking a taxi or the bus. It only takes 35 minutes, although it is extremely windy and at times almost impossible to see anything because of the sand and dust whirling around, my cigarette kept being blown out. I am in front of Vano's office around ten-to-four. Today there are no flowers outside the florists and no newspapers outside the little kiosk. I know Vano is probably not busy inside, but most likely watching *Buffy the Vampire Slayer*, but also that he probably won't leave before 16:00, so I don't text him to let him know I've arrived.

So I just stand waiting in the wind. Next to me a high-rise building is being constructed. Despite the weather a number of workers can be seen way up in the air, on the sides of the building. My eyes wander up and at some point a part of the roof, or maybe a part of the construction, comes loose and starts whirling down towards the street. It's a large 1 × 2 m iron plate and it flies down from the top and across the street, hammering down just in front of a bus on the other side. The bus-driver manages to hit the brakes just before the plate smacks down just in front of the bus. I look at the scene somewhat dumbfounded, and while I'm looking across the street another piece hammers down just next to me – it doesn't touch me, but I can feel the wind suddenly reversing on my cheeks. I look at it and look up.

On the opposite side of the fallen iron plate an elderly man is also looking at it, possibly thinking, as I am, that we might as well have been lying under it. '*Sheni deda*... [fuck your mother...]' he says, shakes his head and walks away.

The minute later Vano comes out from his office. I tell him about the incident, but he just smiles a bit and shrugs his shoulders. We walk towards his doctor's office and Nika meets us on the way. We don't talk much as sand blows into our mouths whenever we open them. Vano get's a new penicillin prescription for his bad eye and the doctor tells him, once again, to take a break from drinking, and Vano tells her, once again, that he probably won't.

We take a taxi to Saburtalo and go to the small shop below Vano's apartment building. Inside, Nika and I buy juice, two bottles of vodka and six packs of cigarettes at one stall, while Vano buys cheese, tomatoes, cucumbers and a piece of ham at another. No bread, as Vano says he has some at home (which turns out to be mouldy, but we eat the good parts as nobody bothers to go out to fetch a fresh loaf). We walk to the entrance of Vano's building and take the lift up. Once inside, Nika and I get ashtrays and glasses in the kitchen, put the vodka bottles in the freezer and take out an ice-cold, half-empty bottle from inside, bringing everything to the living room where Vano is putting on music (we begin with Pet Shop Boys as I remember). We pick sand from our noses and ears and down a few glasses. A bit later Paata shows up.

(Tbilisi, March 2014)

Scene

'If you look for a meaning, you'll miss everything that happens.' – Andrei Tarkovsky (quoted, Strick 2006:71)

I had to admit that I had never seen a Tarkovsky movie before. And I knew instantly that this was a source of embarrassment. If, despite the futility of that endeavour, my aim was in fact to grasp what was going on in this setting, how would I ever perceive anything without having watched Tarkovsky? The question was never posed directly, but I knew it was present. Just like many other things or aspects or relations that 'were there' without me having any clue as to how I was to take note of them, let alone put them into words.

It had been a very straightforward agreement from the outset, that I shouldn't come there and perform my role as a researcher. During the four months of fieldwork that made up the first part of the project, I should come as me. After initiating the fieldwork, this agreement was never again verbalized, but there were times where I felt hints being directed towards me in terms of how I could proceed with both being a researcher and definitely not being a researcher, and how I could establish a method for grasping what was, and what was not, happening. One such instance was when Vano and I watched Tarkovsky's *Mirror*, and Vano directed my attention towards the wind: the one short scene where a strong gust of wind flows across a field, creating waves in the grass along its way. We watched it over and over again. And then again. And at some point I think I got it, I think I grasped what was not being said and how to take note of it. This is what this chapter is about.

Bargain

'Research bargains' are an aspect of many researchers' fieldwork, although of course they vary in degree and consequence (Sluka 1995). My first meeting with Vano took place more than ten years ago. We watched *Drowning by Numbers* (1988) that evening, a film based on repetition and rules of games. I was conducting fieldwork in Tbilisi and we had met by chance via a mutual friend, who at one point took me to Vano's apartment. There were a few other people present that evening, and during the following years I would meet with them whenever I was in the city. By 2012 I learned from another mutual friend that this group of people were described as nihilists, both by themselves and others, and not just by people who knew them but also by various politicians terming people like them as a rising threat to society. These were people who deliberately disengaged from society, and through this posed a challenge to the moral, political and social values of the country (Frederiksen 2018). This made me consider how an anthropological study of nihilism, nothingness and meaninglessness could be conveyed. How could it be done and what would its outcome be? So I told Vano that I had an idea to conduct fieldwork on this theme, and that I would like to base part of it on him and his friends, coming as I had done many times before to his apartment, but this time much more often and with research in mind. Vano was pleased that we would get to see each other more, but he wasn't really that interested in the research itself, even though he had been influential in defining it. He had read the result of a previous project on boredom that I had carried out some years earlier (Frederiksen 2013), and after reading it remarked that, although he liked it's gloomy nature, I was too preoccupied with analytically drowning everything in 'meaning', even in empirical cases where there was, in his opinion, no meaning to be found. I didn't know, in Vano's optic, how to handle meaninglessness – I consistently tried to turn nothing into something. I could thus base part of my study on him under the condition that I would stop doing this. That is, I was given permission for this fieldwork, so long as I would stop trying to make sense of things that did not make sense in themselves. In addition, while I could participate in everything, he did not want to be interviewed and he did not want me to sit and take notes when we were together.

Unnoteworthy

Not being able to take notes while in the field is not something particular to the setting described here. In my own previous fieldwork, note-taking has usually been done during periods of sitting alone in the evening, unfolding jottings, reconstructing events and conversations. Indeed, as Emerson, Fretz and Shaw argue, note-taking often requires the researcher to recall in order to write, something that can be done by 'recalling noteworthy events in the sequence in which one observed and experienced them' (1995:48). This, they hold, may proceed as a stream of consciousness (a principle we will return to later) in which the 'noteworthy' and 'significant' become pivotal points for creating a full set of elaborated notes.

The tricky aspect during the fieldwork on nothingness that I eventually carried out in Georgia in 2014, was that there was rarely anything noteworthy to ignite my memory as I, after an evening or weekend at Vano's, returned to my own apartment in Tbilisi. Often very little had happened, or the same had happened again, or nothing had happened twice. As often before, I had found inspiration in Kathleen Stewart's *Ordinary Affects* (2007) and her wish to capture affects not in terms of 'what they might mean in an order of representation, or whether something is good or bad in an overarching scheme of things' (ibid.:3):

> They're things that happen. They happen in impulses, sensations, expectations, daydreams, encounters, and habits of relating, in strategies and their failures, in forms of persuasion, contagion, and compulsion, in modes of attention, attachment, and agency, and in publics and social worlds of all kinds that catch people up in something that feels like *some*thing.
>
> (ibid.:2, emphasis in original)

But during this particular fieldwork I in some sense wanted to do the opposite of Stewart. I wanted to capture the things that catch people up in no-thing. Not to make sense, but to provide sensations that reflected what was happening (or not happening). And as Samuel Beckett's writings have shown, a lot may be happening when nothing is happening (Weller 2010). The problem I faced, however, when returning to my own apartment, was that I was very obviously not Samuel Beckett. I had no training in writing about nothing or in elaborating something that was almost void of content. I had experience in taking note of the noteworthy, but less so in taking note of the unnoteworthy, which at this time seemed to be all there was.

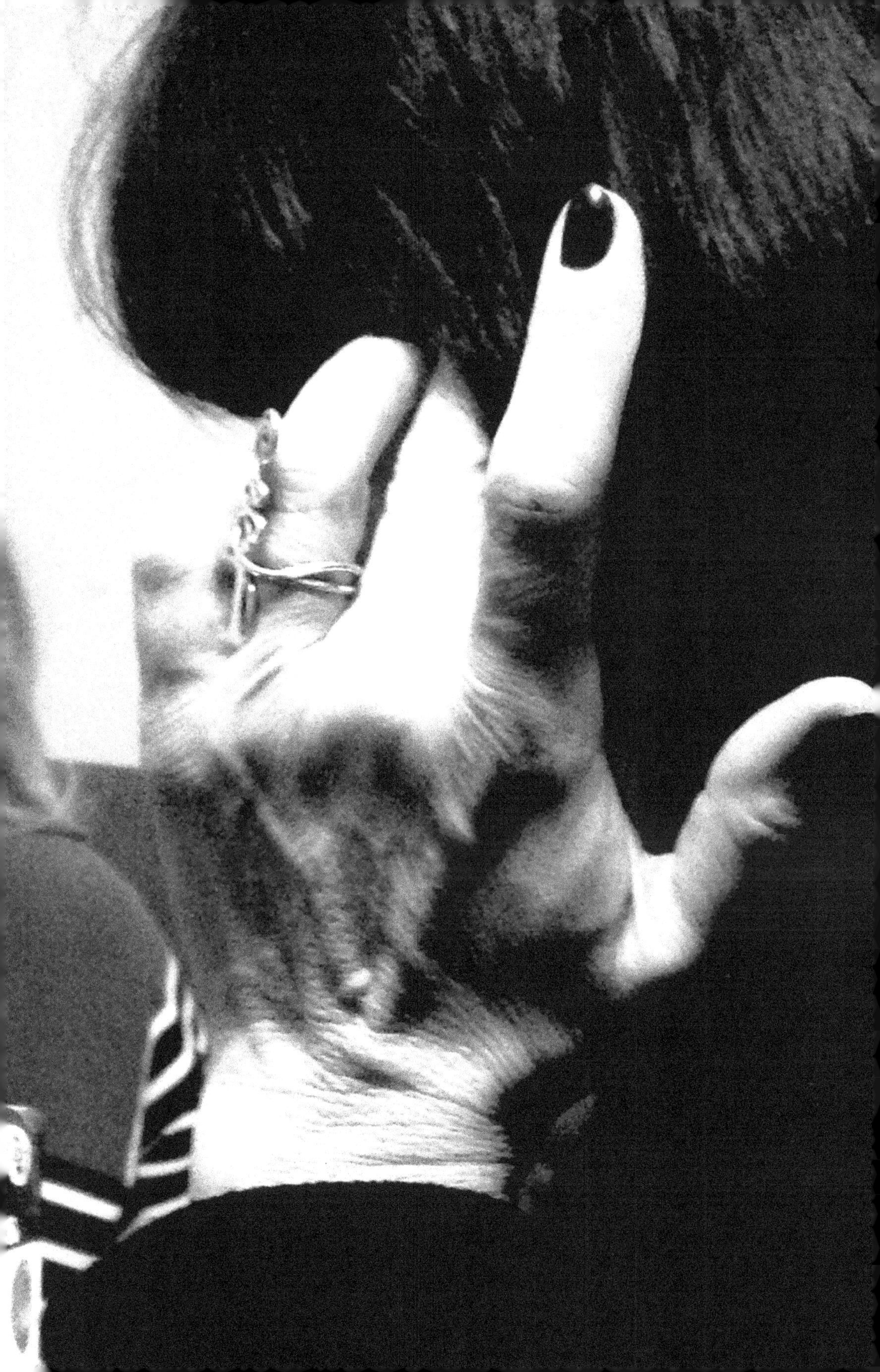

Michael Taussig has argued that a field note or a notebook has its own form and content, 'and should not be seen as a mere stepping stone to the polished end-product of a book or article' (Taussig 2012:515). The challenge for me was thus in a sense twofold: taking note of the unnoteworthy in a way that would also lend it a form or a content that could later be represented in a manner that would create a sensation of it, rather than analytically making sense of it, as the latter would go against my agreement with Vano.

Wind

So, at some point I was certainly done describing the living room that we most often sat in at Vano's:

> Not much seems to have changed from when I first came here seven years ago. The large, red sofa set is the same, as are the paintings on the walls, and the small coffee table in the middle, now, as most times, filled with small glasses, a few bottles of vodka, grape juice, peach juice, cola, various cigarette boxes. The three ashtrays that are constantly filled and emptied. But there is a new device by the TV so that Vano can plug his phone to the TV and listen to music that way.
>
> (Tbilisi, March 2014)

I was also done describing the view:

> we are on the 8th floor and there is a balcony by the living room. It's wide but we never sit here together, but often someone is out there to get a bit of fresh air, when the living room becomes heavily filled with cigarette smoke. From the balcony one looks down into the yard of the Soviet building block we're in. It looks like any other suburb in the city. This could really be anywhere in the outskirts of Tbilisi.
>
> (Tbilisi, March 2014)

And I was done describing the kitchen, the toilet, the hallway, the lift leading to the eighth floor and the small shop downstairs – all spatial aspects and all the people present had been put into detailed notes, as had whatever might have taken place immediately before going there, such as the day when a large piece of metal nearly landed on my head. But I had difficulty in reconstructing what had been said. Often this was because there was a great deal of randomness involved, and I couldn't find a way of putting whatever bits and pieces I remembered into a sequence or narrative.

But then one afternoon, after having spent the night at Vano's place, and the morning in his kitchen eating soup and drinking beer, and midday not taking a walk, he asked which Tarkovsky films I liked. Which was none, as I had never seen any. After what I remember to be a very long silence, he suggested that we start with *Mirror*. Filmed in Russia in the early 1970s, *Mirror* is Andrei Tarkovsky seventh film as director, and it is often seen as a cinematic expression of the stream of consciousness principle most often found in literature, although in a more fragmented manner. Not long after the film had started, Vano froze the frame. The wind scene was coming up and this I should take note of (mentally, that is, not on paper). And so we watched it. And then he played back, and we watched it again. And then he played back. The scene is difficult to describe. I tried many times while in Tbilisi, as Vano sent me a link so that I could re-watch it in my own apartment – 'there is a man walking across a field and as he is midway a gust of wind suddenly appears out of nowhere, creating waves in the long grass. The man stops. And then it happens again – the wind blows through the grass. And then the film continues.' (Tbilisi, May 2014). But others have managed in a more succinct manner, one of them Thomas Redwood, who details it as follows:

> In shot VII of Scene 1, after the first gust of wind ripples through the field past the doctor, the spectator is presented with a close-up image of Masha standing in front of a row of trees and looking to the left of the frame towards the doctor. After a moment´s reflection, Masha then turns to the right of the frame and begins walking to the dacha [...] The next shot (IX) cuts back to a long-shot of the doctor still standing in the field as another strong gust of wind passes through [...] This is followed by another close-up of Masha (shot X) back where she was at the beginning of shot VIII, in front of the trees, once again staring toward the left of the frame [...] Masha then, once again, moves rightwards towards the dacha and at this time the camera follows her. In other words, just as the two shots of the doctor presents a repetition (of the gust of wind) so do the two shots of Masha. Shots VII and X have shown her performing exactly the same action. Viewed attentively, the structure of this brief early sequence clearly negates any sense of straightforward spatial and temporal logic [...] Rather than functioning to represent a linear sequence of events (a sequential continuum of time over four successive shots), Tarkovsky's strategy here serves two explicitly non-linear functions. Firstly [...] the two shots of the doctor in the field establish the wind as a significant motific device. Secondly [...] the two shots of Masha cue the spectator to infer that decoupage sequences in *Mirror* cannot be relied upon to present transparent linear arrangements of diegetic space and time.
>
> (Redwood 2010:105–6)

Non-linear decoupage

Let us dwell for a moment on the notion of 'decoupage' mentioned by Redwood, before we return to Vano's apartment. In French cinema, this is a term that describes the last stage of script-writing, as well as a film's structure after the final cut has been made in the editing room. It may, according to Valerie Orpen, be translated into 'continuity editing': a conceptualization of film 'as a convergence of the spatial fragments of the shooting process with the temporal fragments established in editing' (Orpen 2003:2). It thus differs from the notion of montage, most often associated with Sergei Eisenstein, which is a way of cutting something into sequences, and solely a mode of editing.

Tarkovsky himself was strongly opposed to Eisenstein and the use of montage in film, as he saw montage as a question of fragmenting reality and then reorganizing it into a dialectical framework from which new ideas and new meanings were meant to emerge. Tarkovsky's method (for instance in his use of long takes) was instead one of shifting focus from narrative to duration and thus creating a semantic crisis where 'the meaning is not imposed on the viewer, but is always hidden away or scattered in time. The constant expectation that semantic implications will reveal themselves in the single continuum of the long take tends to exhaust the viewer. No quick-and-easy resolution is available – hence Tarkovsky's notoriety as a challenging or even "boring" director.' (Skakov 2012:7).

Tarkovsky insisted that editing should not be a formative element of a film – a film is not made on the editing table, as montage cinematographers held (Tarkovsky 1986:114). Instead, while finishing *Mirror*, editing 'was a serious test of how good our shooting had been' (ibid.:117). He was critical of montage cinema's belief that bringing two concepts together engendered a third, new one. As he notes, '"Montage Cinema" presents the audience with puzzles and riddles, makes them decipher symbols, take pleasure in allegories, appealing all the time to their intellectual experience. Each of these riddles, however, has its own exact, word for word solution.' (ibid.:118).

Sculpting

Based on the principle of non-linear decoupage, Tarkovsky's alternative to narrativity, linearity and montage, was to conceive of filming as 'sculpting in time' (Tarkovsky 1986). Nariman Skakov writes in relation to this conception that the term 'cinematography' is inherently spatial in that it consists of the terms *graphia* (writing) and *kinēma* (movement), and it becomes a principle of inscribing motion. By referring to his own practice as a question of sculpting in time, Tarkovsky conceived of a process that still retains the question of inscription (through sculpting) but replaces *kinēma* with *chronos*. The objective becomes one of capturing temporal flows (Skakov 2012:8). It is significant here, Skakov mentions, that the word Tarkovsky uses for 'sculpting' is the Russian verb *vaiat*, which is also related to the notion of 'weaving'. This entails that his films 'have a certain texture, a textile labyrinth, where the relationship between individual temporal threads (past-present-future) is not immediately apparent' (ibid.:13). So, again, it is a question of non-linearity and scattered time.

The long takes and the often-time absence of action creates a certain monotony in Tarkovsky's films – there are rarely (if ever) any high points. There are no events that stand out as more significant than others. There are long passages where nothing takes place, and in this Tarkovsky's films have an affinity with Samuel Beckett's writings, and with Vano's apartment; and his viewpoint has an affinity with Taussig's critique of reorganizing an already fragmented social reality (as initially present in a notebook, or for Tarkovsky in the shooting itself) in order to make it make sense later through analysis, or indeed film editing.

Reflection

Mirror is a classic example of the principle of sculpting in time, in that it consists of a series of frameworks that remain un-unified via an overarching narrative line, making any narrative reading of the film impossible. There is no differentiation between past, present and future, and no clear explanations of what is dream, memory or reality (ibid.:100, 102). Tarkovsky wanted to create a reflection (hence the title) without necessarily revealing what was reflected.

My interest here of course is to examine what *Mirror* mirrors in terms of my own fieldwork and note-taking practice. That is, what it reflects in that particular context. As we repeatedly watched the wind scene together, Vano said about the appearance of the wind: 'was it supposed to happen or not? Was it just random and then incorporated or was it carefully planned? All of that doesn't really matter.' Whether or not there was a point, or a form of meaning, was unimportant – if there was one it was hidden away, scattered, and would not add anything if it was ever to appear.

Notes

How does one sculpt a note? Whereas I consistently lacked conversations in my field notes, there was one place where they could be found: online. When not together, Vano and I spent a great deal of time chatting with each other from our respective apartments in Tbilisi when neither of us could be bothered to take a taxi across the city to meet in person, or when Vano was at work. Even these chats were often extremely random, but after having re-watched *Mirror* when I returned to Denmark I began, with permission from Vano, to revisit these communications and work towards highlighting their frequently

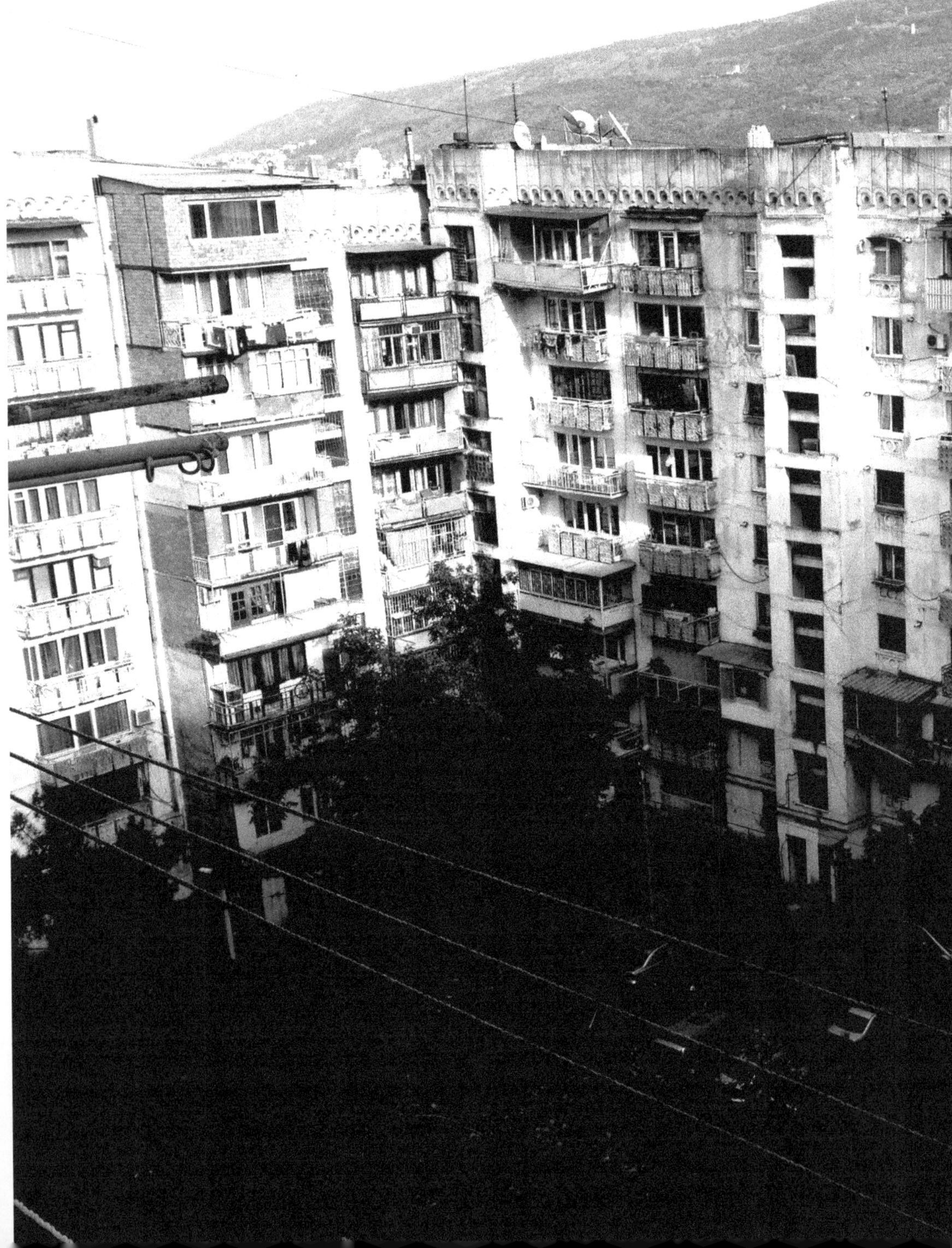

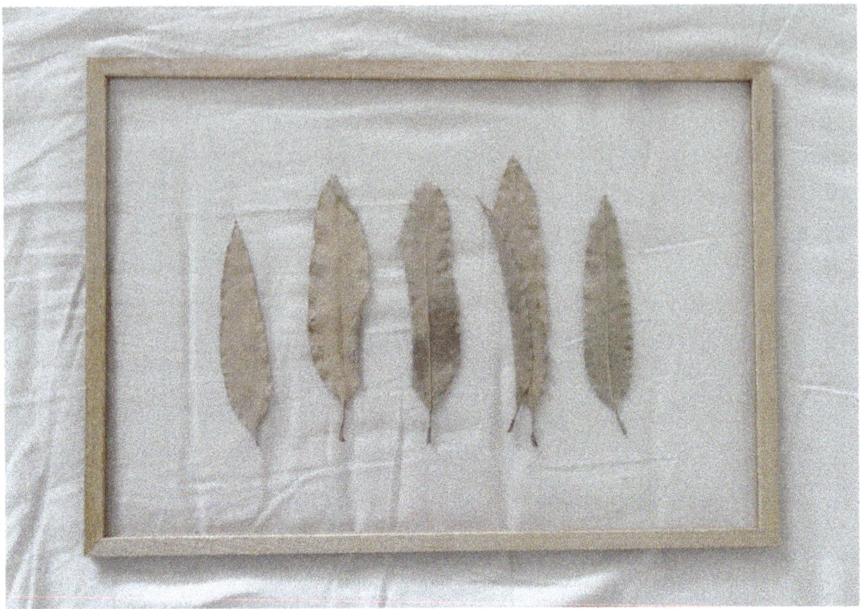

Figure 6.1 Six framed dust-covered leaves. Photograph by the author.

Framing the dust

In Figure 6.1 you see an image of six leaves covered in greyish-brown, sticky dust. Two are clinging to each other, folded over one another, as though they have been glued together by the thin layer of dust. I cut these leaves from the branches of a mango tree on the outskirts of Recife at the end of December 2012. I walked by this filthy tree almost every day for 5 months before I cut off these leaves. Extracting a tiny bit of context from them in my mind with every single passing. After I cut away the leaves, I meticulously wrapped them in a piece of plastic and stuck them inside a book that was big enough to press and conserve them, and solid enough to carry them home safely over 8,241 kilometres of the Atlantic Ocean. The preservation method was natural to me, as both of my parents are biologists, and I remembered how, as a child, I sat atop stacks of old telephone directories to press treasures found in nature – beautiful leaves, flowers or seaweeds. These organic things would be preserved, and I would be excited to discover how different flora changes in appearance after weight, time, and drying made them ready for framing. Therefore, preserving the Brazilian mango leaves was an easy and familiar task. I did not know how the dust would react, though, and only hoped it would stay on the leaves as it was. Fortunately, it did and still remains there now, as the leaves hang on my wall in Denmark.

You may wonder why I seem to be obsessed with dust. Well, what took me on my travels in the first place was an interest in north-east Brazil as a region, random nature. Or rather, towards not highlighting anything, but instead letting them stay as they already were. One attempt involved saving our online conversations and, taking inspiration from Hubert Selby Jr's *Last Exit to Brooklyn* (2011) – a masterpiece in the genre of streams of consciousness – simply deleting who said what, as conversations, both in real life and in chats, were words woven into each other anyway. This was not a question of making it completely impossible for a reader to grasp who was behind which words, but of downplaying it, and of weaving different sections together in a non-linear manner by dissolving their chronology. Hence, rather than unfolding these 'notes' and writing them into a narrative line by explicating what took place, or did not take place, before and after, I would let a series of such notes remained scattered among each other. One example, published later as 'Conscious sedation' (Frederiksen 2016:39–41), reads as follows:

> i'm getting annoyed. now my left ear's plugged or smth. how r u doing? unplug it! i'm good, have just met athos from the four musketeers. will go by the doctor tomorrow before we start drinking. i'm sure we can cure you if the doctor can't. where did u meet which athos? in the park close to where i live. 9 april park. yeah i know where that is. the skatepark? and who's athos? i mean what kind of athos? one of the musketeers. he had a great costume. yes but i mean this specific athos, who is he? have no idea, i think he was russian, now alcoholic/insane/athos. i see. btw the old russian movie 3 musketeers is the best i have seen. i didn't know there was a russian version, lets watch it some time. gladly but i doubt we can get it with subtitles. not that u won't know the story. we can. i think i'll be able to follow the plot. yeah, very likely. otherwise i'll bring athos
>
> to be honest i'm starting to feel too miserable to be glad about anything, but still. how r u?. have a terrible hangover, drank cognac with the artist-group until 6 this morning. i see. yeah i didn't go to my office today either. are you still ill? yes. it's dawning on me. what i did. i don't even know what happened to the paintings. i threw them on the stairs hopefully paata took them. what?! oh you don't know anything about our fight? no. sorry. ok. what happened? can't right now. sorry. no worries, hope you are ok. physically fine. sorry to hear. yeah me too
>
> was calling you i think. at about 6 and just now. yes, i heard it at six but didn't want to get up. and i didnt hear it now. yeah i didn't sleep all night. i mean. really? i went to sleep after that and woke up at 11 or smth. there were things after you left. can't type. will ya come over?. i thought u said something about noon today yesterday. yes, i think i did. i have to spend a few hours packing i think. did you get in another fight with paata? almost. kicked him out twice. tato left on the street. cant type once again. left on the

street? what does that mean. will you come over after packing?. toldya can't type. i have to be at the gallery around 16/17, will let you know when i'm done packing (need to go out and buy some stuff). ok. chances of seeing you today are obviously slim. but anyway it was fun yesterday and all ended well. paata is on his way from gldai already. hehe, you always get in a fight after i leave. (where he stayed at zura's cause i kicked him out, etc.). will be glad to see you if you manage. yeah u always miss all the fun. yeahh. naaa it wasn't really a fight. just a long process of kicking him out and him coming back again. anyway he doesn't really remember anything and all's well. he seemed a bit stoned already when i came. all is perfect in my state of denmark. i think it as just absinthe. was. didn't see any weed last night. not that i looked for it. well, absinth alone can do the trick i think. that he/she/it can, especially 3 of them

havent you gone to bed yet? no. well done. ccant atalk rigjht now\. lol. can even attatck. am unesleep unhaired. haha, ok. and tpoo durnk. and almosyt als[pee.nyway.talk yto ya tomorrow. am pissed aoj tyop of that. aggresivebut non able to spell. unable probably. androwhatever. go to sleep. it's daylight. it's all paatas fault. anyway. hes asleep in my room and im beng stupid heer. anyway. sorry. no worries. will call you tomorrowe. today i mean. yes, do that. okm hope ai w9ill go to sleep. jesus. no I won't its already dayu,igjht but at some point I will. anuway. judging from your spelling i think you will able to. will call you when i wake upo hopefull;y

Unresolved

The above, of course, is merely snapshot of an array of such notes. And as such, I do not expect you as a reader to have been caught up in a stream of consciousness yet. Unsurprisingly, works such as *Last Exit to Brooklyn* are much longer than the 693 words quoted above. What they are intended to do, however, is to work as a representation of a series of scenes that do not immediately have much to say, that do not really amount to anything (or something), but which are still there. It is in this manner that they, potentially, move towards decoupage, in which linear arrangements are dissolved and where, qua Tarkovsky, meaning is not imposed on the reader, but sensations are still present. Indeed, Tarkovsky believed sculpting in time to be a question of 'creating a moment', as time, for him, was not a linear principle related to action, and thus to results or consequence, but a state reflecting a particular reality (Tarkovsky 1986:57).

At this point...

...you might be thinking: 'Weren't there a group of nihilists in *The Big Lebowski*?' Which indeed there were, one of them stating to the main character in a heavy German accent, 'We are nihilists, we believe in nothing.' (Cohen and Cohen 1998:56:01). Or, you might come to think of the philosophy of Sartre or Heidegger, or the writings of Dostoevsky, or the story of how people flocked to the Louvre in 1913 after the Mona Lisa had been stolen to see the spot where the famous painting had once hung, but where there was now nothing – among those going being Franz Kafka and his friend Max Brod (Green 2011:95). Or you might, with the editors of this volume, come to think of the TV show *Seinfeld*. In the episode 'The Pitch', Jerry Seinfeld and George Costanza sit at their local coffee shop and discuss the possibility of creating a TV show, and based on their own conversation George suggests that they pitch a show about nothing, exclaiming to Jerry, 'Who says you gotta have a story!' and following this up with 'Everybody's doing something! We'll do nothing!' (Seinfeld 1992:07:41–08:53).

This is of course a valid point – that nothing, and the related notion of meaninglessness, exists in many different places and contexts. But there is also an important aspect to take note of here. Namely, that just as all the things we can count as being 'something' are obviously different from each other in a myriad of different ways – they are something but not the same thing; so all the things we can count as being 'nothing' are also different from each other. Hence, there is 'nothing' to be found in Sartre, Heidegger, Dostoevsky, *The Big Lebowski* and *Seinfeld*, as well as in a Georgian suburb, but this does not entail that these are the same kinds of nothing. For instance, the nihilists in *The Big Lebowski* represent the principle of creating nothing through destruction, and thus have an affinity with the violent Russian nihilist movement of 1860s. This kind of programmatic search for (or use of) nothing was not the case in Georgia. And although *Seinfeld* is depicted as 'a show about nothing', each episode is still built around a distinct plot in which different minutiae of daily life are put into play, and where the main characters are caught up in details that are perhaps pointless for everyone else around them, but which they themselves cling to. Paradoxes and laughs erupt in *Seinfeld* because of people finding importance in something that others (and we as viewers) regard as nothing, a form particular to representations of nihilism in American popular culture, as argued by Thomas Hibbs (2012). This becomes clear in the final episode in which Jerry, George, Elaine and Kramer are imprisoned for their 'callous indifference and utter disregard for everything that is good and decent' (Seinfeld 1998:46:50) – society blames them for an indifference that they themselves do not acknowledge. Again, this was not the case in Georgia, where indifference was in fact very much acknowledged. As I have argued elsewhere, in the empirical context at stake here, the question of 'nothing' and 'nihilism' may best be characterized as crisis of meaning and an inherent mistrust in end-points (Frederiksen 2017, 2018). We are not dealing with an active nihilism, as associated with the Russian nihilist movement, which in Deleuze's reading of Nietzsche can be seen as 'values without a world', but rather a passive nihilism entailing a 'world without values' (Diken 2009:24). But reaching that kind of characterization necessitates a grounded perspective. That is, it necessitates a perspective on, and a taking note of, how nothing unfolds and how nothing is perceived in the particular context at stake.

Notes, again

This chapter appears in a book about field notes. It presents one facet of the process of writing field notes that can then be singled out and put in a relation to the aspects found in the other chapters of the book in order to make a series of overall arguments and points in the introduction. In the standard process of academic book editing, this chapter is likely to have been situated at a specifically chosen place among the other chapters. This might be a position in which it speaks to similar themes as the chapters before and after; or one in between other chapters that highlights a difference, whereby, through a principle not unlike that of montage, a third meaning might appear. This is done because on an overall level this book is supposed to resolve something about field notes. There should be a take-home message, otherwise what would the point be? My aim with this chapter is of course not to disrupt that effort (though I look forward to seeing where it is eventually located), but rather to bring forth the sensation of the note-taking practices entailed by staying true to the challenge Vano posed, and in this way show the methodological challenges involved in letting the context of a fieldwork directly influence the ways in which notes are taken and unfolded.

Sense unmade

To reiterate, the question for me was to find ways to create a sensation without necessarily making sense. As well as being a methodological challenge, this might also make for texts that are challenging to read. But if there is a point to be made (to the potential discontent of Vano), that would be it. 'Since reality is incomplete, art must not be too afraid of incompleteness', Iris Murdoch once noted (quoted from Kermode 166:130). How incomplete, or how unresolved, can a field note be while still providing a sensation? Tarkovsky insistently refrained from creating meaning but instead worked towards creating a sensation in the viewer when she or he desperately wanted one to emerge. In this way he worked against the principle of creating a full 'understanding' as he believed this mode of film-making inhibited our ways of thinking about or

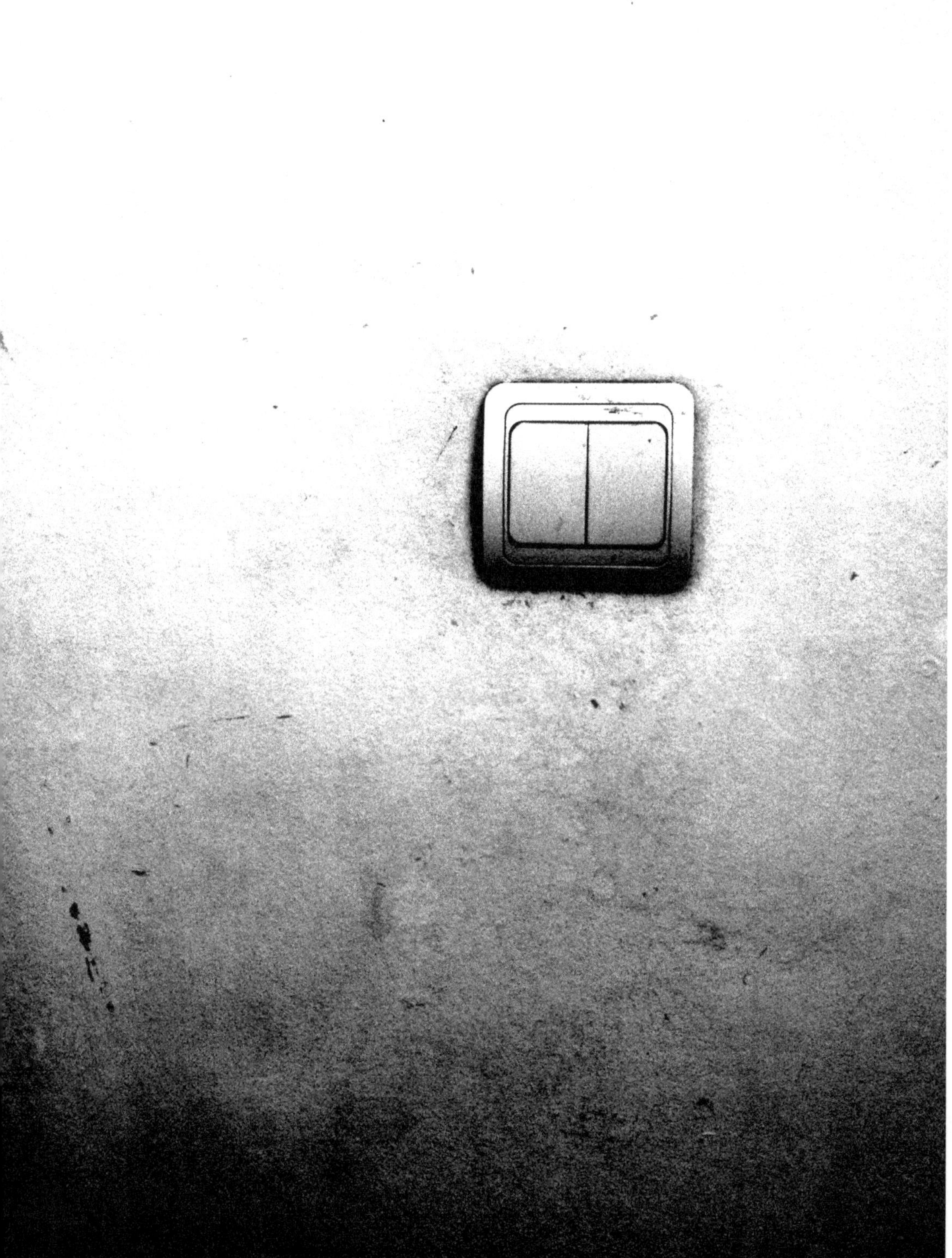

reflecting upon the film. Narrative lines lead to a conclusion, whereas non-linearity leads to considerations that reflect reality on a much deeper and – despite or even perhaps because of the lack of meaning – more realistic level (Tarkovsky 1986).

The entire fieldwork in which Vano figured was premised on the acknowledgement of my own craving for meaning in a situation where it was not necessarily to be found. By watching the wind scene with Vano over and over again, and then later, a long time after having finished the fieldwork, watching it over and over again alone, it suddenly began to make sense to me why Vano had insisted on watching it. It showed me why it made sense not to make sense of anything, and how using particular stylistic measures could, potentially, be helpful for doing this and yet still provide a sensation of the unnoteworthy. The processes of taking note of, or unfolding, the unnoteworthy in the manner done here were not limited to Tarkovsky's principles of decoupage and sculpting. They also came to take shape from (or through) the lyrical universe of Morrissey, Jack Kerouac's *On The Road* (2000) and Peter Greenaway's visual and narrative style – aesthetics that were discussed, listened to or watched during the fieldwork. What *Mirror* came to entail on an overall level, however, was letting the principle found in these aesthetics be reflected in my relation to notes. It may well be that anthropologists are too preoccupied with meaning when we analyze our material (Tomlinson 2006). But the inclination towards carving out meaning or significance may be implied already in the practice of data collection, in terms of what we take note of and what we find unnoteworthy, and furthermore in terms of how we 'edit' our notes when unfolding them.

Random repeat

The weekend goes by as usual. Vano and I text each other back and forth during the day and agree to meet up in front of his workplace in Vake at 4 pm. It's extremely windy and at times almost impossible to see anything because of the sand and dust whirling around, and my cigarette keeps being blown out. I'm in front of Vano's office around ten-to-four. Today there are no flowers outside the florists and no newspapers outside the little kiosk. I know Vano is probably not busy inside, but most likely watching *Buffy the Vampire Slayer*, but also that he probably won't leave before 16:00, so I don't text him to let him know I've arrived.

> So I just stand waiting in the wind. Next to me a high-rise building is being constructed. Despite the weather a number of workers can be seen way up in the air, on the sides of the building. My eyes wander up and at some point a part of the roof, or maybe a part of the construction, comes loose and

starts whirling down towards the street. It's a large 1 × 2 m iron plate and it flies down from the top and across the street, hammering down just in front of a bus on the other side. The bus-driver manages to hit the brakes just before the plate smacks down just in front of the bus. While looking across the street another piece hammers down just next to me. I look at it, and look up. On the opposite side of the fallen iron plate an elderly man is also looking at it. '*Sheni deda*... [fuck your mother...]' he says, shakes his head, and walks away.

The minute later Vano comes out from his office. We walk towards his doctor's office and Nika meets us on the way. We don't talk much as sand blows into our mouths whenever we open them.

We take a taxi to Saburtalo, walk to the entrance of Vano's building and take the lift up. Once inside, Nika and I get ashtrays and glasses in the kitchen. We pick sand from our noses and ears and down a few glasses. A bit later Paata shows up.

Vano and I text each other back and forth, and agree to meet up. I stand waiting in the wind. Vano comes out. We walk and Nika meets us on the way. Sand blows into our mouths whenever we open them. We text each other back and forth.

References

Cohen, E. and Cohen, J. 1998. *The Big Lebowski*. Polygram Filmed Entertainment & Working Title Films.

Drowning by Numbers, 1988 (dir. P. Greenaway; dist. Film Four International).

Diken, B. 2009. *Nihilism*. London: Routledge.

Emerson, R., Fretz, R. and Shaw, L. 1995, *Writing Ethnographic Fieldnotes*. Chicago: Chicago University Press.

Frederiksen, M.D. 2013. *Young Men, Time and Boredom in the Republic of Georgia*. Philadelphia: Temple University Press.

——— 2016. 'Conscious sedation'. In K. Stadler and M.D. Frederiksen (eds.), *A Conscious Issue*. A(4):39–41.

——— 2017. 'Joyful pessimism: marginality, disengagement and the doing of nothing', *Focaal* 78:9–22.

——— 2018. 'Waiting for nothing: nihilism, doubt, and difference without difference in postrevolutionary Georgia'. In M. Janeja and A. Bandak (eds.), *Ethnographies of Waiting: Doubt, Hope and Uncertainty*. London: Bloomsbury.

Green, R. 2011. *Nothing Matters: A Book About Nothing*. Washington: iff Books.

Hibbs, T. 2012. *Shows about Nothing: Nihilism in Popular Culture*. Waco: Baylor University Press.

Kerouac, J. 2000. *On the Road.* London: Penguin Books.
Kermode, F. 1966. *The Sense of an Ending.* New York: Oxford University Press.
Mirror, 1975 (dir. A. Tarkovsky; dist. Mosfilm).
Orpen, V. 2003. *Film Editing: The Art of the Expressive.* London: Wallflower Press.
Redwood, T. 2010. *Andrei Tarkovsky's Poetics of Cinema.* Newcastle upon Tyne: Cambridge Scholars Publishing.
Seinfeld,1992, 'The pitch', S4:E3 (writ. L. David; dist. Columbia TriStar).
——— 1998, 'The finale, part 2', S9:E24 (writ. L. David; dist. Columbia TriStar).
Selby Jr, H. 2011. *Last Exit to Brooklyn.* London: Penguin Books.
Skakov, N. 2012. *The Cinema of Andrei Tarkovsky: Labyrinths in Time and Space.* London: I.B. Tauris.
Sluka, J.A. 1995. 'Reflections on managing danger in fieldwork: dangerous anthropology in Belfast'. In C. Nordstrom and A.C.G.M. Robben (eds.), *Fieldwork under Fire: Contemporary Studies of Violence and Survival*, pp. 276–95. Berkeley: University of California Press.
Stewart, K. 2007. *Ordinary Affects.* Durham: Duke University Press.
Strick, P. 2006. 'Tarkovsky's translations'. In J. Gianvito (ed.), *Andrei Tarkovsky: Interviews*, pp. 70–3. Jackson: University of Mississippi Press.
Tarkovsky, A. 1986. *Sculpting in Time.* Austin: University of Texas Press.
Taussig, M. 2012. 'Exelente zona social', *Cultural Anthropology* 27(3):498–517.
Tomlinson, M. 2006. 'The limits of meaning in Fijian Methodist sermons'. In M. Engelke and M. Tomlinson (eds.), *The Limits of Meaning: Case Studies in the Anthropology of Christianity*, pp. 129–47. New York: Berghahn Books.
Weller, S. 2010. 'Unwords'. In D. Caselli (ed.), *Beckett and Nothing: Trying to Understand Beckett*, pp. 107–25. Manchester: Manchester University Press.

6

The world in a grain of dust

The significance of the apparently insignificant

Maria Nielsen

'Imagine living there. They cannot dry their clean clothes. They cannot even have a meal without dust in it,' Carmem pondered aloud one day, when we passed by the house next to the mango tree. Exactly the same mango tree from which I cut six dusty leaves back in 2012.

Dust clouds

A road lies a few kilometres from the Capibaribe River in Pernambuco, north-east Brazil. The road is virtually 'torn up,' and blends with the exposed earth. I stare out the window in astonishment, as the minibus transports us on a bumpy ride through the bustling scenery. Along the road are several stalls of makeshift materials, set up to cover neatly stacked pyramids of fruit from the hot sun. A group of men in orange coveralls and yellow helmets, equipped with shovels, move about. On the horizon is a seemingly endless area of *mata atlántica*, with its lush, thick, electric-green foliage. On the road, before me, extensive construction work is taking place. I hold my breath when dust enters the wide-open window, and exhale only after we have driven by one of the large road excavations. I notice how the landscape is dotted with signs of investment in the future: bridges are being built, apartment blocks constructed, old roads are widened, and new ones cut across the land. The World Cup arena is being erected, and the site is lit at all times, so diligent workers can labour there day and night. The minibus speeds through the metropolitan region of Recife, the state capital of Pernambuco. The innumerable construction sites make it feel as though the entire periphery of Recife is covered in dust.

In 2012 I was in north-east Brazil to study the way in which changes in infrastructure would affect a suburban town and the people who live there, over time. The clouds of dust made me wonder how local people regarded the investments, the changes they entailed, and the stir the reordering of the roads caused.

To me, the dust came to act as a placeholder for a range of symbolic and iconic meanings that were highly specific to this context. Going over the dusty leaves in the context of this book about field notes, I have come to regard them as capable of taking on an indexical quality with regard to this specific Brazilian setting in the period leading up to the World Cup. I use Peirce's terminology to give the analysis an abstract level of thought on top of the highly subjective feelings that those dusty leaves evoke. To write about dusty leaves in this manner has made me wonder what such a minuscule thing as dust can tell us about temporality, a place, and the people who inhabit that place. And it made me wonder how everything would look after the dust had settled.

Piling up

During my travels in Brazil over the past years I have kept a notebook, and captured thousands of photographs, local poetry, cartoons, brochures, flyers and cuttings from newspapers that caught my attention. All this material piled up on my desk, in my computer and in my mind. These piles of stuff were all part of an ongoing flow of information of interest to the ethnographer, where materials blended with encounters and conversations.

My research is about material changes and their temporal implications in urban spaces; that is, how infrastructure can both expand and confine possibilities over time. In my fieldwork I was in the suburban town Camaragibe, which was undergoing rapid material change because of the construction of the arena for the World Cup nearby. My project was designed so that I visited the field before, during and after the World Cup. I examined public transportation, the use of private cars, the electrical supply, the water supply and security in public spaces. At times this seemed an impracticable programme, as there was no defined, closed group of people that were more relevant to talk to than others. I sought out people who could tell me about different aspects of the city, and usually I ended up with an excessive amount of information and field notes pointing in countless directions. Unsurprisingly, returning with field notes that point in different directions is a rather common experience among anthropologists. But some things always stand out in these piles of information. It is these that end up in our analyses and publications. One thing I brought home from Brazil did not pile up on my desk, it literally piled where I worked. This thing, which seemed to stick in my memory in a different way than all the other material I brought home, was dust.

How did dust catch my attention? This little subject introduced itself because it was impossible to ignore while I was in the field. The whirling, grey-brown, sticky specks of dust became an everyday companion: a highly sensory aspect of doing anything and nothing in this spatiotemporal contiguity. The dust invaded my nose, my eyes, and stuck to my sweaty skin. It infiltrated my wardrobe. It made me force air from my lungs with a sharp short cough, in order to expel dust from my body.

Specks of dust are small and trivial, but nevertheless, they may be telling. This chapter will revolve around dust and notes in anthropological fieldwork, as I explore how the dust on a mango leaf is worth noting. Depending on our definition of 'notes', it may even be considered a note itself. Just as we, as anthropologists, take notes on the pages of our notebooks, we can augment our work by collecting objects from our surroundings and use them as notes. If we take home a physical object that was part of everyday life while we were in the field, it may trigger memories and capture sensations and textures in another manner than the written notes we jot down. Gathering context from the eye of the beholder, we apply our memories to the objects, creating physical notes and aiding our analysis. This is nothing new. Collecting things and bringing them home from the field has been in and out of fashion since the birth of anthropology as a discipline. Dust is surely a thing in itself, but rather than focusing on the thing, I focus on the continual awareness of dust in my field, which allows me to approach urban living in Brazil in a certain manner. This allows me to ask whether such an insignificant thing as dust may in some way encapsulate larger questions. To what kind of knowledge about an area can dust offer access? In short, I will investigate what one of the smallest visible things can tell us about both the field and the fieldworker.

Science commentator Hannah Holmes writes that dust particles, 'too small to distinguish are the individual fragments of a disintegrating world' (2001:1). Next time you wipe down your desk, I would like you to think about what the individual fragments of dust flakes you collect consist of. This will include the everyday things that are found in the local environment around you, perhaps human skin cells, cobwebs, fibres from a woollen sweater, plant pollen, animal hairs, outdoor soil. The world is in a constant state of disintegration (Holmes 2001:2), and dust is the smallest visible thing that holds these fragments of disintegration.

So, in what way can dust tell us something about a place at a specific time? And how can dust specks on a mango leaf transubstantiate and become the focal point of an interpretation? This chapter is about the world in a grain of dust.

and a curiosity about the way in which the outskirts of the metropolis of Recife would be affected by hosting parts of the World Cup, which took place in Brazil in 2014. I collected the dusty leaves a year and a half before the World Cup was held, only a few kilometres away from the brand new arena built for the event. The street where the dusty leaves used to hang is a byway to the main road that connects the city centre of Recife and the urban periphery. The old railway station, a yellow building in the classical colonial style, is situated opposite the road on which I cut the mango leaves. It has been out of use for years and is slowly decaying. There is nothing left of the roof. The yellow and white walls are fading, cracking and turning grey. Slowly, the weeds are growing on top of the railway station, engulfing it and making it disappear. The building stands as a reminder of a time when the railway was a symbol of modernity and progress. The old station sits there, as a thing of a past when goods, mainly wood and sugar, were transported through the area by train. The north-east of Brazil is famous for its sugar production (Scheper-Hughes 1994; Skidmore 2010). However, most production has moved to the more suitable climate in the south. The hinterands of the north-east are notoriously plagued by recurring droughts, making for harsh and unpredictable living conditions (Arons 2004). The north-east is widely known and vividly described as a poor, backward, desert region. For instance, Josué de Castro portrayed the region as 'a stage of 1,500,000 square kilometres, made ready for a huge tragedy' (1967, translation by the author). Although he wrote this many years ago, the north-east remains a place marked by suffering, food scarcity and a lack of water.

More recently, Nicholas Gabriel Arons (2004) has described how droughts have been, and still are, a great concern. They have put people on the move, and migration from the hinterlands of Pernambuco to the state capital, Recife, has made the urban population grow. Many people end up settling on the periphery of the capital, as land there is either affordable or open for squatting (Dalsgaard 2016). Over the past decades, the population has increased every year. Many homes now have an extra floor, even two, and the density of the town continues to increase, as more and more houses, and lately, low-rise blocks, are being constructed. But as Alexandre, who is always full of energy, put it, '*isso é crescimento sem desenvolvimento* [this is growth without development]'. And the last time I spoke to old Donna Biu, she said, '*a cidade cresce, mas o tempo parou* [the town grows, but time is standing still]'. She said this while she sat on her porch on her rocking-chair, facing a two-metre-tall wall her family had recently build around the house in order to protect themselves from intruders. The town and its walls are getting taller day by day. And those who do not build walls around their houses face the walls made by others, as neighbours' walls block the view right in front of people's windows. The population grows, and it keeps growing, and stirring the dust.

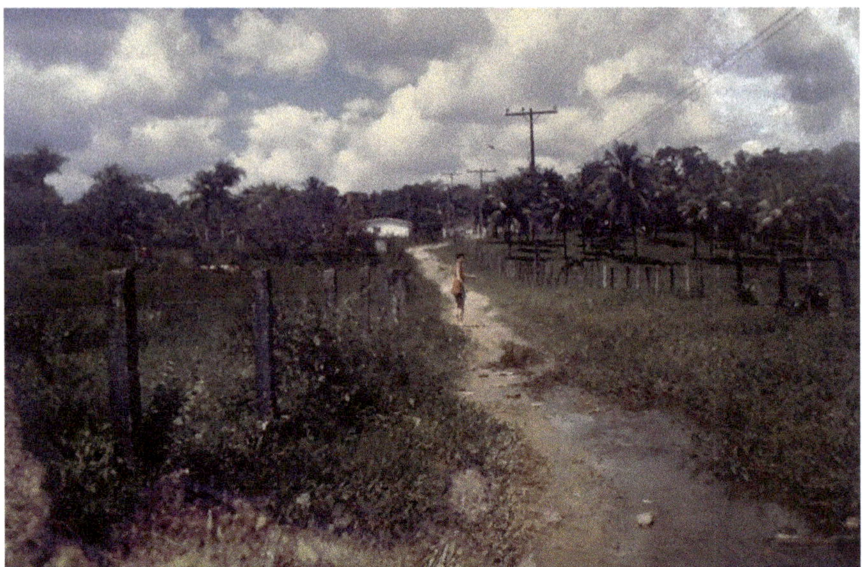

Figure 6.2 A photograph of the area from the late 70s or early 80s. Photograph by Carmem.

Figure 6.3 (opposite, top) Construction site nearby the arena, 2012. Photograph by the author.

Figure 6.4 (opposite, bottom) Dusty mango leaves still attached to the tree, 2012. Photograph by the author.

If you stand under the particular mango tree from which I cut the dusty leaves, you will see older, single-storey houses on one side, and newly built blocks of flats rising on the other side. Some years back, this part of Camaragibe was a green thicket of bushes and trees. Carmem, with whom I stayed, gave me a photograph of how it used to be (Figure 6.2). She could not remember exactly when it was taken. But it must have been about 40 years back. I walked to the place from which the photograph was shot, to observe the changes, and I could barely recognize the townscape. The green thicket had morphed into a flat area dotted with emerging blocks of flats (Figure 6.3).

Construction sites all around me generated the dust I found to be so characteristic of Camaragibe at that time. Some boys were playing football in the afternoon heat on one of the patches of earth the construction had not yet reached. A tail of dust followed the football. Dust was part of the landscape; almost a thing in itself that blurred what was to come. As my attention was drawn to dust, already, in 2012, I began writing down whenever dust was present or a subject of debate, and I noted how it affected the town. I continued this praxis until 2016. The leaves became a way in which I could conserve a tiny part of my field and bring it with me as a reminder of how 2012

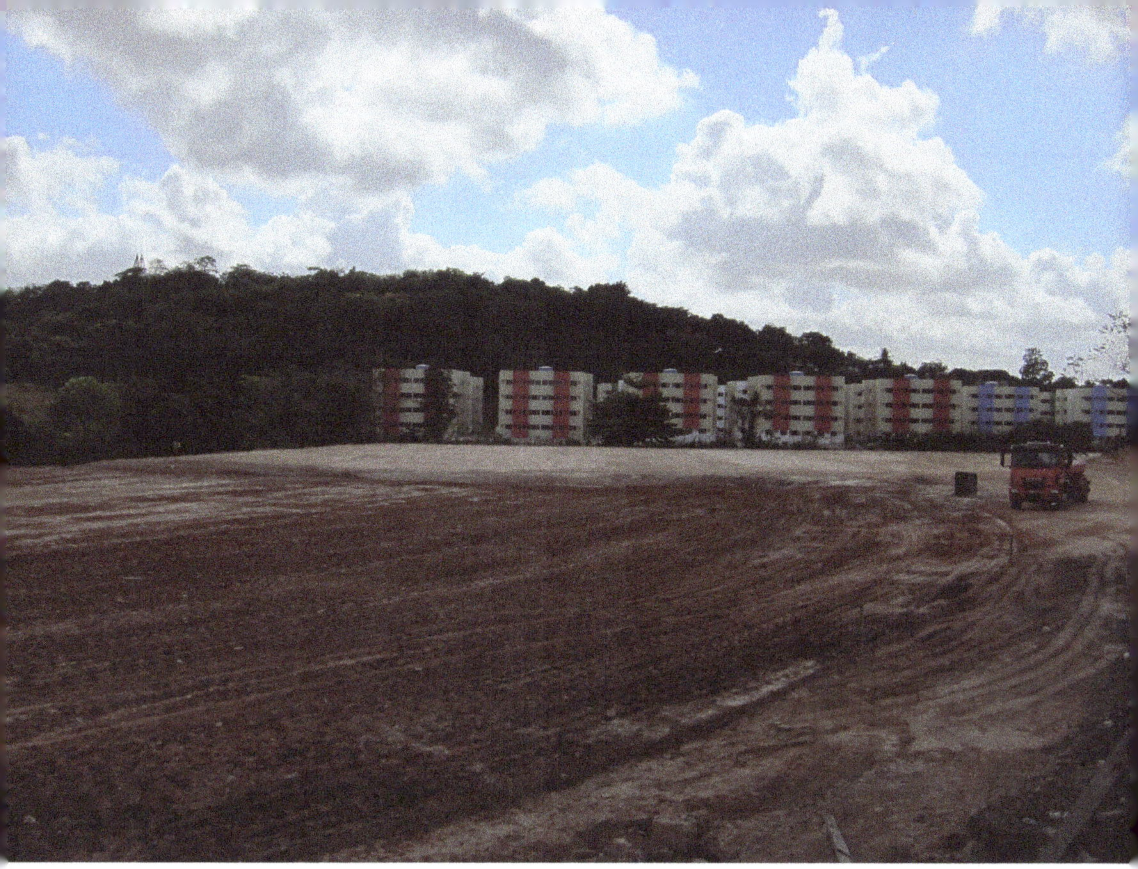

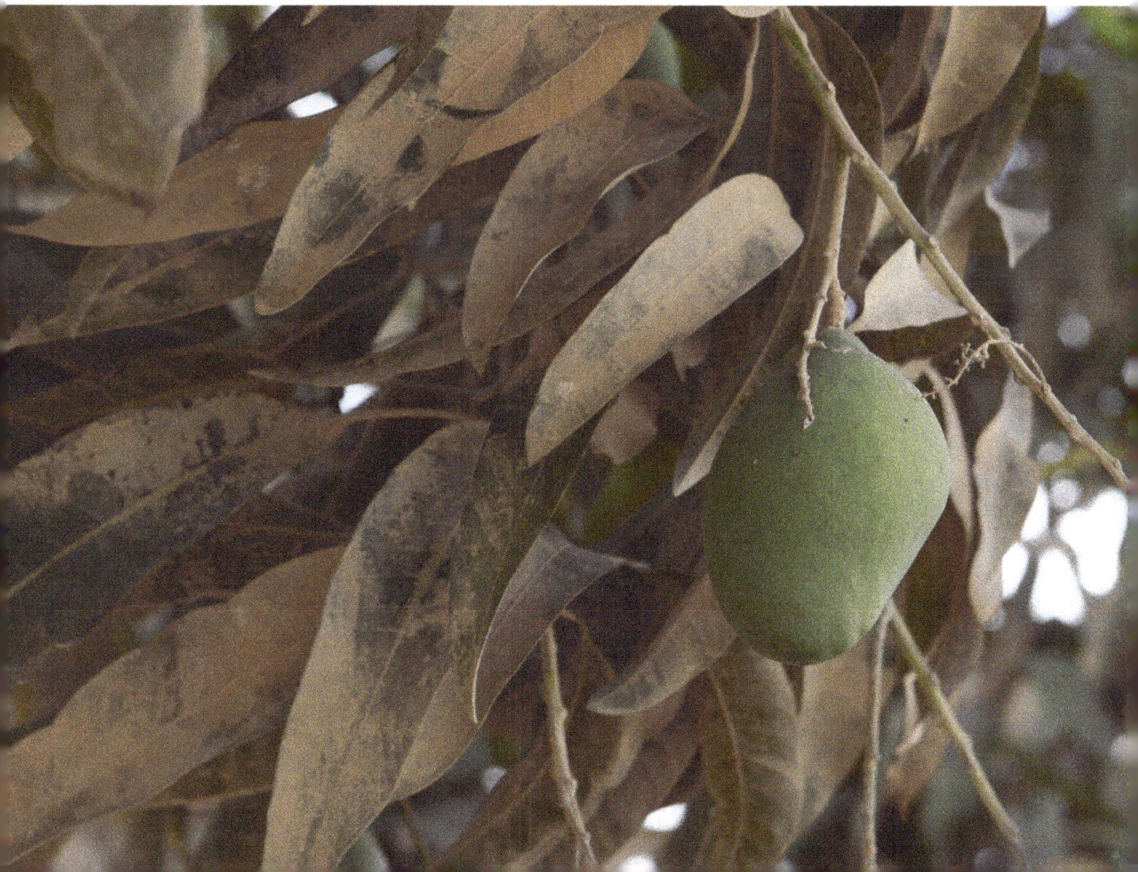

was covered in dust. The conversations I had in the following years, reminded me how dust was no longer such a huge part of the landscape. I brought the dusty leaves home because people talked a lot about '*essa poeira* [this dust]'. The mango tree and the dust that covered it helped me discover and make sense of ideas about the World Cup as an event in the future, and how people related (or not) to this event. In cutting off the leaves, I was trying to preserve the dust. At the time of writing the dust is long gone from the area, but I still have a small sample – maintained, kept and frozen in time.

Small things, telling stories

I cannot count how many times I have been told that Camaragibe was in need of planning, organization and cleaning. Several of the roads were not paved, and this contributed to a dusty environment. The great number of houses with walls without ceramic tiles also added to the quantity of dust, as the exposed and naked brick walls produced dust. Most houses were constructed with an open gap between the walls and the roof, in order to allow the circulation of air. This gap created a constant soundscape of what was done behind closed doors at home, mixed with sounds from whatever went on outside: songs from the local church, crowing roosters, barking dogs, cars rigged with loudspeakers advertising everything from petrol on sale to local politicians, welding noise, running water trickling from a broken pipe, engines of passing cars and motorcycles, televisions running. Besides letting in so many noises, the gap made eavesdropping on neighbours unavoidable. Apart from letting the sounds of the home and the street blend, this little gap also made it easy for dust to travel. Dust is nothing new to either the area or to the people who live there. However, there was something different about the dust that travelled about in 2012. The peculiar thing was that people connected this astounding amount of dust to an event in the future. They said it was dusty because of '*essa copa* [this world cup]'. It made me wonder about dust, and how it may signify different things depending on who creates it, and why. The dust was particularly bad in the house near the mango tree, close to where I lived while I conducted my fieldwork in 2012. Its usually vivid green leaves were completely covered in thick dust (Figure 6.4).

One day, when I walked by this house with Carmem, she noted how awful it must be to live there, in the middle of the dust. The dust dried out the throat, as an elderly woman told me when she offered me one of her throat-soothing pastilles, which she used to battle the dust. It also made people's eyes red, as happened to a young girl I visited, who could barely study for an exam because of her irritated eyes. The increasing amount of dust was also the reason people had to clean their houses more often, as a schoolteacher told me when she invited me to her home. Some told me that the dust from the construction site was making their children sick and allergic, and they held the building of the arena, and the surrounding constructions, responsible. People would spray the unpaved roads with water in an effort to reduce its effects.

In a sense, the dust was a way the future World Cup manifested itself years before it took place. By cutting off the leaves, I brought home a little bit of construction dust, as a reference to, and a reminder of, what Camaragibe was like in 2012. I brought it home as testimony: this dust was connected to the arena and an event in the future. Would photographs not do the trick? Or written notes? Yes, indeed, but only to some extent. The photographs I brought home are snaps from particular days, and when I flip through my notes the word 'dust' does not appear on the pages each and every day. But the mango leaves were always covered in dust when I passed by, during the whole five months of my stay. To me, these leaves are a stronger reminder of how dust really was part of the landscape for an extended period of 2012, and not only on particular days when I happened to take a photograph of it. Of course, the notes and images add another layer to my memory of the dust, but the physical sample is somehow more alive. It can be traced back to the time when it was preserved, providing an extract from a specific time when the area I was studying was undergoing changes in order for it to fit the future. This layer in time is now gone, except for my small sample. It is a material, taken from the field where it used to stick to people's skin and enter eyes, nose and lungs. Dust was on my skin, and under my skin, as it entered my body. It did this in a different way than photographs or written notes could ever record.

To me, notes are what we collect, produce and absorb in the field. What makes dust a note is that it activates my memory. It may be lifeless at first sight, but combined with the rest of my material, dust can act as a memory trigger, a reference to the world as it was when an impoverished neighbourhood awaited the near future. What can dust, for instance, tell us about possibilities and class differences during the time when it was collected? Let us take a closer look at this, aided by a snippet from my notebook: 'The humidity makes the dust stick to my moist skin. It is so dusty here that it is simply impossible for me to stay clean.' To keep oneself clean is essential in Brazil. Being sweaty or dirty, and therefore not presentable, limits one's opportunities, as it has been discussed by, for instance, Anne Line Dalsgaard (2004). The small particles that travel around relate not only to things, but also to people. As Jussi Parikka describes it in 'Dust and exhaustion':

> [...] dust is something that attaches to lungs and expresses a relation of labour: it begs the question of who gets to work in clean spaces, and who

> cleans those spaces. The latter is usually the poorer ones who are easier to expose to dangerous and unhealthy conditions at their workplace.
>
> (Parikka 2013)

Outside of Recife, the exposure to dust was not related to people's workplaces, but to their actual homes. Therefore, the dust marked social relations and revealed not only who had to work in unhealthy environments, but also who had to live with the dust and who did not. If people drive an air-conditioned car, they can arrive without a drop of sweat or speck of dust on their skin. If the mode of transportation is by foot or bus, people are very likely to arrive sweaty and dirty, and then they receive little respect. This division has also been noted by James Holston, who writes that Brazil's public streets have become spaces in which the elite circulate by car, and poor people by foot or public transportation (1999:125). The elite have simply abandoned the activity of walking the public streets. I was told, time and again, by people who lived both in Camaragibe and in the city centre, that I was mad to insist on walking. I was told the city was too dangerous and too hot, and that I should not just walk aimlessly about the streets. Especially not alone. I was simply told that walking was not an activity I should pursue. Similarly, I was told that public transportation was dangerous and something I should avoid for numerous reasons, one being that the ride would make me sweaty and dirty. When I told middle-class people who owned a car that I was going to take the bus, I would be told 'good luck' or 'be careful'.

During peak hours, the buses are overcrowded, and they become awfully hot when little or no air circulates. In the dusty parts of town, dust enters and covers the commuters. Passengers are squeezed so tightly that their bodies rub together, and sweat and dust move from one person to another. The particles find their way from the street onto the bodies, and into people's homes and lives. The dust that was connected to the future event particularly annoyed people, since many of them thought that they would not benefit from the ongoing construction work. There was nothing they could do about it. Paying attention to the smallest things, such as dust, in this way, may reveal social relations and opinions on a much larger scale. The smallest things may sometimes be the most telling ones, providing an avenue to understanding what is occurring. This goes for fieldwork in general, and playing with scale, looking at the tiniest things, may add new and interesting perspectives.

In the case of my fieldwork, dust provided me with a way to perceive my field in a different light. And it made me realize how the meaning of dust changes according to who controls it. Echoing the indexical quality of dust in the context of my field, as I noted elsewhere in my writing, I asked myself and others: is it dusty because of the climate or the way one's house is constructed, because the municipality never paved the roads, or because an enormous arena is being built. People who live in the area had no control over the construction of the arena, something designed as the venue for a party they were not invited to. Riding the bus and talking to people about the construction of the arena, I began to notice that dust was not 'just dust', and I started to observe how different types affected people differently in the town Camaragibe.

Greetings from the future

The word mnemonic derives from the Greek *mnēmōn* ('mindful'), and in English means 'aid to memory'. To anthropologists, field notes are a key mnemonic device, functioning as a reference point that allows us to build a bridge between fieldwork and final product. The notes assist us in remembering what occurred in the field, and as we jot them down we write to our future selves. We take these notes in order to remember what happened, what people said, how the field smelled, felt and sounded, and in order to grasp this, we write. Most anthropologists would argue that being there and sensing the atmosphere is a very important factor, though it is difficult to capture in words. So they seek to aid memory by taking photographs, recording sounds, filming, drawing, or collecting things, in addition to taking notes. The entire body of material collected is part of getting to know the field, and in this process we store information, that can be awakened through memory and the senses. Through this investigation, the anthropologist not only enters the field, the field also enters the anthropologist. As noted by Nadia Seremetakis (1994:28), 'Sensory memory is a form of storage. Storage is always the embodiment and conservation of experiences, persons and matter in vessels of alterity. The awakening of the senses is awakening the capacity for memory, of tangible memory, to be awake is to remember, and one remembers through the sense, via substance.'

Dust relates to the sensory landscape, and affected all my senses and those of my informants. As already mentioned, it stuck to moist skin, dried out the throat, and made eyes itch. It even had a sound. One day Carmem and I sat together in her kitchen, as we had done so many times before, enjoying our morning coffee with corn *cuscuz*, melted cheese and white bread. Birds twittered. Ants marched about and created small trails on the kitchen table, in search of spilt sugar crystals. The heat was not yet forceful, but I could feel that it would gain strength within the next hour. My coffee was pitch black, Carmem's was three parts sugar. Everything was just like any other morning. That is until the calm was broken, and we stared at each other in shock. I had never felt anything like it. By the look on her face, I could tell she felt it too. The air pressure from an explosion some kilometres away was so forceful that we felt it pressing against our bodies. 'It must be *a copa* [the World Cup]'. The explosions and blasts from the construction sites would announce that the dust would be stirred up anew, a small greeting from an event in the future. Not only did the dust have a sound, it also had a scent.

The scent of dust is difficult to put into words and of course it is different depending on the space, place and season. The way I can best describe the dust of Camaragibe in 2012, is that it smelled of a dry attic, if you crawl up there on a hot day. The kind of day where you are met by a wall of heat and dust specks that tumble around in rays of light. It was the smell of forgotten things – a dryness that smells of barely anything. On sunny days the dust in Camaragibe had this particular smell to it. On rainy days, the dust would change. It did not travel. It stayed on the ground, stuck to things, and smelled like wet earth. The feeling of sticky, sweaty skin, itching eyes, blast noise and this dry smell were parts of my physical experience of being in the field. In order to remember these things, it was helpful to me to add dust as an object to my array of notes.

My framed dust leaves can hardly stand alone without some kind of explanation. To strangers, at least, the leaves themselves would not refer to a particular place and time in Brazil. But to me, collecting the leaves, framing them, keeping them and taking care of them, gives them the status of a note. A note that (as probably any note does) refers to something bigger. The framed dust lives on as an object of a bygone time. Whenever I look at it – and not just in the habitual way, but really look at it – that time is evoked for me, in a simultaneity of now and then, as I sit in my office and look at a dust-covered leaf. It refers to a place and a moment when the note was created, and the leaf was plucked, as a product of my eagerness to understand what was at work. And when I tell you the stories that cling to these dusty leaves, you might be carried away by your own imagination. Dust as a 'raw-material note' invites everyone to envision the time and place it was collected. The leaves bear witness to how dusty it actually was, and are evidence of an area that was being transformed.

Dust may indicate decay and oblivion, but it may also indicate change and new times. In 2012 dust covered Camaragibe like a veil, masking the character of the future. It heralded change, and there were expectations of what the future, a future that is now part of the past, would bring. In a sense, the dust is more than what I saw, and more than my informants told me. It holds the potential for interpretation and the unfolding of analysis. As anthropologists, we claim that our knowledge is grounded in fieldwork, that our written notes from the field are the way in which we capture that knowledge, on which we build our analyses. But every time I look at my notes about dust, I am overwhelmed by disbelief. Was it really that dusty? I then look at the leaves and remember it all. Yes, it really was that dusty and the dust was there all the time.

The poetry of dust

At first glance, a landscape covered in dust may seem depressing. In 2012, in the outskirts of Recife, the dust snuck in everywhere. To most people, this picture of a townscape where trees, bushes, streets and houses are enveloped in dust sounds gloomy. But dust does not have to be depressing. There is also something poetic – even magical – about it. As noted by Jussi Parikka (2013), dust is the stuff of fairy tales, stories of deserted places, of places from so long ago that they seem to have never existed. Dust may be stirred up, but it will always settle again. Keeping dust away is an eternal battle against time, and in that repeated activity there is a certain life-affirming circle, like the changing of seasons, like things starting anew.

Before the art of photography was digitized, dust was the photographer's worst enemy. It would cling to the tiny negatives, and become much bigger specks in the developed photograph. Dust would be battled in the darkroom with white gloves and little brushes. I know this because I worked with analogue photography some years back, spending hours to develop a photograph without dust on it. I do not know whether the photographer's battle against dust was something about which Man Ray intended to make a pun, when he made an artwork of dust, in collaboration with Marcel Duchamp. Duchamp let a year's worth of dust build up on a large piece of glass. Man Ray then documented the pattern of the dust by taking a two-hour-long photographic exposure that beautifully seized the complex texture and diversity of materials on the surface of the glass. He titled the artwork *Elevage de poussière* ('Dust Breeding' 1920). After the photograph was taken, Duchamp wiped the glass on which the dust lay almost completely clean, leaving only a section covered with dust. This section he permanently affixed to the glass plate with adhesive, a technique I should perhaps have thought of when I was trying to affix my dust on the mango leaves. Duchamp continued to work on the glass for years and, deliberately, he never finished it. Eventually it was exhibited as the artwork *The Bride Stripped Bare by Her Bachelors, Even* (1915–23), still with the dust on the glass. But to get back to Man Rays photograph – the thing I like about this artwork is that it plays with scale and temporality. It actually looks like an aerial photograph. The dust particles form an entire landscape. In this photograph a year's accumulation of dust created what appears to be a whole world.

Dust does mark the temporality of matter, its piling up tells how long things have sat without being disturbed. It takes a while for dust to breed in forgotten places, such as an attic. But it may also arrive extremely quickly if it is due to rapid changes and construction work, constituting a marker that something is underway. In a sense, my framed dust is the opposite of Man Ray's *Elevage de poussière.* The dust in his photograph bred because it was left undisturbed, the dust on my mango leaf bred because the area in which it was collected was constantly disturbed. These differences between qualities of dust, spanning the poetic and the depressing, the slow and the rapid, have to be sensed and recounted by the people who experience them. Leaves cannot tell stories. But using dust as a note was a prompt that made me pay specific attention to what was said about it.

Some of the people I spoke to in the field did not regard the dust as depressing, but rather as a kind of fairy dust that might finally change their circumstances. To them, the future suggested by dust looked altogether different. They read it as a bearer of change and new opportunities. The changes suggested by the dust made some dream of opening an internet cafe with air-conditioning and glass doors that would not let in the dirt from the traffic. This internet cafe would welcome tourists during the World Cup. The dust made others dream of opening a restaurant that would sell local specialties during the event. For some of the many who dreamt of learning English, this became the reality of actually taking classes.

When dust holds potential and envelops an area in a state of hope and expectation, it is anything but depressing. It becomes the stuff that dreams are made off, evidence that a dream is being built. Richardo, who had an internet café on one of the streets that were to be widened, dreamt of more customers and prosperous times for himself and his family. The widening of the road equalled an expansion of his business, a dream evoked because it seemed plausible, owing to the changing landscape and the construction work stirring up the dust. Others were less thrilled about the future and the dust heralding it. Ana, who had a child that seemed to have allergic reactions to the dust, was one. 'Why all this investment in roads and arenas?' she would ask. 'This will not help my children'. She was hoping for better schools and more investment in the healthcare system instead. The depressing dust and the fairy dust are worlds apart, but both reveal something about the way the future announced itself, and how people perceived this, back in 2012.

The life of the note

In my memory of what the outskirts of Recife were like in 2012, dust plays an important role and it continued to do so in the years following, as I ask people about it every time I return. But its role is somehow dubious. Did dust assume this status after I came home? Is it just my way of trying to make the field come alive in writing? Dust is a physical thing that I brought home from the field, which only acquires the status of a note because I make use of it as such. Combined with stories and statements from my informants, it may reveal a lot about the area where I stayed, but much like a character in a novel, the dust in my field assumed different roles at different times. Once, it was part of everyday life, then, suddenly, it was part of the future, and now it is a thing of the past. In themselves the dusty mango leaves are nothing, they just sit there in their frame, but when they are held together by the stories told about the dust, they become a layer of interpretation. They frame the different atmospheres that shaped the area in 2012. The dust was stirred up by the new infrastructures, and affected simple social routines such as doing homework or cleaning clothing. Part of the story about dust is that such small things – tiny particles – may have an effect on so many aspects of everyday life.

The dust of 2012 seemed to not be part of the world as it was at that point. It heralded the future, and became a sign of the 'not yet, but approaching'. In a sense, dust forecasted potential, creating a space between what the periphery of Recife – or more generally, Pernambuco – was, and what it could be. The dust created a connection between the material changes and the imagined future, and in so doing affected people's lives in the present. A shop owner described the changes and the roadwork as '*isso é uma janela aberta para o mundo* [this is an open window to the world]'. In 2012 a future event made it possible to measure Pernambuco in relation to the rest of the world. Suddenly, its story was the opposite of what people were used to, framing the state of Pernambuco in a way that seemed unfamiliar. The new arena that was being constructed was regarded by people of the area as 'other-worldly', 'an open window', 'part of the future'. In 2012, the familiar stories mentioned in the introduction (Arons 2004; Castro 1967; Scheper-Hughes 1994), with their descriptions of a poor, backward, desert region, seemed to fade.

The dust has settled

On my return to Brazil in 2016 I discover that the mango tree from which I cut the leaves has been cut down. In the felling of 'my' mango tree I hear echoes of the literary cut-up technique, made famous at the end of 1968 with the book, *Minutes to Go* (Burroughs *et al.* 1968), which involves cutting up one text and rearranging it to create another. With its removal, not just of a text, but of a dusty tree from the scene, the main character of my story was excised! The mango tree is gone, the dust has settled, and construction has not been completed. It is as though when the dust settled, everything revealed itself. Numerous politicians in Brazil have been dusting off their hands. Many of them have now been caught, in a period of revelations of extensive corruption within Brazil. What's more, the country has been experiencing political turmoil and the worst recession in its history. The people with whom I reunited in 2016 were no longer concerned with dust, of either the depressing or fairy kind.

In 2012 people in Brazil were looking towards the future; at the time I write this, they fear the past. Even though the dust has settled, it never really leaves. The dust is still there and lingers on, like the past itself. People worry about what will become of Brazil and its fragile democracy. 'It is like we are set back in time,' Carmem tells me when we reunite. 'The rights we fought for are being taken away.' She makes a gesture with her hands, as though she is losing something, as though something is slipping away between her hands. Rights are difficult to gain, they have to be fought for, but they may be lost in the blink of an eye, just like dust disappearing between one's hands.

'What will become of Brazil?' people ask. Much of the population is holding its breath and fearing that Brazil will regress rather than progress. As a Brazilian saying goes, 'Even the past we do not predict.' Where does this leave Brazil and my dusty leaves? It leaves me, and the people I reunited with in 2016, gazing at the past, rather than the future. And the leaves? In the end, everything is made of dust and will return to dust, no matter what we make of it.

References

Arons, N.G. 2004. *Waiting for the Rain: The Politics and Poetry of Drought in Northeast Brazil*. Tucson, AZ: University of Arizona Press.

Burroughs, W.S., Gysin, B., Corso, G. and Beiles, S. 1968. *Minutes to Go*. San Francisco: Beach Books.

Castro, J. de. 1967 *Sete Palmos de Terra e um Caixão: Ensaio Sobre o Nordeste do Brasil, Uma Área Explosiva*. Lisbon: Seara Nova.

Dalsgaard, A.L. 2004. *Matters of Life and Longing: Female Sterilisation in Northeast Brazil*. Copenhagen: Museum Tusculanum Press.

——— 2016. 'Time will tell: temporalities of debt in an urban neighborhood in Northeast Brazil', *Ethnos* 82:(3)458–74.

Holmes, H. 2001. *The Secret Life of Dust: From the Cosmos to the Kitchen Counter, the Big Consequences of Little Things*. Wiley-Blackwell.

Holston, J. 1999. *Cities and Citizenship*. Durham: Duke University Press.

Parikka, J. 2013. 'Dust and exhaustion: the labor of media materialism', *Journal of Theory, Technology and Culture*: journals.uvic.ca/index.php/ctheory/article/view/14790/5665 (accessed 15 February 2016).

Scheper-Hughes, N. 1994. *Death without Weeping: The Violence of Everyday Life in Brazil*. Berkeley: University of California Press.

Seremetakis, C.N. 1994. *The Senses Still: Perception and Memory as Material Culture in Modernity*. Boulder, Colorado: Westview Press.

Skidmore, T.E. 2010. *Brazil: Five Centuries of Change*. New York: Oxford University Press.

7
Life notes
When fields refuse to stay in place

Morten Schütt

This is a story of unexpected ethnographic success. I will tell it from two perspectives: in retrospect, from my present position; and as it happened to me, with all the emotions and questions that not knowing the future involves. Together these two perspectives compile my experience of having my field invade my life, and consequently turning everything in it, including myself, into field notes.

It begins with being caught on film.

March 2013

'This is really a beautiful scene, with you there right in front of the painting of Nikolay Chudotvorets. And the way you bow your head there makes you look like a real Russian icon!' I look at Arunas in slight surprise, then turn my attention back to the computer. He's right, I see. He really caught me there, though you need to pay a little attention to catch my moment with God underneath my unceremonial-looking green down coat and grey woollen hat. I'm standing there in the congregation, with the others dressed as mundanely as me for this Sunday morning liturgy, in the wing of the small wooden temple. I'm clearly listening to the choir, my eyes bright and concentrated and my breath rhythmically manifesting itself as two long tails of steam in the cold winter air. Then, suddenly, my eyes close and my head tilts forward. And is that a tear running down the side of my nose?

I try to recall the situation from the inside, as Arunas plays the scene again. It wouldn't be the first time I've been moved to tears by a simple liturgy. This time Arunas may have caught me during one of my more intense experiences.

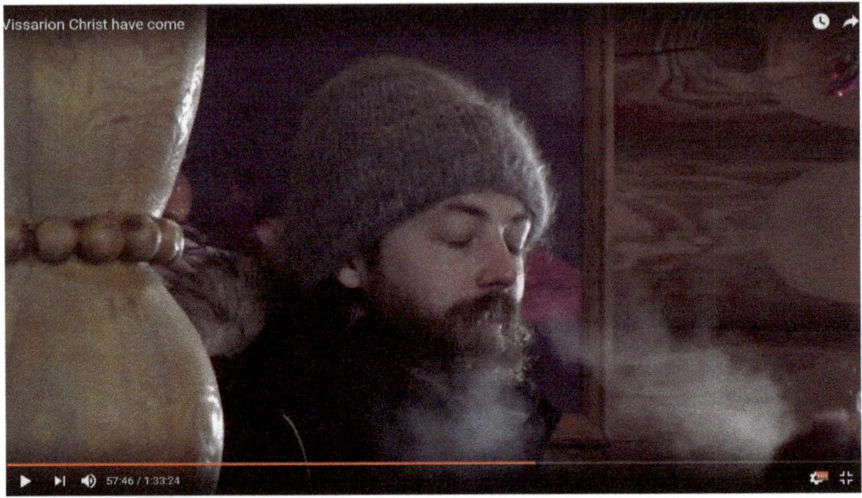

Figure 7.1 Caught on camera with The Holy Spirit? Arunas Machulis.

The booming voices of the men repeat the same line several times over. And standing here, I suddenly understand what the heavily ecclesiastical words actually mean: 'We sing your glory, and the Holy Spirit we summon into our hearts!' And just as I realize the meaning of the words, I feel a rush of chilly, prickly energy passing through me, as if entering me from the ground at my heels and surging up my spine. It reaches my chest, filling it and making me gasp for breath before rapidly moving up my neck to my head, where it finds its only possible outlet. I bow my head and cry, trying to control myself in the middle of the crowd, but obviously not quite able to.

It doesn't look as dramatic from the outside. But then again, nobody seemed to take any notice when I was there, either. But whatever it was, Holy Spirit or something else, I can't deny its presence.

My thoughts are interrupted by Arunas suddenly giving me a concerned look. 'Should we leave this out? You know, when you show this to your colleagues, they might just say that now you've become one of us and that you can't ever be taken seriously as a scientist anymore!' I smile in relief at his naïve concern, and shake my head vigorously. 'No. I'm an anthropologist. You remember that stuff I told you about participant observation and feeling things on your own hide? Well, this is it. It's cool.'

June 2019. What's being 'cool'?

Six years have passed since I had this conversation with Arunas, in the room in which he still edits the footage he has shot with his small camera in various locations in The Promised Land, the new religious community he joined some twenty odd years ago. His aim is to make documentaries that show humanity the error of its ways and the alternative that his Teacher, the Christ Reborn, and his community in the Siberian countryside, are offering. It's five years since he finished this particular film and uploaded it to YouTube.

I'm not as 'cool' about the film as I thought I would be. My reassurance to Arunas that experiencing the Holy Spirit first hand was just what I needed for sparking a vital discussion about God back home, was definitely the excited bravado of a fledgling anthropologist finally being let loose in the field after years of study, and discovering that all this writing on anthropological methodology actually has merit. That yes, you can indeed actually place yourself bodily among people who at first seem decidedly strange to you, and then, given time and effort, go on to have experiences not unlike theirs. Contrary to my initial scepticism about whether I would become able to feel the presence of the divine just by participating in the daily lives of believers, immersive ethnographic method really does seem to work, and this is a quite exciting discovery the first time around. However, what to make of the visceral knowledge gained from this kind of experience was not obvious to me at the time. How to live with it was even less clear. It seems like I had expected my new understanding to just heap itself on top of everything else I already knew. But it didn't. Being touched by the divine changes everything and nothing. I clearly had not anticipated the way this experience would assume a life of its own away from the field.

My coolness with the film after returning from the field is definitely belied by my less-than-eager efforts to make good on my promises to Arunas about showing the film to others and securing funding for further film projects. Sure, I did ask here and there; but to be honest, the film took a long time to resurface from beneath the usual day-to-day workload I had, perhaps as an unconscious act of sabotage on my part, buried it under in the office. I see now that I had come to see the interest of others as unlikely; which in my defence, is perhaps unsurprising. The film was clearly made by an amateur. The cutting is quite abrupt at times, the rather quaint English subtitles come thundering into the screen from the right, and the insertion of popular Western music and cinema, clearly in violation of copyright and complete with Russian dubbing over the still audible English soundtrack, positively screams bootleg montage. It's Russian garage cinema. Even if I still like it myself, it's understandable if I had second thoughts about who in Europe would really be interested in funding the films of an unknown Lithuanian member of some sect in Siberia. Who would fund someone whose aim is clearly to tell us all about the return of Christ to a place most Westerners would see as the frozen edge of the world?

Without actually showing anyone the film, I asked a few colleagues and did a few internet searches. My doubts were confirmed. So, what else could I do?

I felt guilty for a long time. I see now that I salved my conscience with the fact that while participating in Arunas's film was important to the process of getting access to, and building social capital with, the religious community he lives in, one of his goals in including me was to use what he saw as my authority as a scientist to rubber-stamp his message and to use me as a crowbar to gain access to the heaps of money he imagined to be locked away in funds in Europe. I was, and am, under no obligation to push his agenda further. Still, this did little to abate my nagging feeling of betrayal. Was I just holding out on a half-baked promise to a friend, who will surely do fine anyway? Or was I denying my own part in a project which I myself felt frighteningly strongly about, and which still touches my heart in deep places?

Ironic sympathy

Looking back on my experiences in the field and my reluctance to tell others about them, it's quite strange to think now that my choice of The Promised Land for my PhD fieldwork initially seemed to be a matter of convenience. I was quite fond of Russia, having travelled there several times over the years. As I speak the language quite well, it was an obvious region for me to pick.

But there were few places in Russia that I felt like taking my wife and children. City life would get lonely and boring for them, and social life in the villages often involves frequent use of vast amounts of alcohol. Having visited the Church of the Last Testament (as Arunas's community is officially named) as a backpacker a few years earlier, choosing it for my field location seemed like the solution to my problem. The Promised Land is definitely in the countryside, a large area of pristine birch and evergreen forest covering the softly rolling Sayan Mountains in the southernmost part of Krasnoyarsk Territory. The around five thousand inhabitants, many of them members of the Church, live in small villages of wooden houses sprinkled around the area, mostly on the banks of shallow rivers. It is a beautiful place. In addition to being teetotallers, most of Teacher's followers are well educated, having moved here from cities all over the former Soviet Union. So, it was likely that my wife would be able to find English-speaking friends of her own. Also, as, according to the statistics, the community, has one of highest birth rates in Russia, my children should be able to make some friends too, especially given that children roam around freely in the villages.

I only had one problem. Notwithstanding the beautiful setting, I felt annoyed by the place. Sure, I found appealing many of the community's ideals, such as the idea of producing your own food locally and organically, and the Waldorfian inspiration evident in the schools, and the notion of trying to live together in a close community instead of within the atomized social structure I pictured as predominant in the West. Learning to not just act kindly, but to stop thinking badly about others altogether, which I had been told was fundamental to the way these people saw spiritual practice, also evoked my sympathy.

However, sympathy is one thing. Taking seriously other people's belief in what I saw as a utopia is quite another. On my first visit as a backpacker, I had found the overwhelmingly positive attitude of these utopianists nauseatingly hypocritical and, most of all, naïve. Their self-congratulatory stories about themselves just seemed too good to be true. There were also a few things that ran directly counter to the ideals I would follow, were I, hypothetically, to dream up a utopia for myself. Not the least, the idea of placing someone on a pedestal as the Christ Reborn, all dressed up in red robes and surrounded with Christian imagery. Besides being incomprehensible, this is kitsch. And then they had ideas of ideal gender roles, with men being in charge and women following, supporting and not arguing. Not my utopia either. I liked the thought of women being as strong as men, and men as soft as women, and prided myself on being empathic and reasonable with the women in my life. Given how strong and bossy I generally found Russian women to be, I was quite surprised, no, dismayed, that they would agree to this backslide into patriarchy. Oh, and their humour, all friendly and good natured with no hint of sharp teeth. How could one stand living without the occasional provocative tingle of a well-placed cynical or sarcastic remark to keep matters straight and real?

Looking back, rather than convenience, it was this dual sympathy and aversion that was instrumental in pulling me back there for research. I had used my experience in the community as a good traveller's tale on social occasions up to that point, always getting myself some good laughs by ironically alluding to the futility of the utopianism of this Siberian Christ and his followers. That was, until a colleague called me out on it. Why did I want to do research there, if I found it so ridiculous? Was there really nothing in what these people were doing that I could relate to?

This was a good question, with embarrassing poignancy. What kind of anthropologist sets out for the field full of irony? My kind, apparently. I decided to accept this fact as an anthropological challenge. Seeing these people as modern, well-educated city dwellers such as myself, but holding beliefs I saw as outlandish, would I be able to reach across the chasm of understanding where it seemed the widest, and grasp their experience of the divine itself?

Let's return to the moment when I arrived in the field.

September – December 2011: unshareable knowledge

On entering the field, the challenge I had given myself turned out to be harder than I thought.

My new informants welcome me kindly. But even though they find my sympathetic approach commendable, they're not terribly interested in what I'm going to write about them. Their project is to discover and refine the soul, they tell me, a process so subtle and fine that it defies any kind of scientific inquiry. So, from their point of view, my project of scientifically understanding them is doomed from the start. My questions about how they came to this conclusion, how they 'know' all this, are deftly deflected back towards me. They're obviously quite reluctant to talk about themselves.

Instead, they tell me that by living in their community I'll eventually begin to feel my own soul come alive. After a while, I'll realize the futility of my research and put it aside; and in due time, I'll abandon my place out in 'the other world' to settle with them in The Promised Land. I'll fit right in. They can see it in my eyes. Not only will I realize I belong there, it will become clear to me that I can stay in 'the other world' no more. They tell me about the secret 'world government' that has enslaved the planet through to its liberal do-as-you-like ideology, all of which runs counter to spiritual growth and snuffs out the soul. The Promised Land is the only place to free your mind from this. Besides, the aggression accumulating from this subtle tyranny will likely soon cause a global karmic backlash, wiping out most of the planet's population. So, it's high time to join their Noah's Ark, as they, with a good-natured laugh, call it. Unless, of course, I want to queue up for reincarnation with seven billion other souls, they jokingly add. Oh, and about my wife: she'll follow me, with our children. If she doesn't, that's her choice. My task as a man is to lead the way by following the call of my soul. Hers, as a woman, is to follow.

Their seemingly casual placing of me in their grand narratives unsettles me. Their retelling of them as if they are plain facts that they already know, seems downright heartless. How annoying, to be included in their irrational conspiracy theories without being asked! But I'm not alone in feeling like this. Along the way, they present me with journalistic documentaries about their community, in which I get a palpable sense of the same ironic, at times even hateful, distance I myself feel towards what I'm witnessing here. It's a good reminder of my own methodological goal, and of who I am, an anthropologist. Unlike these journalists, with their agenda of uncovering the 'truth' about this place, if that's what it is, I'm here for the native's point of view. I can do better.

I just have to realize that the ontological abyss is wider than I had imagined, and that there are ethical constraints. Should I, in the name of participant observation, leave my wife to move to Siberia? The question is absurd. But how to understand the existential stance of my informants without somehow circumscribing or explaining it away, when real access to participating in their world seems so far out of reach? Day after day, I ponder what it would take for me to believe what they believe. But apart from small patches of agreement that there are definitely many things wrong with the world today, the gulf seems unbridgeable. I'll have to get it from them. Get some interviews.

But even as I prudently start out with innocent requests to leave my recorder running while casually chatting, in order to better remember our conversations, I run into a wall of indifference. My gear turns my otherwise lively and cheerful conversation partners into, at best, patient teachers of religious ideology, giving me the information they presume I need to complete a task they have a hard time seeing the relevance of, apart from it obviously being important to me. At the first opportunity they excuse themselves, obviously not finding my company terribly interesting anymore. I decide to postpone interviewing until I've built more trust, using my recorder from here on in to just talk to myself on my long walks around the villages.

Liminal friends

Arunas is an exception. In many ways he is an outsider in his community, and meeting him was no accident. In a similar but different way from me, I have found him also to be a liminal character, and our interests have converged and clashed in ways which have taught me things my ironic self might have wished left unlearned.

Arunas has a sharp eye for the hypocrisies of his community, and with our growing friendship he has become a rich source of jokes portraying the paradoxes of communal life in the footsteps of Christ. Not right away, though. His critical gaze comes from deep commitment, and his wit he reserves for those he deems capable of understanding it as such. It took a while for me to understand this. Seeing in him a fellow critical intellectual, in the beginning I habitually threw in the occasional clever bit of sarcasm at the expense of those we talked about. However, my attempts to joke usually only elicited a slight frown and a quick change of subject.

I quickly feel our connection during a few chance meetings, and my first visit for tea confirms it. As darkness descends on the cold winter's afternoon outside, I learn of his background as a practitioner of Zen Buddhism in Soviet Lithuania, and the longing of his soul for a life of fuller manifestation.

He shows me one of the most significant films he has made on life in the community. He explains how he uses the form of an unfolding story, seen through the eyes of a main character, to examine key concepts that people try to live by here. This one is about the concept of *prazdnik*, celebration. It's about a clown wandering around the community talking to various people during the preparations for the summer festival. All the while, his inner child, played by a friend of Arunas's son, insistently keeps asking him the inconvenient question of what an inner celebration of the soul really is, forcing him onto a quest to clarify what this apparently self-evident concept actually means.

I, in turn, share the ambitions of my research, my predicament as an agnostic in understanding what people are doing here, and my frustration at the reluctance I meet when doing interviews. He understands, and confirms what has been dawning on me already, namely that people here don't care for what they see as unengaged conversations, but need to see the gleam of soul in my eyes. He feels the same way, but as a documentarist he doesn't think that soul, recording equipment and research necessarily rule each other out. Moreover, he thinks he can see the soul in my eyes as we talk. He can. He's a sharp and witty conversation partner, and frustrations notwithstanding, not accepting my own cynical attitude at face value these last few months has set off a train of reflections I'm happy to share with him.

January – April 2013: a documentarist and his subject

Having taken to each other, Arunas and I agree for me to rent one of his two houses for my next period of fieldwork. Thus, we become neighbours, friends and mentor–apprentice, and I often return to his small office once my family is asleep, for help in interpreting the experiences I've had during the day. Among other subjects of conversation is a sequel to the film with the clown, which is causing him a bit of creative frustration. He has already shot quite a few scenes with him, but now the clown has left for the city to pursue his career as an actor. Arunas is trying to persuade him to come back for further filming, but is by now becoming resigned to the fact that he probably will have to make do with the fragmented material he already has. But as he muses over this, a new idea begins to take form in his head: 'Have you ever tried being on film?', he asks one day. 'Can I just try filming you?'

I hesitantly agree, wondering what he's up to as he quickly sets a chair for me to sit on. He sets his small camera upon a tripod and starts asking me questions about my research project and anthropology in general. I quickly loosen up and start talking. Even as I struggle to translate my complicated theoretical jargon into the still rather plain Russian I have at my disposal, I can't help but notice how quickly the tables have been turned. Arunas is a really good interviewer, better than me. As he goes on extracting information from me, I wonder how come I still haven't worked up the nerve to ask him for an interview, when he, seemingly without any problems, is doing one with me, on camera no less. My informant is studying me, and I can't help feeling that he is more proficient at this than I am at studying him.

Arunas is enthusiastic about my performance, and suggests we make a film on the community together. Actually, we could make a documentary

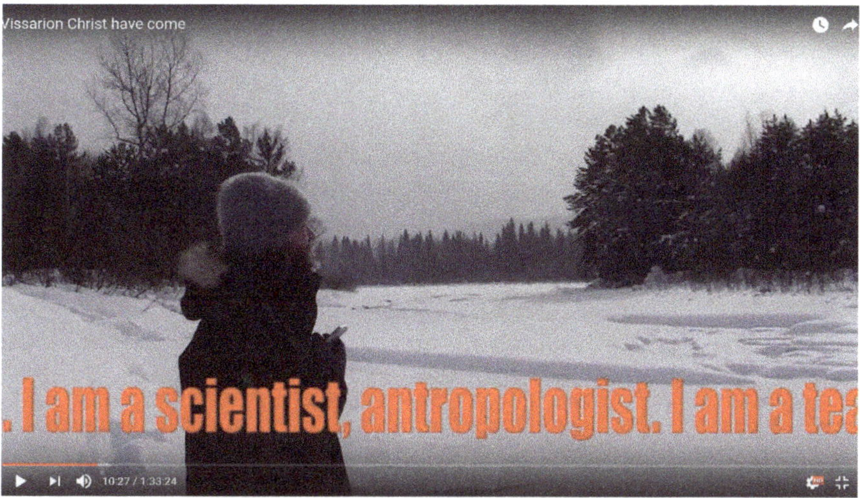

Figure 7.2 Introducing myself and my research to my viewers. Arunas Machulis.

about me! Even if people here don't fancy being investigated personally, they still find the idea of somebody coming here to explore the community scientifically kind of neat. It could result in a really interesting film for people here. I hesitate, but he reassures me enthusiastically that he already has a lot of ideas about scenes to shoot and people for me to interview, like my Belgian friend, Gert, or that former member of the Ukrainian parliament, Vasya. He'll arrange everything.

I can't help thinking to myself that this would be a rather crude, journalistic way of going about interviewing people. Then again, even though I know that ethnography may be done without interviews, and even though I am trying to come to terms with relying almost exclusively on participatory methods, I still feel a frustrating longing for the reassuring feeling of validity that having the voices of my informants on record should give. But I think I should let my informant take the lead. Arunas is offering me a gift, and I'll be reciprocating with a gift of my own. It's a win for both of us.

So, I accept. And from that day, Arunas's camera becomes a more or less constant presence in my daily life. When I'm talking to somebody outside his house, he suddenly jumps out with the camera in his hand. When I am taking part in the liturgy, I suddenly see him observing me through his lens from the other side of the temple. He begins rearranging my schedule to shoot specific scenes, often taking cues from things I tell him. Having told him about my experience of hacking holes in the ice with an axe to get water from the river, I find myself ordered outside and spending two hours walking up and down to the water hole with my buckets to ensure the perfect shoot in sunny weather. He prompts me to visit Gert, asking me to ask him some questions in Russian, after politely asking our wives to vacate the room along with the children. It's absurd and artificial, as Gert and I usually communicate in English without any pretence of me asking him anything. But despite the absurdity, I find myself enjoying it, and the setup does get Gert to say things he otherwise wouldn't. Besides, doing obviously staged scenes in other places gets us a lot of positive, curious attention. Somehow, playing the scientist the way these people imagine it's done, but doing it with Arunas, gives me increased credibility. Working with a local pays off. Besides, our film project being quite open-ended, it's interesting to witness how it unfolds and what it will mean for my research.

March – May 2014: sinking in

Our filming carries over from this fieldwork period to the next one, a year later. Limiting my obvious presence as an anthropologist to my time on camera, I concentrate on participant observation. I chop wood, sing in the church choir and drink an awful lot of tea. And I talk. Quite often, the subject returns to the topic that puzzles me the most: opening my soul and becoming unable to go back to live in 'the other world'. Even if I can't really imagine this happening to me, it seems to have happened to almost everybody else here. Though they seem unwilling to share their stories, I feel that this narrative makes sense of their own experiences of converting. So, sharing my own reflections on it, in a roundabout way, gives me access to theirs.

It's not only doubts that I share. I begin to see the appeal of this place. The people here are actually really nice, the countryside is magnificent, and there's little rush. As I let myself sink into the quiet local rhythm of life, for the sake of the argument, I try to picture myself having a future here. Taking care of my own land would be interesting, and I've already established myself as a useful person to the community with my musical and linguistic skills. It would be a good place for my kids. I already have plenty of friends, and would probably have a much more active social life than at home. It could be all right, actually.

As I participate in the rural life, the contemplative practices underlying it are gradually revealed to me. Through Arunas I learn that Teacher's doctrine has many things in common with the Buddhist notion of attachment. Freeing your soul means becoming aware of your attachments to your false ideas of yourself. In my conversations with Arunas, this converges subtly with my own ideas of my ethnographic enterprise. I marvel at discovering that those I saw as delusional sentimentalists, are actually dedicated to critical practices of introspection that at first glance look quite similar to my own project of uncovering the arbitrariness of my own position.

It's exhilarating to discover this level of interaction with my friends, and to share my discovery of my false selves with them. I begin joking that they're actually anthropologists. They, for their part, joke back that it's the other way around: I'm a believer – and my anthropological training, with all my professional tools for dissecting my own cultural background, makes me a much better believer than them.

They're right. Or they could be. For their joke poignantly points out the difference in what we find when we take ourselves apart. They find soul. I find layer upon layer of anthropological interest. If I found soul, would I believe it, or would I analyze it?

Is that what my irony is all about? Refusing to take seriously in my own life what they claim to have found in theirs?

As, day after day, I get down on my knees in the temple, I allow irony to dissipate. It melts away as I realize that those same choir psalms I initially despised for their naïve praise of God, now possess a simple, but otherworldly, beauty; and that the happy, now familiar faces around me no longer evoke my feelings of contempt, only sympathetic joy. I close my eyes, my soul bursts forth. Is this who I really am? My tears start flowing in release as all sorts of feelings wash through me. Among these, is fear at the ground now shaking beneath my feet.

Resistance from vanity

Arunas gets plenty of ideas as I bounce my experiences and reflections off him. He shows me his attempts at putting the scenes together, which also involve his unused clips of the clown. I'm a bit surprised, as in my vanity I had thought the film was strictly about me. Now there's a juxtaposition of me and the clown: the clown finishing his visit to the community and despairing upon returning to his illusory and alienating life in the city; and me coming to the community and, during the course of my ethnographic investigation, moving closer to God. One of the highlights is me, on Arunas's request, playing the guitar and telling a group of followers about an incident in which playing the guitar made me cry and feel my soul. This was a real incident, but its recounting was staged. Arunas wants me to do a contrasting voice-over, in which I talk about how my rationalistic European background makes accepting Teacher as the living word of Truth seem impossible.

I feel somewhat uneasy at this proposition, seeing that this film is turning into a piece of not-so-subtle propaganda for his community, and uses my statement to give an authoritative scientific stamp of approval to the entire project, at the same time as it cements the inferiority of science in grasping for higher truths. Even worse, the blanket statement Arunas has prepared for me is rather crude. It makes me look uneducated. Then again, I did say something to Arunas to that effect, so in all honesty I can't be against it. But at least it

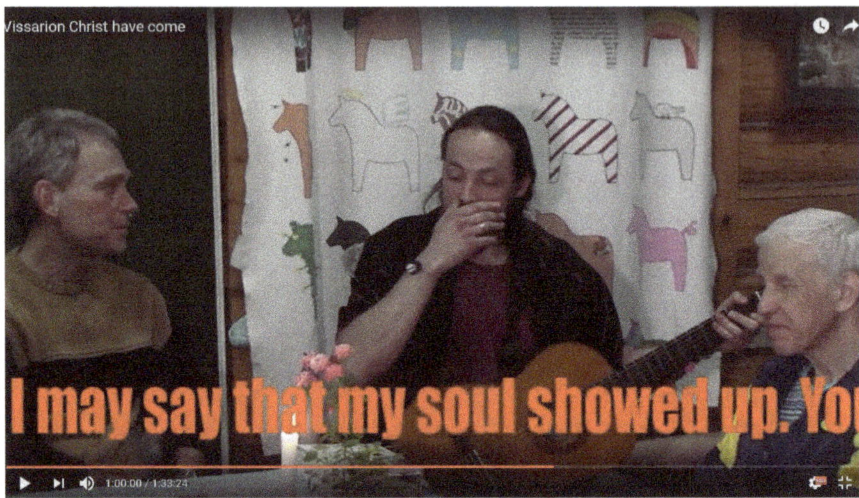

Figure 7.3 Relating my experiences of soul to fellow believers for the benefit of the camera. Arunas Machulis.

should be formulated more accurately! So, I reject Arunas's draft, and insist on writing my own words.

I hand over almost two pages of precise and carefully thought-out formulations, meticulously understated, with hedges in all the necessary places. It's a lot longer than Arunas's proposal, and I watch him a little anxiously, feeling a bit guilty about running his layman's version into the ground with my more professional one. But he hands it back with a slight tilt of his head to the side, saying it looks good, but that I'm still not writing with blood. 'Blood!' I frown, taken aback. 'I thought you wanted my anthropological take on all this, what does blood have to do with it!' He says calmly that he can't really recognize what I've been telling him about myself and my experiences in my writing, but anyway, it's too long and complicated for the film, so I should try to shorten it to maybe one-quarter of its present length. Well, that's hard to argue with. He is the producer after all. All right, I say, a lot calmer than I feel. Who the hell does he think he's dealing with, some bad poet aspiring to sell fiction in airport kiosks? Blood, really! I take my paper, go back indoors and try reformulating it.

After a while, I give up in frustration. Yes, I can write a shorter piece, but then it becomes even more complicated. Considering the broad audience, it seems like Arunas's words actually fit better than anything I can come up with. It's not as if what I said is unrecognizable in his text. On the contrary. But the broad brushstroke of the statement still annoys me. I guess I could just refuse to cooperate, or insist on saying something completely different. But why? Is my professional vanity, or the fact that he has an agenda with the film, a good enough reason to take away his commission to represent me, while I am actually living under his roof with the explicit intention of writing about him? He has an agenda, but he's not being dishonest. But maybe I am. My hypocrisy leaves a nasty taste in my mouth. No; I have to go along with it.

April 2013 – May 2015: away and safe

Back home, safely away from Arunas's scrutiny, I write my own things. But somehow, I find it difficult to write. The field feels far away, and as I treat it through the lens of etic terminology, the tingling, tear-provoking sensation of my soul slips through my fingers. Was it ever really there at all, as anything but a learned impulse? How am I supposed to answer that? I'm not... because I can't. But describing the learning process itself, discussing cognitive versus embodied perspectives, is feasible, at least, and provides me with a direction for writing in the form of answerable questions. Listening to my field recordings, I recall pleasant days of praying in the sun and moonlit nights of seeing visions of our future utopia, and I write it out with respectful methodological agnosticism. This becomes an anthropology of religious conversion based on participant observation, with all the due referencing, understating and hedging that Arunas so dislikes. I get a few pats on the back for it from my academic colleagues.

In hindsight, something is amiss. Could I have written it any differently? That's hard to say. I've often felt like grabbing my younger self by the collar and forcing him to tell the truth. I still do, at times. But I'm beginning to recognize the personal constraints on what he wrote, indeed lived, at the time, and to accept with a certain gentleness what, at other times, I've felt like labelling as cowardice, in order to distance my current from my previous self. Like it or not, that guy's still part of me. I wrote with all the courage and integrity I could muster, doing my best to push my own understanding of the limits of what anthropology can do in the process. The resulting writing was sympathetic and humanizing, and implied that the religious radicality that I had initially perceived, was actually a social construction of my own that was irrelevant to my informants' lives; and that conversions entailed no madness, only prolonged exposure, like that I had endured.

I was wrong. Probably against my better judgment, but not wilfully. I can see now how, in telling others about my adventures, I chose to emphasize the academic interest of using myself as an ethnographic tool to understand the Other, disarmingly throwing in a few jokes to satisfy the gleam of irony I thought I detected in the eyes of those to whom I told my improbable story of a frozen Christ in Siberia. This wasn't honest to my own experience. But using anthropology to normalize what I used to see as crazy, was still a big step, both in courage and humility, and pretending that participant observation always carries a tinge of make-believe shielded me from many uncomfortable existential questions that I wasn't ready to answer.

Now to use my well-earned access to the field to validate my findings. I needed some interviews to get the native's point of view from the natives themselves.

June – August 2015: falling in, coming out

I return to the field for final checks. It should be easy, but I feel a strange resistance to going. I meet resistance from my Siberian friends as well. They still prefer talking about me, and how my practices of the soul are going. Somehow, they seem more radical in their beliefs than I remember them to be. Besides, the mosquitoes are killing me. I just want to go home.

Then reality sends me a reminder of just how little say I actually have in all this.

The reminder's name is Anya. She's beautiful and dances like a dream, moving her naked feet deftly through the grass under the flowing folds of her long dress. Her eyes dance with the same elegance, coquettishly darting back and forth to mine, and she shows her care for me by picking me blackberries, knowing that they're my favourite. She exudes a femininity so strong that I'm surprised at myself for not laughing it off as I usually would, for it being so trite and stereotypical.

I used to see through these things. I used to know that a woman like Anya was just performing the gender ideology of this place. Not any longer. If anything, I finally see through my own alleged 'seeing through' these things. She has obviously chosen to live her feminine soul. I have chosen nothing, least of all to be the man whom she now, by her presence, forces me to see. Seeing is all I allow myself to do. But that's more than enough.

I'd felt the ground shaking before, but now there's an earthquake under my feet, as I realize how steadfastly I've been lying to myself while away, hiding behind academic explanation, burying my budding understanding of my own false ideas about myself. This is real. And if this is real, how many other lies am I still believing? What kind of machine am I – ignorant, emasculated and powerless – serving back home? I can't live like that!

I stop caring about the interviews I came for. I stick to recording myself, because it's a comforting habit on my long walks, but any idea of using these recordings in the future dissolves in the face of dealing with the present. Yes, now I seem to understand my informants, but I really don't give a damn about it. This isn't about them anymore. To the extent it is, it's in the inverse way of it being all about me. Now I finally have an informant who is willing to open up about facing the heartbreaking choice between incompatible realities, truth and illusion: me. But any idea of using this for anthropology seems absurd.

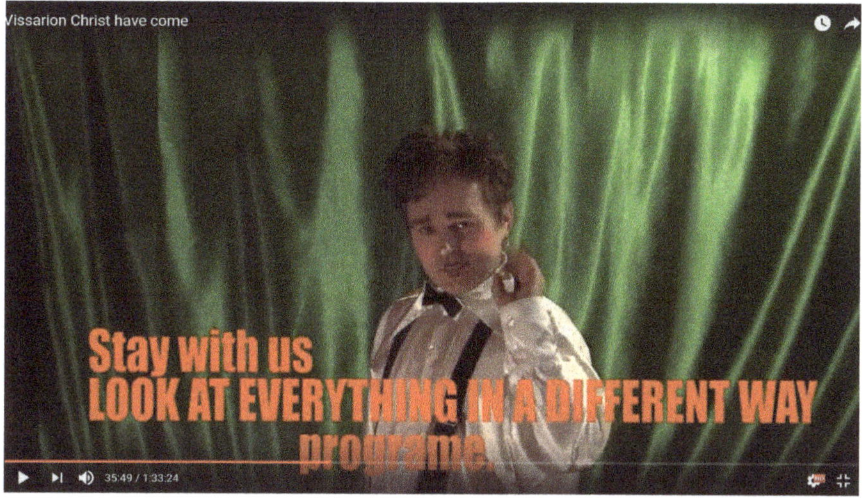

Figure 7.4 Dima the clown urging us all to reconsider our relation to reality. Arunas Machulis.

Again, I find myself dissolved in tears on my knees on the temple floor, realizing my impossible position. My children's faces look back at me behind my closed eyelids, wonderingly, as if at someone they used to know but can no longer recognize. I'm not who they think I am. Or who my wife thinks I am. Nothing is as we thought it was. They might be better off with somebody else, someone they can know, somebody who isn't feeling the pull of something they will never understand. The force of this pull is tearing us apart.

Oh, and Anya! She's calling to the man in me. To stay.

It's all beyond my control. Tears streaming down my face, I pray. I pray that if nothing else, my children will be okay.

My friends pick me up. To my surprise, there are no casual remarks about how the time has now come for me to find my place here. On the contrary, they express deep concern for my children, citing Teacher on the importance of safeguarding children at all costs. Sure, my soul has opened, even explosively so. But it's only natural that the realization of your soul's masculinity manifests in sexual attraction to the feminine. Chasing after this attraction is a mistake. On the contrary, masculinity is found in responsibility and self-control. If I really mean to take Teacher's words to heart, here is an excellent opportunity to practise them, by going against myself.

They hit my existential vulnerability precisely. It's hard to swallow, but I know they're right. Accepting the call of my soul means letting go of my attachment to Anya, Teacher and Siberia, and taking responsibility for my life where it is. Doing the right thing. The rest is fate, wherever that may lead me.

I go home. Except for a feeling of strong resolve in my belly, I don't know exactly what I need to do. Only that it needs to be honest. One of the first opportunities surfaces a few days after returning. It's a seminar I signed up for long ago, to give a talk on Arunas's film. An act of courage, I thought at the time, would be to show it to my colleagues. I see now how my courage was belied by my abstract, a meta-discussion of the way we can use the Other's constructions of us as anthropologists, to say something about the Other. I'm dismayed by my own intellectual move, to honour my promise to Arunas, while deftly flipping the spotlight from me to him. It seems very clever. However, really it is arrogant and dishonest, a pretence to be a disembodied brain talking to other disembodied brains, selling my friend and my engagement with the film and the community to bolster my intellectual ego, all while staying out of sight myself.

We're anthropologists, I remind myself. We feel in order to understand. Indeed, grasping the divine through my own body was what I set out to do four years ago. Now I'm about to disclose myself as a follower of the latest reincarnation of Christ in Siberia. Damn me if I don't.

Can anthropology meet and bear my new perspective? Do I want it to? What's the point? I have no idea. I just know that the thought of going to the seminar scares the living daylights out of me, and that I have to go.

I arrive late, having spent my morning frantically searching the film for good parts to show, in a sudden inexplicable urge to honour the original proposal for my presentation. The sick feeling in my stomach radiates all the way out to my hands and feet as I take the floor, filling them with a prickly, nervous energy. I begin showing clips from the film while I talk about my unease at revealing my complicity in this piece of religious propaganda. A series of good laughs from my audience calms me a bit and urges me on, until it suddenly strikes me what I'm doing. I'm joking. I cringe inside, realizing that I have fallen back into the groove of my tried and tested presenter persona. This is not me, I hear myself saying. I'm denying my engagement with the film.

As I finish my presentation and the questions begin, I break out of it. I talk about how I finally understand how people come to leave their families behind and move to Siberia. About how I don't know where I'm headed. And about how I see my marriage breaking up. The room falls quiet. I get some comments commending my openness, and some questions underscoring the immense anthropological interest of this.

I don't know what to do with the sympathy. I feel estranged. The questions seem to fall on me from another planet. I try to answer, but somehow my replies gravitate their own way, towards my own hazy understanding of something I want to share, though my words somehow fall short of the faces behind the tables.

I stay for lunch and some more nebulous talk about falling in love, feeling my masculinity awake and riding through life like a madman. Then I beat a hasty retreat in my car, feeling weak, stupid and out of my element. What did I do this for? To out myself? No matter how sincere the sympathy, I have the feeling that my audience didn't quite understand how insane this all feels. Probably because, in the end, I lacked both the courage and the words to disclose its reality. For what is it, really, this thing I've taken with me home from the field?

I have no idea what I'm doing, and I have no idea how, if at all, anthropology fits into all of this.

July 2019: my field is my life

Four years have passed. To me everything has changed, though from the outside most things probably seem similar.

I'm still married. After the seminar, I came clean to my wife: about Anya, about wanting to be a man, and eventually about my spiritual longing. Unsurprisingly, things erupted between us. More surprisingly, they quickly calmed down again. As it turned out, she had for a long time secretly detested my insistence on total marital equality, sensing it as insincere and cowardly on my part, without being able to put her finger on exactly what was wrong. She actually welcomed change. She doesn't want a stereotypical patriarch, but neither does she want equality. She wants polarity. Among other things she longs for, is for me to be the decisive one, the one who takes charge, and to be able truly to see me and what I want for the both of us. Frankly, this is what I want too, even if it's no laughing matter to turn that boat around. The soul takes no prisoners. You don't need to go to Siberia to make scary changes in your life.

Speaking of which: I've been to Siberia again, and still keep in touch with Arunas, Anya and my other friends. They kept me going in the first long period of feeling lonely and misunderstood after coming home, and they still teach me a lot. I'm deeply grateful. Anya's naked feet dancing around the meadows were one of the greatest turning points of my life. I've found that with patience, perseverance and courage, I've found no less abundance of beauty and dancing skill in the feet I've been married to all along.

I wonder, then, what coming home from the field really means, anthropologically speaking. It certainly doesn't mean sifting through my field notes, trying to tease out an understanding of my informants' lives. None of my notes, not even my emotional self-recordings, can relay this to me. Sure, they can reconnect me with specific events that may serve as illustrations of points I'd like to get across. But extracting any understanding from my field experiences comes through integrating learned practices into my life, for example, in relating to my wife in new ways; or through meditating on the portrait of Teacher. Is he Christ? I don't care. Like most of my Siberian friends, I have put that question aside, as attempting to answer it would merely be an intellectual exercise. In practice, I find that whenever I come across Teacher's words, I pay attention. Most of the time they make deep sense to me, and they usually serve as timely reminders to stay awake and keep my life on course.

Which brings me to my point. What initially was thought to be just a convenient choice of place for fieldwork, with an added interesting methodological challenge based on the irony I brought to the field, has resulted in a continuously life-changing event, turning what was particular about the field into an unfolding aspect of me as the ethnographer. In other words, the field as a fixed geographical locale has transposed itself onto me as a living and changing entity. My field is my life. Consequently, whatever I produce or encounter may take on the status of notes or observations. Examples include the first seven drafts of this story, all displaying differing attitudes to what I've been going through. Other examples are feedback and peer reviews, which prompt me to do things to my texts that I would previously have found to be of utmost importance, but which now often seem quite irrelevant to me. Contextualizing The Promised Land, for instance. Such promptings help point out to me where I'm headed – or just as often, just where I'm not – and force me to consider my relation to this profession of mine, and what to do about it. It's inescapable if I'm to write anything at all. Which it seems I am.

Context, to take that example, really is not the issue here. I won't say that contextualizing in order to understand the conditions of the lives of our informants does not have merit, if that is your goal. But for me, what is of importance is existential experience, transcending the field and the notes ostensibly taken home from it. The Promised Land is not the issue here. The issue is something intangible that I'm carrying with me from my encounter with that place that continually shapes and is shaped by my encounters with life at home, physically away from my so-called field. We might call this 'something' the experience of soul.

However, my thoughts on soul are for another time. To return to the beginning of my story, Arunas's film might be seen as a note produced by an informant that tells me something about his perception of reality, through his perception of me. It certainly does do this. But beyond its descriptive qualities, the film was a testament to, and an agent in, my personal change in the field, without which I would not have come to understand the main lessons my informants, in their roundabout way, were trying to impart. Even though much of the action in the film is staged, as Arunas's representation of my process of change, it is nevertheless based on hours and hours of open discussions of this process in the small room in his attic. While the film's representation is far from exhaustive, and definitely not neutral, I still clearly recognize myself in his gaze, though even at this stage in the process there are times when I shirk from it in gut-wrenching embarrassment. At those times I'd still rather not make use of the film. But that's the point. How could I not?

Refraining would not just be breaking a promise to my informant, friend and collaborator. I realize that it would be a betrayal of myself, and of the anthropology I'm trying to write. By showing the film to others, I've allowed Arunas to drag me kicking and screaming to the point of no return in my struggle with the irony I so like to hide myself behind. He likely didn't know this, but he's forced me to at least try to be honest with myself, something I found much harder to do while working in isolation with field notes, recordings and interviews. In so doing, he has in a most unexpected way helped me see the masks that I wear, an insight that has proven indispensable in understanding what my informants are trying to tell me. This progress has entailed self-disclosure, to myself and to the gaze of Others, in the field and at home.

This has changed my life and changed my writing, and it continues to do so. I don't yet understand how, and most likely I never fully will. So what? What I write is, to the best of my ability and courage, truth as I see it, even though such truth is always liminal, temporary, and constrained by my mind's limited ability to overcome its own desire to make sense to itself. My life is a field note. I am a field note. This paper is a field note. Does it also qualify as anthropology, then? I don't know. But whatever I write must come from this place.

References

Vissarion Christ Have Come (dir. A. Machulis): www.youtube.com/watch?v=WqQ3hZarSXM (accessed 16 July 2019).

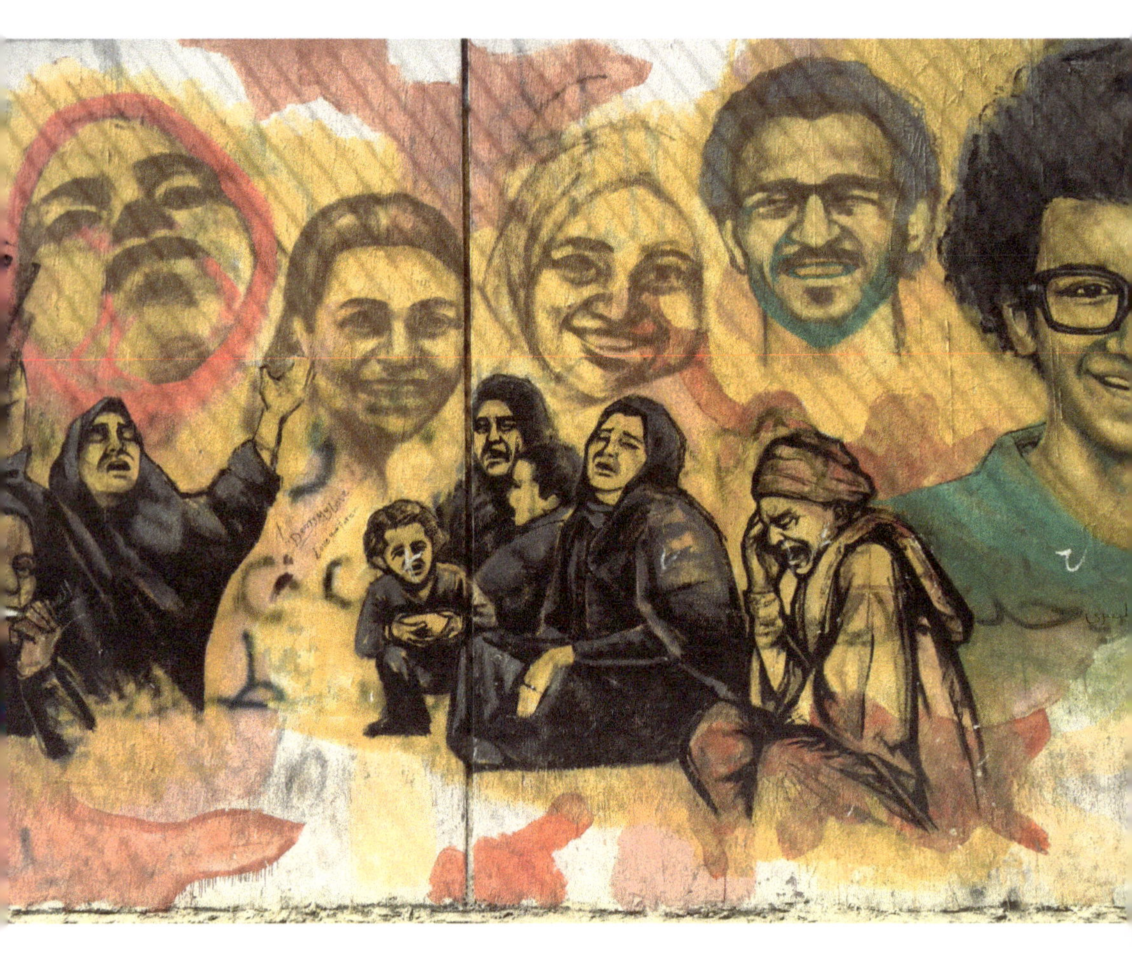

8

Risky notes

Reading tense situations in Cairo 2015

MILLE KJÆRGAARD THORSEN

'There is no reason for us to fight,' Rania says. She looks at Fatima, a woman in her forties with type 2 diabetes. Rania, one of the doctors in the diabetes clinic, adds: 'You have to know what you can eat and what is forbidden.' Fatima starts arguing again. She is shouting in a loud shrill voice. The air-conditioning is humming in the background, keeping the Cairo summer heat at a far distance. I am cold. I pull on my sweater while trying to keep up with Rania and Fatima's conversation in my notebook. Fatima is talking and talking. I don't quite understand her. Rania sighs and opens Fatima's file on the computer. Rania starts ticking off several symptoms, without asking Fatima about them: 'weight gain', 'fatigue', 'excessive thirst'. Fatima is still talking, arguing that her blood-sugar levels are too high because she is 'upset' and 'sad', not because she is not eating correctly. Rania doesn't respond, but keeps checking off symptoms in Fatima's file. A nurse opens the door and walks across the consultation room. She is drinking a Coke, straight out of the shiny red can. She picks up a stethoscope and leaves the room without speaking a word. A patient abruptly opens the door and walks in. Rania tells her to leave immediately. Rania closes Fatima's file on the computer, and tells her to lie down on the examination bed. Rania slowly gets up from behind the desk to examine her. On her way to the examination bed she tells me in English: 'Bad habits, one of the main causes of wrong treatment. Write that down...' She points to my notebook. Rania quietly examines Fatima before suddenly exclaiming in Arabic, so Fatima

Figure 8.1 (opposite) *Graffiti on Mohamed Mahmoud Street, Cairo. Photograph by the author, 25 May 2015, artist Essam Eiss.*

understands: 'She claims her measurements are too high because she is sad. But that is wrong!'

14 August 2015: at the square

I get off the train and walk straight towards the stairs of the metro station that leads to Mohamed Mahmoud Street, just off Tahrir Square.[1] A police officer blocks my way. 'Your bag,' he says in Arabic. I look at him, surprised. He points me to a desk that has been set up in the middle of the station. Several police officers are sitting behind the desk, drinking tea, occasionally stopping people passing by. I walk over to the desk. I open my purse and the police officer rummages through everything inside. He smiles and waves me towards the exit. I smile back at him and quickly leave the station. The square seems peaceful and quiet. I pass the colourful graffiti walls on Mohamed Mahmoud Street, leftovers from the political turmoil of the past five years.

An old man is selling magazines and local newspapers from a stall in the middle of the street. I scan them for something interesting. The man points to *Egypt Today*, an English-language magazine. I tell him, in Arabic, that I am looking for Arabic women's magazines. He smiles at me and starts picking out different ones from around the stall. Most of the covers show women in wedding dresses. I ask him if they are all about getting married. He laughs and says they are about 'fashion.' I pick out four magazines to buy.

I walk straight to McDonald's down the street. A couple of young boys dressed in McDonald's uniforms are fooling around behind the counter. I ask for a sundae. 'We have no more sundae,' one of them tells me in Arabic. I ask for a McFlurry. 'We have no more McFlurry,' he adds. One of the other young boys interrupts and says in Arabic: 'There is no more sundae, there is no more McFlurry, there is no more milkshake. It's a problem.' We all laugh. Cairo is out of ice cream.

I leave McDonald's and decide to go to visit Mohamed. On the way back to the metro station I pass a couple of soldiers on guard in Tahrir Square. They all look young, and drenched in sweat in their black uniforms. Back on the metro I watch the city pass by. Several young boys enter the women's carriage selling all kinds of stuff: hairpins, underwear, a toothbrush, colourful stickers, jewellery, colouring books, batteries, tablecloths. I buy a paper fan, 'only three pounds.'

1 Tahrir Square (known as Liberation Square in English) is one of the main squares in downtown Cairo. It has been one of the central gathering points for protestors since the revolution of 2011, and is heavily guarded by police and soldiers.

14 August 2015: in the garden

Mohamed and I are sitting in the garden drinking our sugary mint tea. Mohamed is taking a break from his work as a gardener. I am taking a break from downtown Cairo. We are talking about my research. Mohamed argues that the high prevalence of diabetes in Egypt is caused by increasingly hard living conditions. 'Let me tell you something…', he keeps saying while explaining how stress and concern can cause diabetes. He specifically mentions triggers like depression, feeling upset or sad, worrying too much, and feeling nervous or aggressive. He wraps up his argument by telling me this is why it is important to laugh a lot and not 'think too much'. And why you should drink tea: 'you can't drink tea when you are angry', he explains as he sips from his cup. I nod while I drink my tea. I ask Mohamed if factors such as weight and food intake can cause diabetes. Mohamed laughs and explains that I have it all wrong: 'You can't get diabetes because you are fat!' he says. We both laugh at my assumption. I ask Mohamed how exactly life conditions are worsening in Egypt. He says, 'Politics are really bad, there is a lot of corruption', he says and adds that I surely know this already. I ask him if he believes the corruption is worse today than before the revolution. Mohamed points to a wooden garden gate in front of us. 'Before the revolution, the President would maybe take a piece of wood for himself. There would still be a door. Today the President will take the whole door. He doesn't care.' We laugh at the comparison. I ask Mohamed to elaborate: 'So, what you mean is…' Mohamed laughs and asks me to stop. 'Enough!' he exclaims, hands in the air. 'You are going to give me diabetes with all these questions.' We laugh again.

Introducing my field

This chapter tells the story of a collection of written field notes and of how they came to life in Cairo in the summer and autumn of 2015. In the above and in the following pages I present the reader with excerpts from my field notes taken during my fieldwork on diabetes in Cairo, Egypt. These excerpts (followed by my reflections) illustrate what it is like to take field notes in a field of political and social unrest. They show how conducting fieldwork in a tense setting may affect the practicalities of writing field notes, such as their format and ethical considerations. In addition, they show how a specific ethnographic context, such as the one in Cairo in 2015, may magnify more general questions related to ethnographic research due to a growing sense of paranoia in the researcher. They raise certain questions, such as how to interpret atmospheres and moods (rarely spoken of) in the field, how to depict such ambiguous atmospheres in one's field notes, and, finally, how to interpret these notes upon returning from the field.

I arrived in Cairo to conduct the first phase of fieldwork for my PhD in the beginning of May 2015. This was four years after the revolution of 2011 that formed part of the Arab Spring, a series of political revolts in the region of North Africa and the Middle East. My fieldwork was to focus on diabetes, a chronic illness with very high prevalence rates in the region.[2] In my project proposal I had stated that the political situation in Egypt would not affect my fieldwork, as I was focusing on a very 'apolitical' topic, diabetes. But as it turned out, nothing is really apolitical in Egypt (or probably anywhere).

Following the ousting of Hosni Mubarak in 2011, Mohamed Morsi was elected as president in 2012, only to be ousted in 2013 and replaced by Abdul Fattah Al-Sisi in 2014. From my Egyptian acquaintances I quickly learned that the political atmosphere since 2011 had gone from one of great optimism to one of political fatigue. Whereas most of my interlocutors had participated in the demonstrations and political discussions back in 2011, few were engaging in political discussions (even among friends and family) four years later. As one of my interlocutors told me, she was 'depressed' about politics. Despite this reluctance to openly discuss it, or the state of the country, politics seemed to be everywhere.

When planning my fieldwork I had initially arranged to stay with an Egyptian family I knew well from a previous stay in Egypt in 2010. The family lived in a rather poor, tight-knit community a little way outside Cairo. They quickly agreed to me staying with them, yet expressed some concern as to the possible consequences of my stay. Mostly they were concerned about what the neighbours might say about me and about them, but they were also worried about whether or not they had to report to the police that they had a foreigner staying with them. Finally, they decided to ask someone they knew in the police force before my arrival. Once I arrived, the family never let me leave the house on my own. Because I was a woman and a foreigner they felt it was 'too dangerous' for me. Out and about with my Egyptian family, we were frequently stopped by people in the street: 'Who is she? What is she doing here? Why is she staying with you?' Relatives would likewise call my host family to ask about the girl from 'outside'. To me, these inquiries often felt more suspicious and sceptical than friendly. For example, I was quickly reminded of the Arabic word '*gasusa*', spy, as it was often mumbled by people passing us on the street. After a month with my Egyptian host family I moved to a more central base in Cairo in an effort to walk the streets more freely and on my own.

---

2 The prevalence rate of diabetes in Egypt is around 15.5 per cent of the total population, compared to for example 8 per cent in Denmark (International Diabetes Federation 2014).

As I focused on my fieldwork on diabetes, slowly expanding my network to include several families with diabetic members, diabetic clinics, doctors and pharmacies, other issues seemed to be focusing in on me. Everyday life went on as usual, but the atmosphere of the city at times seemed thick with tension. On a daily basis, both my interlocutors and the media would report alarming stories about raids, illegal detentions and disappearances of members of opposing parties. Laws were passed to limit the freedom of press and a 'shoot-before-you-ask' policy seemed to be prevailing among the security police.[3] Foreigners and Egyptians alike were arrested for taking pictures in public places, or were detained by locals and brought to the police station for looking suspicious. Some foreign researchers were arrested and deported for associating with the 'wrong crowd', namely political activists or journalists. Finally, explosions and shootings, especially targeting police and military roadblocks, were happening at least a couple of times a week around Cairo. I myself was challenged by security several times, either for taking a picture of something that was not 'allowed' (e.g. a flower in the street) or for waiting for someone too long on a street corner. As one of my interlocutors put it: 'I feel like the streets in Egypt are for movement only. If you stop, someone will ask you why and who you are.'

Despite these ongoing incidents, business went on as usual. Men and women showed up for their appointments at the diabetes clinic, they would have their ice cream at McDonald's, shop for wedding magazines, pity the young conscripts standing outside all day in the heat, buy hairpins and tablecloths on the metro, drink their sugary mint tea and chat in the cool afternoon breeze. But more often than not (it seemed), certain words were spoken without further explanation, and emotions would change rapidly. This raised new questions for me and led me to regard incidents I had previously described in my field notes in a different light. What was this 'worry' or 'stress' everyone was talking about that would lead to diabetes? Why were the police suddenly checking people leaving the metro station, as opposed to entering it? Did the police officer really smile or did he look at me with suspicion? Why was the square suddenly so quiet and not bustling with activity? Was that young conscript really a poor young man, or was he out to arrest me? Should I maybe cross the street to avoid passing him?

---

3 For example, twelve people were killed and ten injured when the Egyptian air force opened fire on a tourist party in the Western Desert in September 2015. The Egyptian authorities argued that the area was restricted and that the group appeared to be driving in vehicles similar to those used by a known terrorist group in the area.

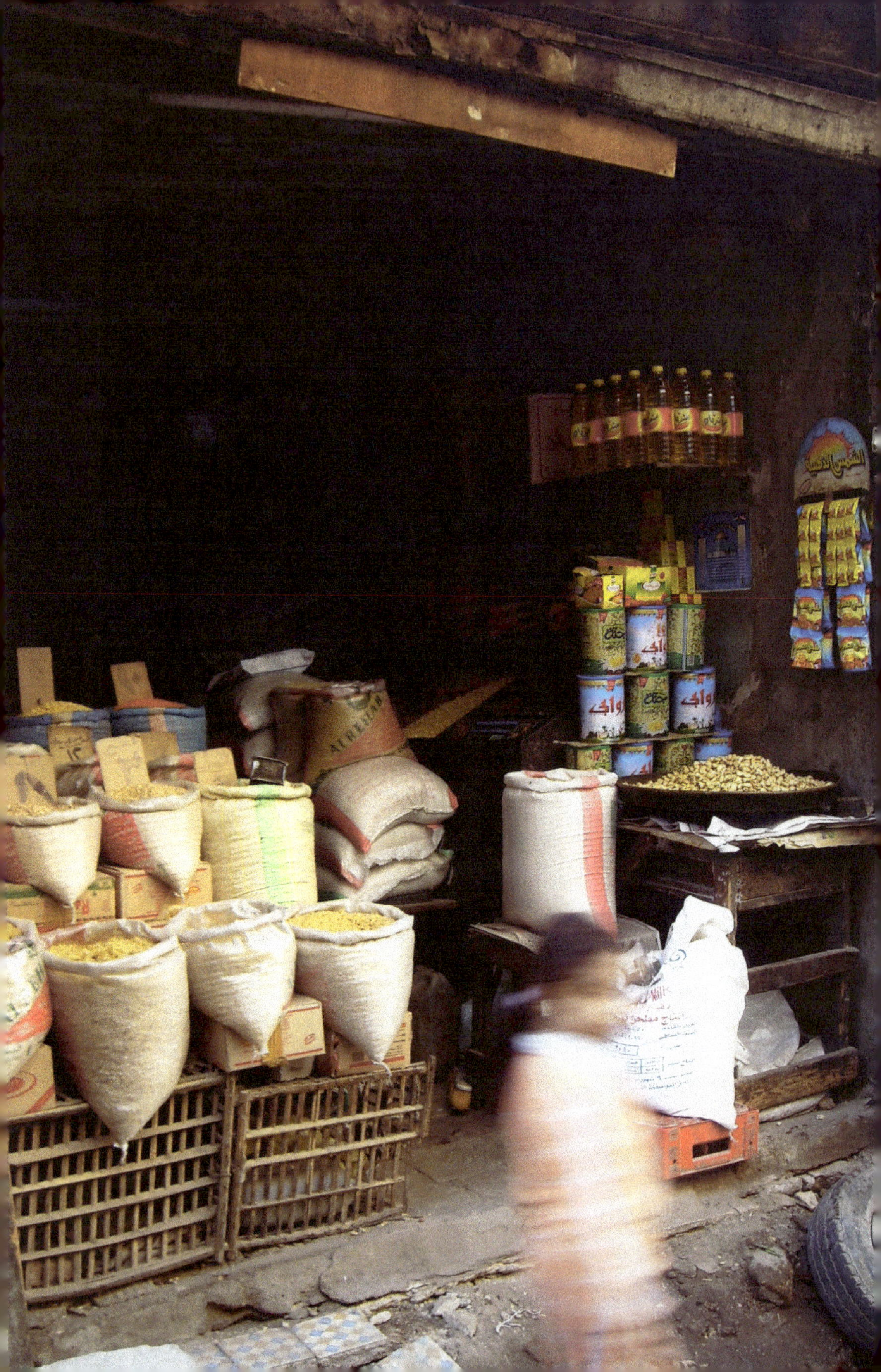

During my first months of fieldwork I would often switch in and out of these contradictory feelings and experiences – between peaceful normalcy and fearful paranoia. In fact, when I go through my field notes, I find that most of my early notes revolve around me feeling rather bored with my field, finding it hard to come up with something to write about – yet my notes capture a gradual sense of unease with what is going on around me.

Risky notes

Two ethical considerations were especially relevant during my fieldwork in Cairo. The first revolved around risks I might be imposing on my interlocutors when involving them in my research. The second concerned putting myself at risk when associating with certain people. These ethical considerations were closely related to the trust and mistrust displayed between my interlocutors, and between my interlocutors and myself. Those who showed me great trust had me consider how I could best protect them from the possibility of trouble with the authorities; while those who displayed little trust in me, had me considering whether or not I should make an effort to protect myself.

These issues of trust and mistrust, and the ethical considerations that followed, had some very specific consequences for how I came to conduct my fieldwork and write my field notes. For one thing, very few of my interlocutors let me record our conversations, as they were concerned the *mukhabarat*, the Egyptian intelligence service, were 'listening in' on my dictaphone or would somehow get hold of the recordings. The few interlocutors who did let me record an interview would at some point ask me to turn off the dictaphone in order to elaborate (in greater confidentiality) on something specific.

When it came to writing notes in the field, I would always ask my interlocutors if they were comfortable with me taking notes. Some would question why it was necessary, others agreed willingly. Often I would show my interlocutors the contents of my notebook, pointing out how I mostly wrote down facts or Arabic words, so as to not forget them. Several times I tried including my interlocutors in the note-taking process by asking them to write something out in Arabic, a word or a quote I wanted to make sure of getting down accurately. My notebooks are thus mostly jottings of numbers, random words and quotes, as well as brief chronologies of my day. None of the pages have information such as dates and locations. A typical page from my notebooks would be a list of Arabic words indicating the content of a conversation I was having with an unspecified person at an unspecified time. One page lists the words in English and then in Arabic: 'extremist', 'to harm',

Figure 8.2 (opposite) A girl passing a shop in central Cairo. Photograph by the author, 25 October 2015.

'to frustrate', 'optimism', 'pessimism', 'global', 'bribe', 'qualified'. Another list goes 'sterile instruments', 'uterus', 'foetus', 'vaccination', 'to bury', 'coffin'. Other pages contain more specific renditions of observations or bits of conversations. The more detailed observations and dialogues in my notebook mostly stem from visits to hospitals and clinics, as the atmosphere there was less tense and my role was more focused on observing than participating. Here is an example of these kind of notes, from a visit to a diabetes clinic (the dialogue is written in Arabic in my notebook and is between the patient and the doctor):

> PATIENT 14
> Eman, 40s, chubby face, black clothes with beads.
> 'First time here?'
> 'Mmm...'
> 'What do you take?'
> 'Pills' [Note to myself in the margin: not taking the pills right.]
> 'What do you eat?'
> 'I eat everything.'
> 'Do you drink a lot of Pepsi?' [Note to myself in the margin: measurements are high.]
> 'Your diabetes is not as it should be. You have to learn how to eat correctly and take your medicine correctly.'
> Checklist: drinks a lot, pees a lot, tired, problems with vision.
> 'Please lie down on the bed.'
> Examine her. Examine her legs. Feel her pulse. Fix her medicine.
> 'The eye doctor is next door.'

On getting home I would type out my actual field notes on the computer, assisted by my memory as well as notes like those above written in my notebook. In my typed-up field notes I would stick mostly to Danish, though I always kept quotes in their original language (English or Arabic). Most of the time I made sure not to type out the exact locations I had visited during my day, trying to keep companies, pharmacies, hospitals and so on anonymous in my notes. I changed the names of my interlocutors. The excerpts from my field notes throughout this chapter, such as those that open the chapter from the diabetes clinic, the square and the garden, more or less show these typed-up field notes in their original form. The notes have only been edited to the extent of fitting them to the chapter by, for example, cutting out long descriptions of places or people, or putting in descriptions necessary for the reader to understand the excerpt. They have also been translated from Danish/Arabic to English.

When in Cairo, I would keep my physical notebooks on my bookshelf in my apartment, not too worried that anyone would find them interesting. Sometimes I would cross out what I felt could be compromising to an interlocutor. I would send my typed-up field notes to my university email and, when the internet allowed it, I would save them on my home university server. I made sure not to save any documents on my desktop. As my fieldwork went by and my network expanded, I made sure to take a mental note of anyone I knew of some importance in Egypt. Who could get me out of a potentially bad situation with the authorities? As I was doing my fieldwork, I realized that most of my interlocutors had such people in readiness: connections to friends or distant relatives who had positions in different ministries, the police force or military, someone higher up the social and political ladder than themselves.

I took all of the above initiatives in an attempt to protect my interlocutors and myself from potential trouble. To this day, I am still not sure if this reflects my growing paranoia or the actual dangers of conducting fieldwork in Egypt in 2015. What I do know is that the politically tense situation blurred my sense of reality, making it difficult to interpret and understand what was going on around me. Issues of trust and mistrust were magnified, as everyone (including myself) seemed to either show too much or too little trust in one and another. As a result, in retrospect, moments in my field notes that are characterized primarily by mistrust appear almost silly and laughable. Contrarily, some of the moments characterized by great trust come off as risky and dangerous. In the remaining parts of this chapter I present the reader with two encounters – one with a pharmacist and one with a young conscript. Both illustrate moments of trust and mistrust and point to a question to be asked of all field notes: how do we, as ethnographers, interpret both our notes and the contexts in which they play out.

20 June 2015: at the pharmacy

I am sitting behind the desk. Ibrahim, the pharmacist, is sitting next to me looking intensely at his hands resting in his lap. Business is slow. It's midday and it's Ramadan, and most people are at home sleeping. Ibrahim keeps his answers to my questions short. I find it difficult to keep a conversation going with him. Ibrahim just told me that the general state of health is very bad in Egypt, but he seems reluctant to elaborate. I start suggesting answers: 'Because the life conditions are hard, or?' Ibrahim asks me how long I have been in Egypt. I tell him I have been here a while, and was here for six months before that as well. He briefly looks at me and says: 'So you know the life conditions are hard….' I smile at him and say: 'Yes, I know they are very hard.'

We sit for a while in silence. I try to strike up the conversation with Ibrahim again. I ask him how one becomes a pharmacist in Egypt. He quickly responds: 'We have a faculty. Nothing is wrong with our education.' I try to clarify that I don't doubt it's a fine education, I am only asking as I don't know where and how long and so on. I start asking specific questions: how long does it take to become a pharmacist? 'Five years.' Is it possible to open a pharmacy once you finish your education? 'If you have money.' Do you need a licence? Ibrahim looks at me and says: 'I don't understand your questions. Why are you asking all these things?' I try explaining yet again that I am asking these questions because I am curious and don't know the answers. I emphasize that it is background information for my research, but I find him very suspicious of me. Several times I tell him that I can come back another day when one of the other pharmacists is here. He tells me no: 'Please sit down…' A woman enters the pharmacy. She wants to buy some formula milk for her baby. She briefly looks at me, then back at Ibrahim. She asks him why I am not wearing a hijab. He mutters something. The woman leaves the pharmacy and Ibrahim sits down behind the desk again. I ask Ibrahim what are the greatest health risks in Egypt. He says: 'The water is dangerous. Please don't drink the water.' I laugh, trying to loosen up the tension a bit, and respond that I have already been sick from the water twice. 'So you know,' he says, disinterestedly shrugging.

I ask Ibrahim if many people get sick when fasting during Ramadan. Ibrahim looks at me and responds with a question: 'Are you a Christian?' Surprised, I say yes, and feel like giving up on this man and this pharmacy altogether. Ibrahim continues: 'Fasting is good. It won't kill you. You get tired, but then it's okay…' Trying to keep the conversation going for a bit, I tell him that I am asking because I know several people with diabetes and one who is pregnant, all of whom are fasting – and they seem very tired and ill from it. Irritated, he responds: 'No, fasting is good. They will fast and be tired, but then it's okay. It won't kill them.' I don't respond.

We sit for a bit, neither of us speaking a word. I feel that Ibrahim is misinterpreting the intentions of all my questions. He asks a bit about my research. I try to explain – yet again – what it is I am doing here in Egypt and at his pharmacy. Ibrahim laughs at me while he looks at the ceiling. He comments that many people have studied what I am studying: 'But you want to do your own study? Even though it has already been done?' I tell him there may be many numbers and statistics, but not really any studies where the researchers 'talk to people', 'qualitative studies'. Trying to keep it simple, I tell him again that I wish to talk to people and understand from their perspective what it is like to live with diabetes in Egypt. He looks at me directly and says: 'Be careful. You are too pretty to be talking to people.' I quickly respond: 'I am careful!' I feel angry and embarrassed. For five minutes we stare at the TV in silence. Ibrahim occasionally changes the channel. Finally I get up and tell him I have to go. I thank him for his time and quickly leave the pharmacy.

Mistrust

Miscommunication and misunderstandings are part of all fieldwork. The words exchanged in the above encounter were – on paper – no worse than I had experienced in previous fieldwork (e.g. in Denmark), but the situation felt worse. I found myself nearly running out of the pharmacy, thinking I would never return (I did), trying to shake off some kind of fear. In the days that followed I realised that the general paranoia that I had observed among my interlocutors, and often found exaggerated, was taking its toll on me. I was getting quite paranoid myself.

As was evident with my host family, most of my interlocutors at some point expressed concern about being associated with certain people (e.g. colleagues, relatives or me), because associating with the wrong crowd could get them fired, arrested or worse. 'I am not in touch with a lot of my family. I don't know what they do or think. Maybe one joined the Muslim Brotherhood,' one of my interlocutors said, rather concerned that her distant relatives might reflect badly on her and her immediate family. As mentioned previously, most of the people I talked to in relation to my fieldwork were reluctant to let me record any interviews as they were concerned the Egyptian intelligence service was 'listening in'. Some were not even comfortable with me taking notes of our conversations. All my interlocutors at some point – and often more than once – expressed the feeling that they were being watched closely by the authorities.

When I wrote up my field notes from the pharmacy, the encounter seemed to come across more silly than scary. I had been scared of something during my visit, but what exactly was hard to recount to others (and to myself). I struggled to capture in words, how I had in fact experienced the encounter as intimidating. It seemed there had been no real exchange of words or actions between the pharmacist and myself that I could point to in order to justify my fear, and later I found myself sounding a bit hysterical when trying to explain 'what had happened' to others. Both writing and talking about my visit to the pharmacy, I would doubt my own sense of reality. Had I perceived the situation correctly? Or was I perhaps exaggerating the grounds for my fear and the pharmacist's suspicion of me?

Adding to the story is the fact that I had originally had an appointment with a different pharmacist working at the same pharmacy, but she had already left work when I showed up. Instead, Ibrahim insisted I stay with him, a warm and typical gesture in Egypt where visitors (even those who are not entirely welcome) are rarely turned away. I knew that the polite thing would be to insist that I would come back another day, but at the time I felt as if my fieldwork had ground to a standstill. Basically, I was finding it hard to get anyone to talk to me. I thus convinced myself to stay with Ibrahim to get some useful notes and insights, even though my knowledge of Egyptian customs told me to turn

AFTEN KL. 21 I AWACH

down his offer. In retrospect, Ibrahim's reluctance to answer my questions might actually have stemmed from my overstaying the visit, rather than any doubts as to who I was or the intent of my questioning. I will never know.

My fear of the pharmacist (and perhaps his fear of me) seemed mostly to stem from the context, as opposed to what specifically played out between the two of us during my visit. We both were mistrustful and doubted each other's intentions: Who is she? Why is she asking all these questions? Who does she report to? Who is he? Why is he so defensive? Who does he report to? Reading through the field notes from my pharmacy visit, I understand that the encounter was colored by incidents that happened prior to meeting the pharmacist, and which were completely unrelated to this specific person. Feelings of fear were in general difficult to put into words without undermining them, and that was probably why at the beginning of my fieldwork I had considered the paranoia of my interlocutors to be exaggerated – only to eventually experience that others found me to be exaggerating my own fears. It only added to the general confusion and blurred sense of reality that most days seemed completely normal and safe (as evident in my field notes opening this chapter), only for this normalcy to be suddenly ruptured without notice by alarming stories or personal observations of seemingly random detentions, raids, shootings and explosions.

4 July 2015: at a party

We are standing on the terrace. I am talking to Mustafa. He is in his late twenties and is currently doing his mandatory military service. He tells me he has to serve for a year, but has only just started. Mustafa says he hates the army. He is plotting how to get out of his military service early. We both laugh. I ask him what exactly he is plotting to do. Mustafa tells me he will try to act mentally unstable. He has already started, havings told his superior that he does not want to stand guard with a gun because he is fantasizing about turning it on himself. Mustafa laughs, and explains that he doesn't want to stand guard at checkpoints or other exposed police posts, as the conscripts there are frequently targeted in drive-by shootings and bombings. 'They believed me,' he says of his superiors and the army psychiatrist. He then explains that he has to go back for an evaluation in two weeks.

We go inside the apartment to grab some food. I pick out a piece of pie. Mustafa and I go into the living room to find an empty spot. We sit down. I ask about different strategies for getting exempted from military service. Mustafa mentions gaining a lot of weight just before the draft, or paying a bribe. He adds that you have to know the person you are about to bribe well or you might get into trouble. Mustafa comments that very few people try to fake mental instability. 'It's dangerous,' he adds. He explains that others get exempted if the intelligence service has them listed as political opponents to the regime: members of the Muslim Brotherhood, for example. Mustafa tells me he tried to hang out a lot at the synagogue downtown in order to come off as just that, a political opponent to the regime: 'But apparently it wasn't enough to get me exempted,' he laughs again.[4]

Trust

As is evident throughout this chapter, the paranoia among my interlocutors seemed to slowly seep into me, and as my fieldwork went on, moments of mistrust and paranoia ruptured my sense of a peaceful everyday life ever more frequently. The mistrust seemed to bloom in my consciousness. Because my questions were often interrupted or turned down by my interlocutors, I felt it was increasingly difficult to gather any data about what was 'really' going on. But on returning home and going through my field notes, it became very obvious that this was actually not the case. Just as normalcy had been ruptured by moments of fear and paranoia, so had moments of mistrust been ruptured by moments of great confidence and trust. In fact, my field notes are full of moments like the encounter with Mustafa presented above. I realize that from an outsider's perspective the encounter may come off as rather harmless, but Mustafa showed great trust in me when he confided stories and sentiments that could get him arrested (or worse) for treason.

A couple of weeks after talking to Mustafa, I received a party invitation from him on Facebook: an 'I-GOT-EXEMPTED-FROM-THE-MILITARY PARTY'. Those were the exact words that headlined the online invitation he had sent out to everyone he knew in Cairo. I remember laughing when I read it, but also finding it rather bold to send out an invitation with such a headline on Facebook (who was watching?). Then I reasoned that maybe I was exaggerating, and the thing to do might be to handle this paranoia of mine with some humour. Later that same day I met up with a mutual Egyptian friend who commented on Mustafa's Facebook invitation. I noted that he called it 'rather dangerous'. I decided I was probably going to be busy on the day of the party and chose not to go.

The encounter with Mustafa reveals that those who showed great trust in me during my fieldwork contributed just as much to my confusion about how to read and understand my field as those who had shown mistrust. An encounter like that with Mustafa made me doubt my understanding of

4 Mustafa indicates that the activities at the synagogue in Cairo are surely under surveillance by the Egyptian intelligence service, and that an obvious affiliation with the Jewish community in Cairo would mark him as a political opponent of the regime.

other interactions, such as that with the pharmacist (Ibrahim). The Mustafa and Ibrahim episodes represent the ongoing processes of trying to read and understand the situations I found myself in during my fieldwork in Cairo – and how, throughout my fieldwork and upon returning from it, I was left with quite different ways of interpreting the same encounters and incidents.

At my desk[5]

I sit at my desk in my apartment in downtown Cairo trying to type up my field notes from the day at the pharmacy. The power is off and it's incredibly hot. I go back and forth between the kitchen and my desk, picking up things to eat and drink. I write some, then eat some. Write some and drink some. I am finding it hard to concentrate. I check the local news on my phone. Nothing new has happened since the last time I checked. I try to focus on my notes again, looking back and forth between the scribbles in my notebook and the words on my computer screen. Recounting the visit to the pharmacy makes me feel uncomfortable. I don't want to go back there. I text my boyfriend in Denmark: 'The pharmacist was weird.' Suddenly the power is back on. Someone shouts with excitement next door. The fan on my desk starts spinning and feels nice. I finish the day's field notes and send them to my university e-mail server in an attempt to get them off my computer.

Later, I decide to write my supervisor back in Denmark. Included in my e-mail are: 'People here are suspicious and don't trust each other.' and 'It is difficult to explain the atmosphere here completely, but people are afraid they are being watched by the authorities or that someone might report them for something. What's worse is – it is contagious, I am getting suspicious and insecure of people around me as well.' At the end of the e-mail I try to pin down the political situation to give my words more force: 'People are getting arrested and sentenced for all sorts of strange things. This past week we had several bombings around Cairo (one across the street from where I live). The state prosecutor was also assassinated last week and there have been fights between the military and militia groups (ISIS affiliated) in Sinai, more than 100 people were killed.' I send the email, subject line 'Greetings from Cairo!' I get a text from my mother, asking me how I am doing. I pick up the phone and reply: 'Everything here is fine! I had a really exciting day visiting a pharmacy. I might go back. How is everything back home?'

5 This particular story of me writing field notes was written specifically for this chapter, and is thus not an excerpt from field notes in line with those presented above. It is based on actual e-mails and text messages, as well as excerpts from my personal diary.

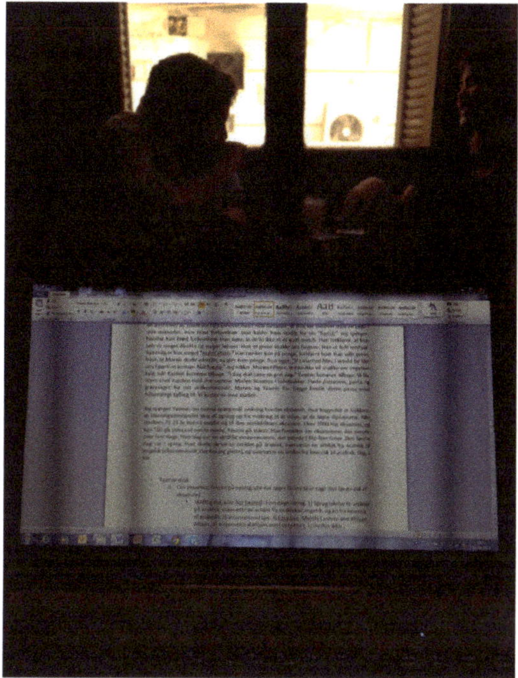

Figure 8.3 Typing out my notes in the dark corner of a café. Photograph by the author, 12 September 2015.

Concluding remarks

In this chapter I have focused on several aspects of the written field note, drawing on my experience of writing them in a field of political and social unrest, and showing how this can affect not only the practicalities of writing, but also the analytical process of trying to make sense of one's notes.

Clifford Geertz has discussed the many ways of interpreting the wink of an eye – as a flirtatious gesture, underscoring a sarcastic comment, or just as a physiological twitch. The key to understanding the wink is to be found in the context surrounding it (Geertz 1973). As is evident throughout this chapter, this was essentially my challenge when in Cairo, which continues as I try to make sense of my notes at home. In Cairo I was frequently insecure about the contexts in which interactions played out, and would thus doubt my understanding of the 'winks'. This doubt led to further difficulties in assessing whether or not my notes posed a risk to anyone (which notes, why and to whom?). This prompted several ethical reflections and caused me to send my notes into a virtual space, some might say out of paranoia, others out of caution.

As is evident in the above excerpts, I never explicitly commented on my uncertainty as to how best to interpret my field. For me the ambiguities were present in the contexts surrounding my notes. Was the square quiet because it was a peaceful day, or because something unspecified (but surely frightening) had happened? Was the pharmacist suspicious of me and my intentions, or would he just rather I left him alone with his TV and his Ramadan soap opera? The fact that I rarely felt completely confident about the contexts of my note-making left them with an inherent ambiguity. Such ambiguousness is present in all fields and all written field notes (take Geertz's wink of an eye as an example of this), but in my particular case this was made more extreme by the circumstances of political tension.

Rena Lederman has observed that written field notes 'may give us the sense that, for the moment anyhow, they contain the basis for all that can be written about a place' (1990:89). But when we move from taking our field notes to actually using them in anthropological writing, we learn that they are 'not a fixed repository of data from the field but a reinterpretable and contradictory patchwork of perspectives. We rightly fear that immersion in them might cause us to doubt our conviction of what's what.' (ibid.:90). This realization came to me already in the field, in the very process of writing up my field notes, and stayed with me as a reminder throughout subsequent attempts to analyse my data.

To conclude: the dynamic nature of written field notes leaves them open to interpretation long after they are written. The process of both interpreting our field, writing our field notes and analysing our data thus becomes an open-ended (and risky) process that may tilt our understanding in many different directions.

References

Geertz, C. 1973. 'Thick description: toward an interpretive theory of culture.' In *The Interpretation Of Cultures: Selected Essays*, pp. 3–30. New York: Basic Books.

Lederman, R.1990. 'Pretexts for ethnography: on reading fieldnotes.' In R. Sanjek (ed.), *Fieldnotes: The Makings of Anthropology*, pp. 71–91. Ithaca: Cornell University Press.

International Diabetes Federation 2014: www.idf.org/diabetesatlas (accessed 8 September 2016).

9

ethnoGRAPHIC field notes

On drawn notes and their potentials

METTE LIND KUSK

I have agreed to be a bridesmaid at a wedding, as one of my interlocutors' relatives is getting married. I have never met the happy couple, but I have been assured that this will not be a problem. I enter the women's dressing room, where I have been told that a dress and people who can help me put it on are waiting. In the small, concrete room I become absorbed in the crowd of busy women who guide me through the process of dressing up in a gomezi, a traditional women's dress with pointed shoulders and lots of satin fabric. People assure me that I will look 'very smart!' – the usual compliment for a nice outfit. Some girls are half naked, while others are busy adding lipstick or eye shadow to their own or another's face. In putting on the gomezi, my intimate space is completely dissolved – one girl wraps a blanket around my hips while my friend tightens the strap of my bra. My body is touched and commented upon very candidly. I could not help but picture myself from the outside, in the middle of this liberating circus, into which I was dragged rather randomly, and I felt a need to describe it. Afterwards, I made a field-note drawing (Figure 9.1).

This chapter revolves around drawn field notes such as Figure 9.1, which I made during my fieldwork, carried out in Northern Uganda between 2014 and 2016, on the intimate connections between people and land, and local land conflicts. I use the drawn notes in a twofold way, which I will try to spell out in this chapter: methodologically during fieldwork, and concurrently as a means of communicating stories from my fieldwork, at first through my blog and currently in my further writings, in which I am trying to incorporate some of them.

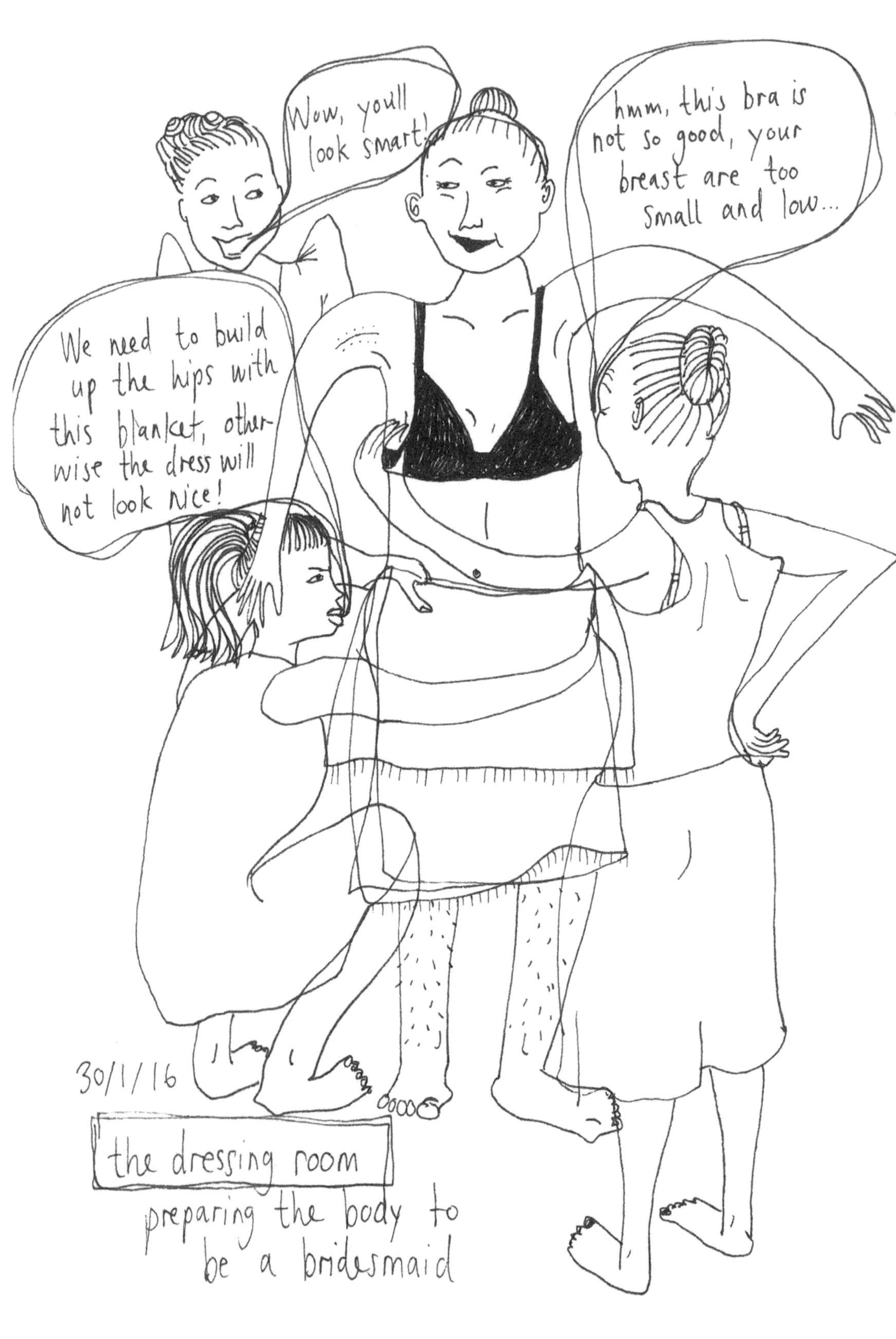
Wow, youll look smart!
hmm, this bra is not so good, your breast are too small and low...
We need to build up the hips with this blanket, other-wise the dress will not look nice!
30/1/16
the dressing room
preparing the body to be a bridesmaid

When doing fieldwork as anthropologists, we engage with both our bodies and minds, and are constantly exposed to interactions that provoke dilemmas and questions. We become incorporated into different people's agendas, which make sensuous and social experiences in new settings – such as the situation in the dressing room – part of the daily routine. The knowledge we gain is largely experiential and interactional, prompted by the 'stranger effect' (Taussig 2011:144), in which the role of the outsider is part of what stimulates stories and interactions. I think most ethnographers need a mode of expression that leaves space to include themselves, and their first-hand experiences and interpretations, in a way that does them justice. Not just for their own sake, but also because of the ideal that anthropologists should be reflective and open about their role and positioning in relation to the knowledge they gain – an ideal expressed in the ground-breaking debates on representation within the discipline begun in the 1980s (Marcus and Fisher 1999). This is how our work as anthropologists becomes credible: by making our role in knowledge production transparent.

Some anthropologists are good at interweaving these personal details and experiences into their regular, written field notes. Others keep a separate diary as a vent for things they feel are too personal or emotional to go into their analytic field notes. Some express themselves in poetry. Upon ending my fieldwork I realized that for me, drawing is a mode of expression that enables me to include myself in descriptions of social situations in a way that feels more straightforward, or unfiltered, than my attempts to translate my experiences into writing. Producing drawings and revisiting them later enables me to 'hold on' to the person who agreed to be a bridesmaid at a stranger's wedding, who I regard as 'my (fieldwork)self'. This is a particular version of me: an ethnographer consciously striving to achieve and maintain good relations during fieldwork; a person who was used to the role of an outsider, and who sometimes enjoyed being thrown into unfamiliar social events. Writing feels like a tedious way to describe my subjective experiences and the way I felt in a particular situation. When I draw, it feels like play, like telling a story to a friend, and it feels sincere.

Additionally, I discovered another useful aspect of describing situations in drawings: they focus my attention on the material details of the particular physical surroundings in which I found myself – sometimes consciously, other times intuitively. When I describe situations in drawings I always base them, to some extent, on material details, and this adds another dimension to the potential of drawn notes within ethnography. They can be used to notice, hold

Figure 9.1 (opposite) 'The dressing room'. Field-note drawing on the process of becoming a bridesmaid.

on to and communicate material particulars of the field that could later turn out to be analytically important.

Drawing has been a mode of expression for me for as long as I can recall. When I was younger, I passionately drew an endless number of horses: naturalistic, shaded drawings in black and white, and colourful cartoons. People responded with great enthusiasm, and I think their recognition and encouragement made me continue to draw when most other children stopped. Fashionable women, miserable faces and stylish couples replaced the horses as I grew older. When engaging in fieldwork, which is an extremely rich experience, it felt meaningful to draw notes as well as writing them.

In the first part of this chapter, I will describe the practice of drawing during fieldwork and explore how it expanded my attention in new directions. In the second part, I will focus on the products, the drawings, and how I use them to create ethnographic accounts, both on their own and in combination with text.

Doing fieldwork: the sketchbook as a friend

The self-portrait (Figure 9.2) shows how I created most of my drawn notes: sitting comfortably at a desk with a cup of coffee when I had time on my own. I did try drawing in public, sitting on the veranda of my hut in the village where I stayed with a family, allowing people to peek over my shoulder while I tried to make my hands move across the paper, unaffected by the looks, laughs and comments that this activity attracted. This could have been a great opportunity to interact with my interlocutors in a new way, providing the kind of entry point to their curious questions that Manuel Ramos (2004:149) describes following his experiences of drawing in public during fieldwork. But I rarely drew on my veranda. I needed some space for reflection in order to consider what had made an impression on me, and to reflect upon my role and my understanding of a particular, often ambivalent situation. Even though it may sound paradoxical, portraying an experience in close detail required some degree of distance. And, on a very practical level, I needed a chair and a table. As I like to use watercolours in addition to thin, black pens, drawing without a desk is impractical. The colours add to the atmosphere I want to convey, while shading a room in grey tones emphasizes the time of day as well as the way I experienced a particular situation, as in Figure 9.2, in which the darkness has crept in and filled the room, making me feel quite lonely. But as can be seen, I had my head torch to send down a cone of light from my forehead, allowing me to write and draw despite one of the recurring power cuts leaving the town of Gulu dark at 8 pm.

My sketchbook was like a kind of friend with whom I shared stories during my fieldwork. If something made an impression on me, or felt

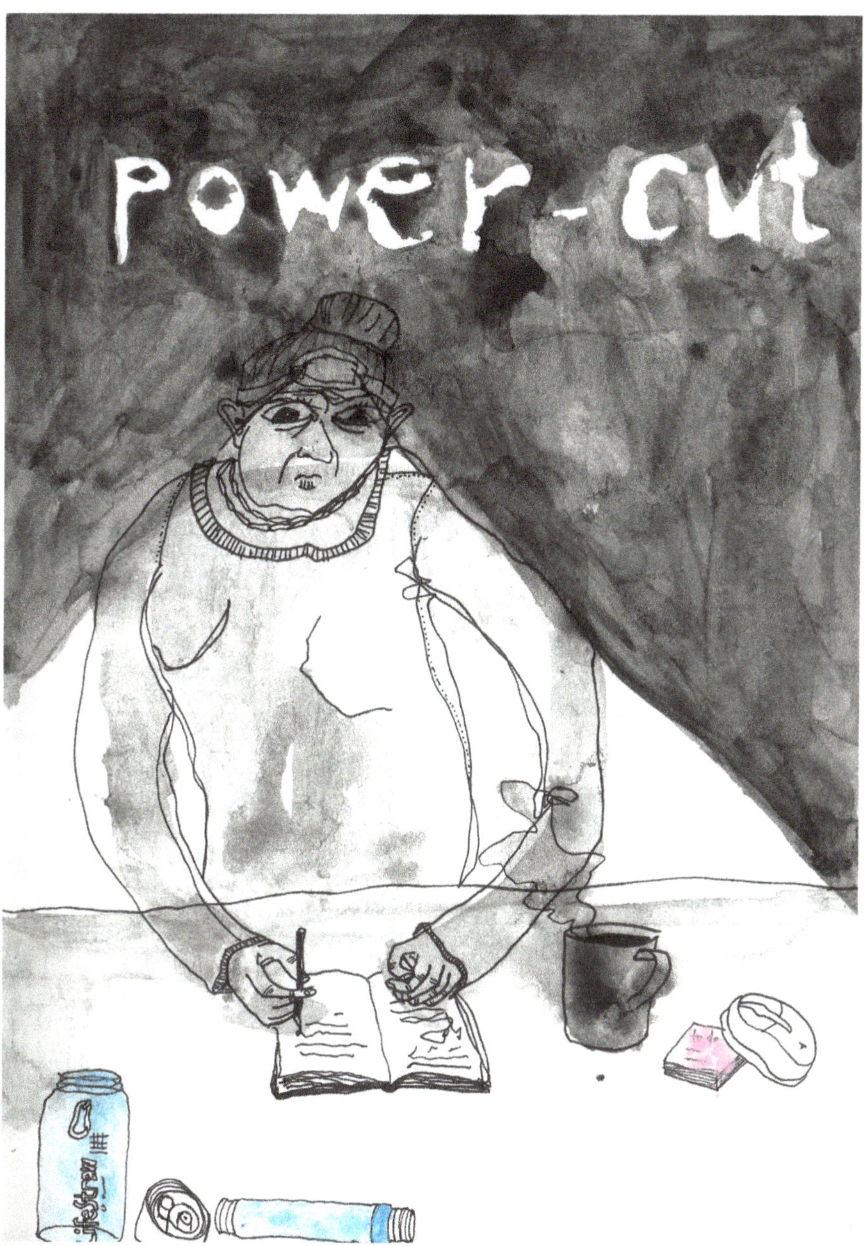

Figure 9.2 'Power cut'. Field-note drawing illustrating one of the recurring power cuts in Gulu town.

important or puzzling, I would draw it, sharing it with my notebook, just as we share experiences with friends. Often, I would also have actual people in mind, close friends that I knew would understand, without further explanation, what a particular drawing showed. The drawing of fieldwork situations became a way of telling stories centred on small and intimate moments. It became a way of focusing attention in a different way than writing, and a way of holding onto myself in the situations I experienced. In this way, my drawing book resembles what Vincent Crapanzano terms 'the Third' in fieldwork (2010:73–4): a reference point, often outside yourself and your interlocutors, which can help you hold onto your (fieldwork)self during and after intense experiences. Whether or not the Third is an actual person or, as in my case, an artefact, it creates a space for pondering on experiences and emotions. In addition to being an anchor during fieldwork, it serves the same purpose in the times that follow. As the American author Joan Didion phrases it, a personal notebook is 'crucial in the way it helps us reconnect with our former selves' (see New 2005:9).

Serious playfulness

It is difficult for me to pinpoint why I choose to draw one situation and not another. I have not defined any systematic restrictions on what to describe in drawings and what in words – instead, I tend to work intuitively. Allowing myself to draw notes was a way of including play in my fieldwork, whereas writing field notes felt more like real work, a daily task – a distinction Taussig also points out in his writings on fieldwork drawings (2011:73). One aspect of play is that it is not structured around what you ought to do, but around what you feel like doing. The space of play is not restricted by a specific end goal or product. Play is an activity that is meaningful in itself. Describing what I do as 'serious playfulness' is meant to highlight the potential relevance of drawing within ethnographic practice, as well as my growing dedication to the activity as I began to publish my drawings online.

Retrospectively, I can discern some common patterns regarding what I drew. Most of my drawn notes try to capture a feeling or an atmosphere in condensed fashion, or portray something I found funny, annoying, fascinating or provocative. Generally, there were some visual aspects of a situation that I found appealing or particularly revealing. There is a drawing of me (Figure 9.3) getting ready to sleep in the round hut of my field assistant, alongside her, her two boys and my colleague Hannah. We do not talk. The boys are already asleep, snoring next to a solar lamp, and Hannah and I are reading, using our head torches to light up the pages. I imagine us from above, with the five of us

Figure 9.3 (opposite) 'Night in the village'.

comfortably resting in each other's company, protected by the round walls that are still warm from being heated up all day by the intense sun, even though they are now surrounded by the dark, cool night.

In my mind, in the depicted scene, the only things that existed were us and the universe. The small, intimate and everyday moments, in which the occasionally lonely feeling of fieldwork arise, have been replaced by a sense of strong connectedness to the people with whom I was sharing a sleeping space. There was probably nothing special about that evening for my interlocutors. It was just another normal night's sleep (although there were two anthropologists in the hut with them). But I was moved by the experience, and wanted to hold onto it. I think small moments like this would have slipped my attention when revisiting my written field notes if I had written a few sentences about the situation. Such words would not have captured the moment as I experienced it. To try to capture it with a camera would not even make sense. But drawing it made it possible to sustain the magical atmosphere of that moment, and having the drawing enables me to recall it now, several years later. It stands out, perhaps not as an 'ethnographic moment' that becomes the starting point for a developed analysis, but rather as a small ethnographic account in its own right. It constitutes a self-reflexive, methodological note that reminds me of myself in the field, and of the relations that I cultivated during that time, and which formed the basis of the knowledge I had gained. Surely this is an important part of what field notes should do, enabling us to recall such moments, so that we stay true to the relationships on which our insights are based?

Capturing material details

During fieldwork, I would sometimes make a small list of ideas of things to draw when I had some time on my own, and occasionally I would make a quick sketch, on the spot, to remember details of a particular place or situation. For example, I visited some of my interlocutors in prison, when they were arrested in connection with a land conflict that got out of hand (to put it mildly), and I drew Figure 9.4 while waiting outside.

I made the sketch because I wanted to be able to recall what the prison looked like, roughly, so I could draw it later on. Drawing notes made me think in images, prompting me to take note of material details in a new way, because I would need the details later. I agree with Ramos, who has pointed out that 'a trained eye and a skillful hand are useful instruments for documenting both material culture aspects and varied instances of social life' (2004:149). But you may ask what the purpose of inscribing such material details was? When I was making the drawings, I am not sure I could have answered this question. As ethnographers, we are trained to remain somewhat 'unfocused'

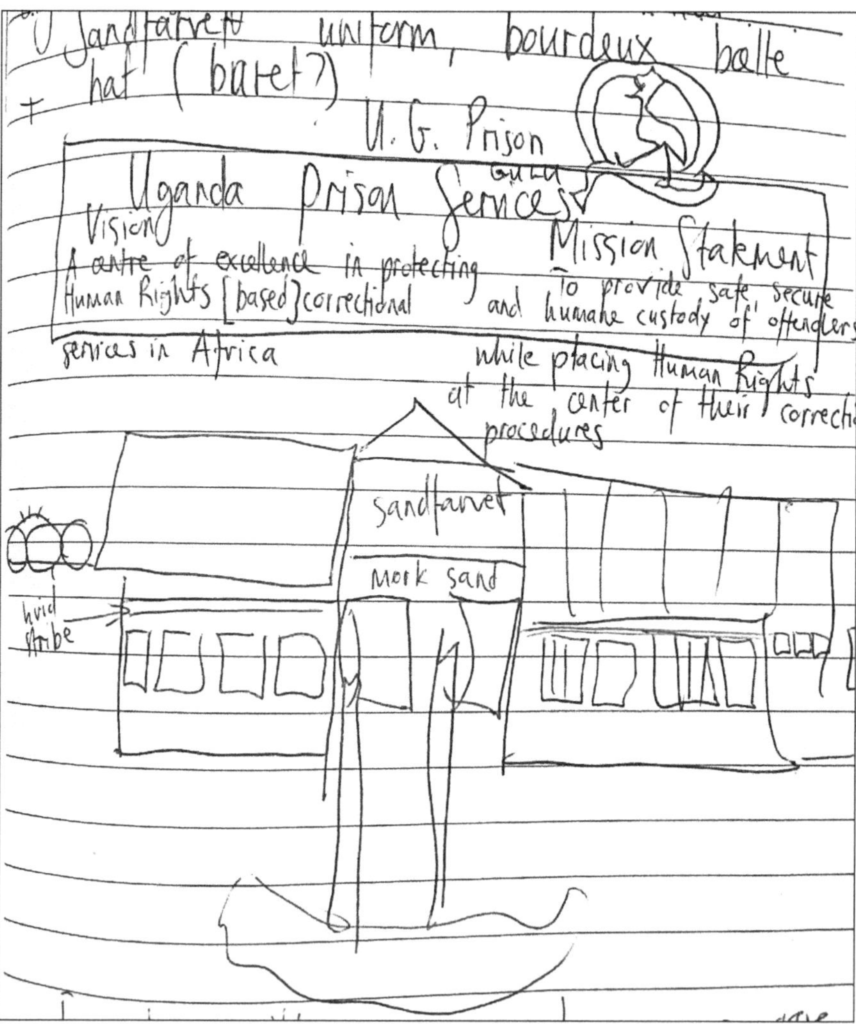

Figure 9.4 Quick sketch made outside the prison.

during fieldwork, so as to avoid imposing preconceived ideas on the worlds we engage in. This approach influences our note-making practices, which are often marked by excess. We produce more field notes than we need; and when we make notes, their future analytical relevance is not yet apparent. But the inclusion of material details in my drawings created the potential for subsequent analytic elaboration.

I did not always make sketches like those shown here. Sometimes I used photographs or just my memory. I consciously tried to remember details that, to my eye, were characteristic of the place of my fieldwork: like people's clothes, slogans on buses, buildings or T-shirts, the ways people sit and stand, light and colours, furniture, and so on. The process of drawing stimulated my attention in a way that using a camera could not achieve, even though the two processes could capture some of the same material aspects. I take photographs, but make drawings (cf. Taussig 2011:21). Snapping a photograph does not require me to take note of any of the elements captured by the camera lens (although skilful photographers do this, of course). Taking a picture with a camera happens in the blink of an eye, in all its detail, without really paying attention to it or letting it get under my skin, and without making myself present or intervening in the scene. But when I draw, it takes time, and requires me to take note. As Taussig points out, drawings, or at least my field-note drawings as well as his, intervene in the reality they describe more explicitly than photographs (ibid.:12–13): they are more selective and less naturalistic.

My drawings do not result in the kind of realistic, spatial descriptions that a camera can produce. On the contrary: in my drawn notes only a few characteristic details are included, while a lot of context is left out. Michael Taussig describes this fragmented character of drawings, their incompleteness and their pointing away from full, realist descriptions as their strength, and the thing that enables them to capture invisible and inarticulate aspects so well (ibid.:13). By simplifying and filtering, something vivid can be captured and made to stand out. In my drawings, that 'something vivid' is often a combination of some material details, a brief interaction, and something non-verbal: an atmosphere, or implicit and inarticulate aspects of how I experienced a particular situation.

After the prison visit, I drew Figure 9.5, which describes my interaction with the staff before being allowed to enter. Part of the drawing (the figures and furniture) is reproduced from memory, but the prison building is based on the sketch. Despite taking careful descriptions of the colours, I never got around to actually adding any. Even so, thinking in drawings made me take note of them, and they are still present on the initial sketch as a potential that may or may not be realized in further writings or drawings, depending on what direction these take.

In addition to the sketch, I have around ten pages of written field notes from this prison visit, describing the procedure for visits, who I talked to, and my interlocutors' descriptions of the complex events leading to their arrest, their interpretations of these events, and updates on their current situation. In my written notes, I do not write anything about how the prison staff made me feel. But in the drawing, my frustrations, over one more restriction imposed by a person in power, are emphasized. At this point in my fieldwork, I had spent many weeks trying to understand this particular land conflict, which led to the imprisonment of nine people, and had spoken to lawyers and police officers who avoided my questions and repeatedly referred me to other officials. By the time of the visit, I was exhausted by what had turned out to be an extremely

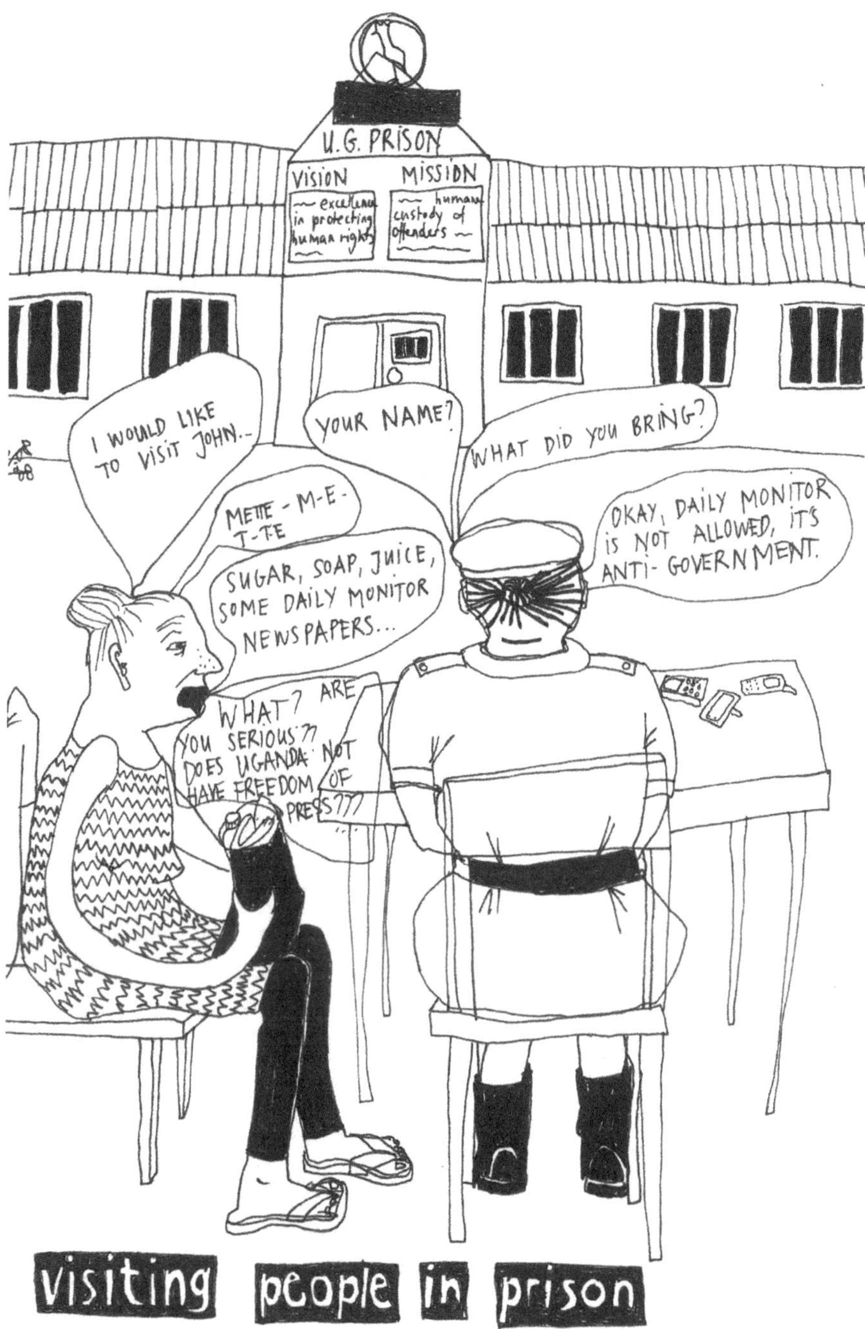

Figure 9.5 'Visiting people in prison'. Field-note drawing made based on the sketch of Figure 9.4.

frustrating experience. The officer's claim that *Daily Monitor* newspapers are illegal in prisons seemed like one more ridiculous and frustrating power play in an endless stream of them.

The depiction of the interaction with the prison officer records just one brief moment, capturing a small interaction taking place outside the prison building. In this way, my drawn notes can be described as being organized spatially, whereas my written notes are organized narratively. The drawing describes a moment in space, whereas my written notes describe the visit as a whole, as it unfolded over time, and are structured narratively: beginning when I entered; moving through my meeting with my interlocutors, listening to their stories and asking questions about the events; and ending with our reaching an agreement on when my next visit should be. The dialogue I had with my interlocutors was too complex to be conveyed in a short exchange of words, which is why I continuously alternated between drawing and writing field notes. When taking notes of things that are spoken, writing them down seems like a very straightforward way to capture them. But if you want to hold on to a moment in space in which inarticulate aspects are just as important as the words that are spoken, drawing seems like the best option.

'Do you grow pasta in Denmark?'

Hannah Vestergaard Thoustrup, an anthropologist colleague,[1] and good friend, narrated a scene to me over a cup of coffee. In the village where we had both done fieldwork, she was served pasta for breakfast, and someone asked her if we grew pasta in Denmark. The question gave rise to a variety of images in my mind, and we both found it funny and absurd at the same time. I can imagine Hannah's facial expression, surprised and doubtful about how to answer, and I wonder what other ideas our interlocutors have about Denmark. After all, it is a far-away place, and Hannah and I are the only source of information they have. I also find this question charming, and very revealing about the place in which I did my fieldwork. In the rural areas of northern Uganda there is hardly any processed food in the daily diet. Most households grow a variety of subsistence crops – cassava, sweet potatoes, beans, peas, groundnuts, sesame, maize, greens and millet are among the most common – which they process in their homes, drying them in the sun and processing them on their grinding stone, or perhaps on a local grinding machine. People

1 Hannah was one among numerous Danish and Ugandan colleagues contributing to the collaborative TrustLand project, funded by DANIDA, led by professor MSO Lotte Meinert and lecturer Stephen Langole. The project ran from 2013–17 and explored various perspectives on post-war land relations in northern Uganda. See trustland.me.

buy very few things that are not locally produced – salt, sugar and cooking oil, as well as sweet biscuits and fizzy drinks – and these are available in even the smallest and most remote shops. When an unfamiliar product like pasta is introduced, it is only natural to assume that it is a crop from elsewhere in the world that happens not to be grown in Uganda. Like apples. My interlocutors had no reason to know that pasta is the result of a long, industrial process, an idea that seems alien and quite absurd to them.

I remember having the inclination to draw this scene, but for various reasons I chose not to. Perhaps the fact that it was Hannah who had experienced the situation, not myself, caused part of the hesitation. But more importantly, I was worried that it would be misunderstood, making my interlocutors look foolish, whereas what I actually found bizarre, from a Ugandan viewpoint, was the Western food industry. So, some self-censorship took place, and this was partly because I had decided to share the drawn notes publicly on my blog, 'ethnoGRAPHIC fieldnotes' (ethnographicfieldnotes. blogspot.dk). To share notes with the world beyond face-to-face encounters and my physical notebooks, by publishing them online, made me censor out drawings like the one about the pasta. The story could not be shared without adding more words and explanations than I wanted to my drawings.

Turning the inside out: making field notes public

Why would I share my drawn notes publicly, on a blog? And what difference, if any, does it make when you publish your drawn field notes? Upon reading Michael Taussig's wonderful book *I Swear I Saw This: Drawings In Fieldnote Books, Namely My Own* (2011), I was inspired by his call to see our ethnographic notebooks not as mere tools for later publications, but as lively and valuable products in themselves. He views it as deceit to turn what are essentially stories and personal interactions into generalized 'information' void of subjectivity in order to develop abstract theories, which is what often happens when we publish our work. This propensity, according to him, makes our fieldwork notebooks extremely important, as they have 'at least one foot in the sensuous immediacy' (ibid.:49), and remind us what ethnographic knowledge is actually made of: observations, stories and interactions captured in a variety of ways, via words, drawings, photos, newspaper cuttings and so on. Taussig's points made me begin to view my own drawn notes as products in themselves, which could make up meaningful publications in their own right. Instead of structuring them into a narrative with a plot after completing my fieldwork, I decided to publish them as my fieldwork progressed.

The second inspiration for sharing drawn notes on a blog came from my former drawing teacher, the renowned illustrator and artist Signe Parkins. Since 2009, she has kept an online sketch blog (signeparkins.blogspot.dk), where she posts sketches of her everyday life in Aarhus with her partner and two children. She observes and describes her own life through drawings and small fragments of conversations and thoughts. Even though what the drawings describe is mostly mundane – everyday stuff mixed with dreams and emotions – they communicate something recognizable and captivating in the way they dwell on small moments, poetic and imperfect as they are, to make up a fascinating family portrait seen through Signe's eyes. Had she written about her life, I am not sure I would have followed her blog. But the sketches keep me curious.

So, I too created a blog, and I shared some drawn notes on it. At first I only shared the URL with my husband. I had to overcome my own insecurity, and vanity, before sharing more widely. What if somebody told me to stop, or told me that what I was doing was extremely inappropriate, unprofessional, unethical or un-anthropological? Or what if they revealed something I had not thought about? After all, anthropologists do not usually make their field notes publicly accessible, and drawings are not a common field-note format.

I sent the link to my supervisor, family and colleagues. As I started sharing the blog, I felt it begin to have some kind of agency. It came alive and had an effect on me, calling me to 'feed' it with new drawn notes regularly, increasing my commitment to drawing notes, and making me take what I had regarded as a relaxed and playful activity more seriously. It made me think more in terms of visual notes, how experiences could be captured in this modality, and I allowed myself to dedicate more time to drawing.

My sister said she preferred looking at my drawings instead of reading about my fieldwork (which did not offend me, perhaps surprisingly – after all, I too love to look at drawings). The drawn notes seem easier to access, or more appealing. Perhaps this is connected to the difference between abstract text and concrete images. Text has to be read from the top left corner down to the bottom right corner in order to decode the contents of the abstract symbols. Conversely, drawn notes mainly consist of concrete, visual imitations of what is being described. The content is immediately available for the person looking at the drawings. There is no particular order in which they should be 'read'. You can dwell on one detail, move across the page to another, and there is no predetermined direction to the 'reading'. To me, this is part of what makes drawings and other images appealing: they spur the curiosity and free movement of your eyes.

Another aspect, and I think part of the trick of captivating the viewer, is that the drawer is present in such drawings. Drawings reveal the drawer. In most of my drawn notes, I have depicted myself: in the dressing room, with the police officer, and with my field assistant and my colleague. But in the drawings that do not include such explicit self-portraits, I am still present; the analogue

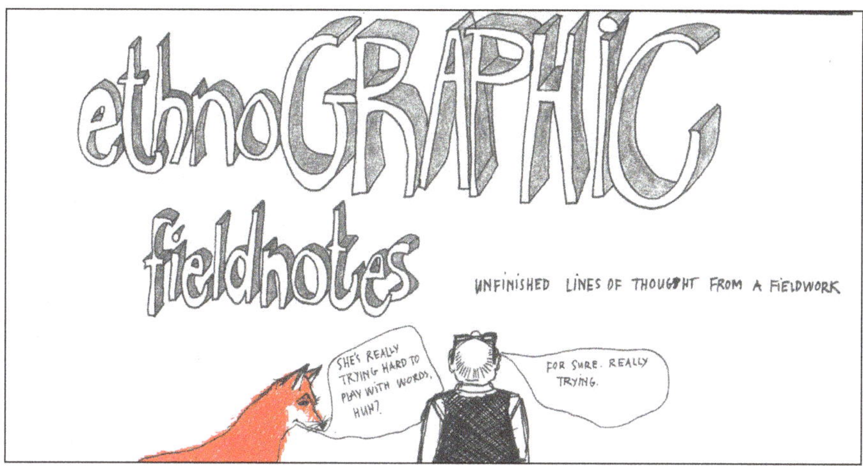

Figure 9.6 *'ethnoGRAPHIC fieldnotes'.*

lines do not leave an impression of coming from nowhere, they clearly stem from a human hand, from human movement. Text written in a digital font, like this one, sometimes makes us forget the human hand behind it, even when the content is highly personal. A drawing invites the viewer into the world of the drawer in a very intimate and immediate way. As Jennifer New points out in her book *Drawings From Life: The Journal as Art* (2005), the appeal of visual journals to outside viewers lies in the opportunity they offer for seeing how a person operates (ibid.:10). Drawings offer concrete, visual windows into the drawer's being-in-the-world. When I look at other people's drawings – or look with them, as Ingold formulates it, emphasizing the importance of reliving the moment described in the lines (2011:1) – they allow me to start imagining the situations beyond the picture and the thoughts and personality of the artist. It is often said that reading books without illustrations allows the reader to create his or her own images. But in counterpoint, when you 'read' drawings with a minimum of text, you can add your own stories to them.

Naturally, questions of representation were part of the reason why I was at first hesitant to publish my drawn notes. What kind of a portrait of my interlocutors was I posting? What impression would it leave with people? It was beyond my control. What made me feel comfortable about sharing the notes, despite these concerns, was that the drawings so clearly come from a subjective perspective, from my hand. Anyone could see that this was not an attempt to create an objective representation of a place or of people via 'a view from nowhere'. The drawings were portraits grounded in my personal observations and experiences, fragmented, subjective and ambiguous, and open to various interpretations. When I visit Signe's blog, I do not think of her drawings as reflecting her partner or her girls in a neutral manner. Clearly, the descriptions of their everyday life are filtered through Signe's experiences, and I trusted people to conclude the same about my drawings.

Concluding remarks: towards a more graphic anthropology?

I will use Figure 9.7 as an introduction to my writings about the struggles people face with regard to their land. My aim is to make drawn notes something more than mere illustrations of written words, by instead making them the starting point from which the text evolves.

I sit to the left, next to one of my interlocutors, and we are, once again, being told that his court case concerning a land conflict is being postponed. In fact, this man will later lose part of his home and get arrested, based on dubious accusations. He is one of the people I visited in prison. The drawing sets the scene and serves as the point of departure for my analysis, which revolves around the unpredictability of the Ugandan court system and the insecurity it generates: most days you wait around for a considerable length of time, only to have your case adjourned. But suddenly, as happened in this case, the waiting time may be replaced by the opposite: intense and brutal court action, depriving people of their freedom and their land for reasons that are far from clear, and leaving them in another waiting space, in prison, for an indeterminate period of time until their case is heard.

In this drawing, I am again reminded of my own experience of the situation. I felt so frustrated, because of the many hours that the people in power made less powerful people wait. It felt unbearable when, after a few visits to court, I learned that this is mainly what people do there. The focus on the clock, on hours wasted, was not something my interlocutors complained about very much. The waiting time was something that frustrated me, not them. They were frustrated about the money wasted on transport and lawyers each time they had to show up in court, only to hear that their case was adjourned; and they were frustrated by the fact that the court system treated them as playthings, adjourning cases again and again for no obvious reason. 'Legal bullying' is what one of my friends jokingly termed it. And the unpredictability rendered them insecure. Their frustrations concerned resources, lack of closure on the cases, and the unpredictability of the powerful system; whereas my immediate frustrations were connected to the waiting time. The drawing reminds me of this.

Regardless of the niche status of drawings in anthropological writings, I want to round off this chapter by drawing attention to other strands within our discipline in which scholars play with graphic genres and their potentials

Figure 9.7 (opposite) 'Court, day two, four hours of waiting'. Field-note drawing from one of several visits to court marked by waiting time.

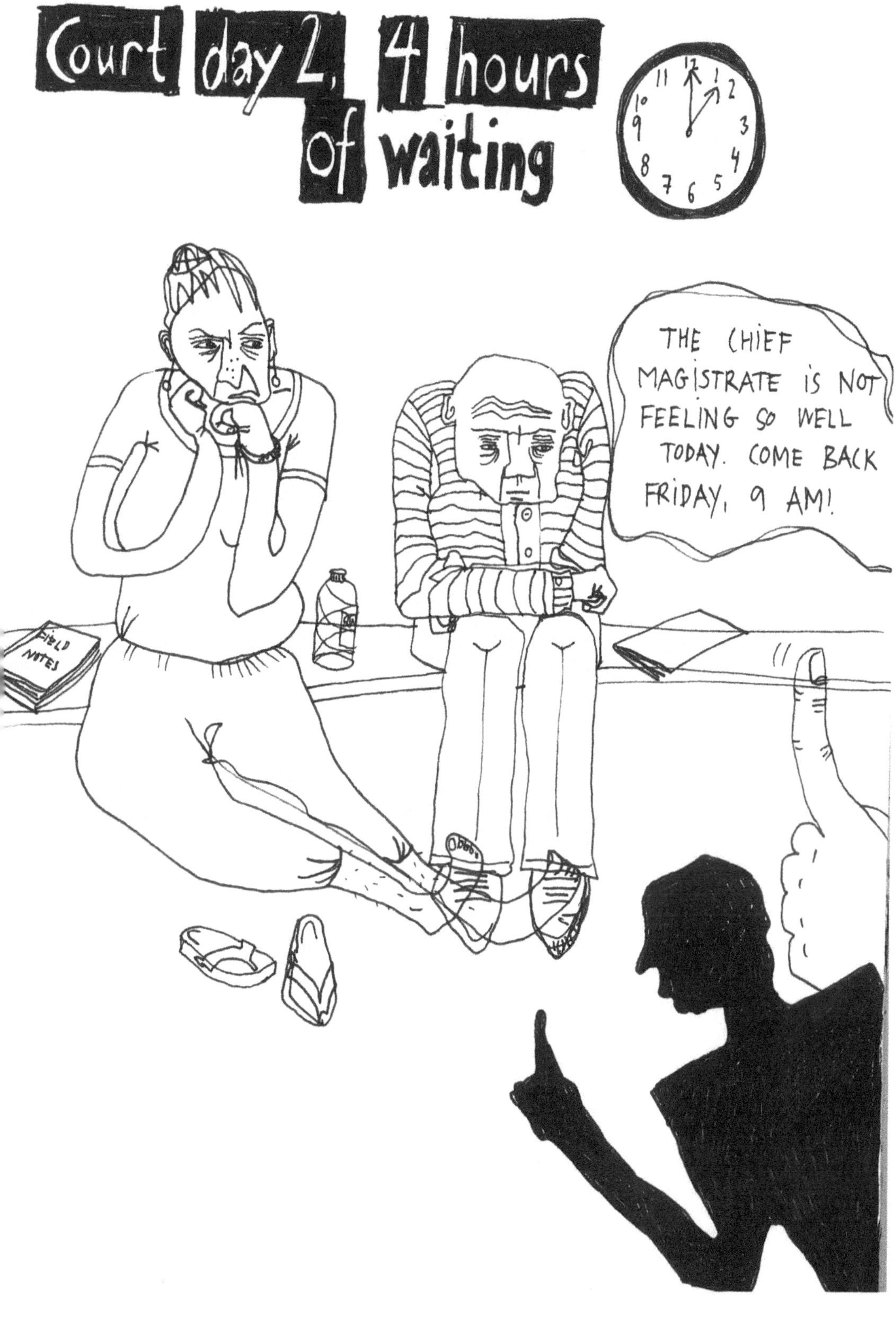

Court day 2, 4 hours of waiting

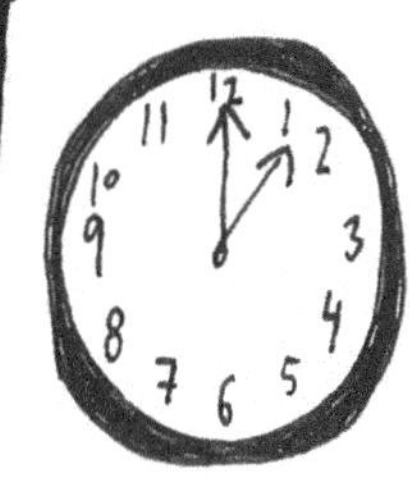

THE CHIEF MAGISTRATE IS NOT FEELING SO WELL TODAY. COME BACK FRIDAY, 9 AM!

FIELD NOTES

for anthropological research as well as representation. Such scholars call for anthropologists to create and include analogue sketches in their publications. Michael Taussig has dedicated a whole book to exploring a particular drawing from his field-note book, and he argues that more drawings, and field notes in general, should be included in what anthropologists write (2011). Manuel Ramos (2004, 2015, 2018) combines his skills as an anthropologist and as a graphic illustrator to record, interpret and communicate ethnographic accounts; and one of his publications includes a series of beautiful sketches from a week in *Musée des Arts Premiers* in Paris (2015). He describes this as an effort to 'free [anthropological production] from its boring, academic format' (ibid.:5). In *Redrawing Anthropology: Materiality, Movements, Lines,* Tim Ingold and colleagues call for anthropologists to engage in drawing because it connects ways of making, observing and describing – the core of what anthropologists do – in one movement (2011). The University of Toronto Press has announced a book series called ethnoGRAPHIC where they encourage anthropologists to publish their work in graphic novel or comic format,[2] and the book *Drawn to See. Drawing as an Ethnographic Method* by Andrew Causey (2017) has already been published. Additionally, seven blog posts under the headline 'Graphic Adventures in Anthropology' have been published on the University of Toronto's blog on teaching.[3] In *Working Images* (Pink *et al.* 2004), a variety of visual formats, including drawings, are explored to see how they can be used in the process of creating and representing ethnographic knowledge.

The fact that a variety of different types of field notes can make us take note of things in new ways, and bring about lively and rich ethnographic accounts, is clear from the various contributions in this volume. Drawing is only one of many approaches. Throughout this chapter, I have shown how drawn notes are useful during the course of fieldwork and as a means of communicating ethnographic accounts. For me, doing fieldwork with a sketchbook as a much needed friend, a 'Third' to whom I can tell unfiltered fieldwork stories, has created a space where I can reflect upon and describe some of the intense experiences that fieldwork inevitably exposes one to. It has enabled me to hold onto my (fieldwork)self – the bridesmaid, the one who was sick of waiting, the one who (sometimes) loved the intimacy of sharing a hut with four others. Furthermore, drawing situations during fieldwork stimulated my awareness of material details and made it possible to capture small but revealing moments spatially, supplementing field notes produced in the form of written narratives. As products, my drawn notes constitute

2 www.utpteachingculture.com/announcing-ethnographic-a-new-series

3 www.utpteachingculture.com/tag/graphic-adventures-in-anthropology

small and inconclusive ethnographic accounts on my blog, inviting others to gain glimpses into my field site and my experiences there. At the moment I am using some of my drawn notes to set the scene for and guide my further writings. My aim is to evoke the readers' curiosity, to make my own presence in generating the empirical material transparent, and to convey a sense of the physical settings in which fieldwork situations play out. Despite their modest presence in anthropology, drawn field notes are relevant both as a descriptive format when conducting fieldwork, and when communicating ethnographic research. Drawing and looking at analogue lines produced by other people helps to draw our attention in new directions.

References

Causey, A. 2017. *Drawn to See: Drawing as an Ethnographic Method*. North York, Ontario: University of Toronto Press.

Crapanzano, V. 2010. '"At the heart of the discipline": critical reflections on fieldwork'. In J. Davies and D. Spencer (eds.), *Emotions in the Field. The Psychology and Anthropology of Fieldwork Experience*, pp. 55–78. Stanford: Stanford University Press.

Ingold, T. (ed.) 2011. *Redrawing Anthropology: Materiality, Movements, Lines*. London: Routledge.

Marcus, G.E. and Fisher, M.J. 1999. *Anthropology as Cultural Critique: An Experimental Moment in the Human Sciences*. Chicago: University of Chicago Press.

New, J. 2005. *Drawing from Life: The Journal as Art*. New York: Princeton Architectural Press.

Pink, S., Kürti, L. and Afonso, A.I. (eds.) 2004. *Working Images: Visual Research and Representation in Ethnography*. London: Routledge

Ramos, M.J. 2004. 'Drawing the lines: the limitations of intercultural ekphrasis'. In S. Pink, L. Kurti and A.I. Afonso (eds.), *Working Images. Visual Research and Representation in Ethnography*, pp. 135–56. London: Routledge.

——— 2015. 'Stop the academic world, I wanna get off in the Quai de Branly: of sketchbooks, museums and anthropology', *Cadernos de Arte e Antropologia* 4(2):141–78.

——— 2018. *Of Hairy Kings and Saintly Slaves: An Ethiopian Travelogue*. Canon Pyon: Sean Kingston Publishing.

Taussig, M. 2011. *I Swear I Saw This. Drawings from Fieldwork Notebooks, Namely my Own*. Chicago: University of Chicago Press.

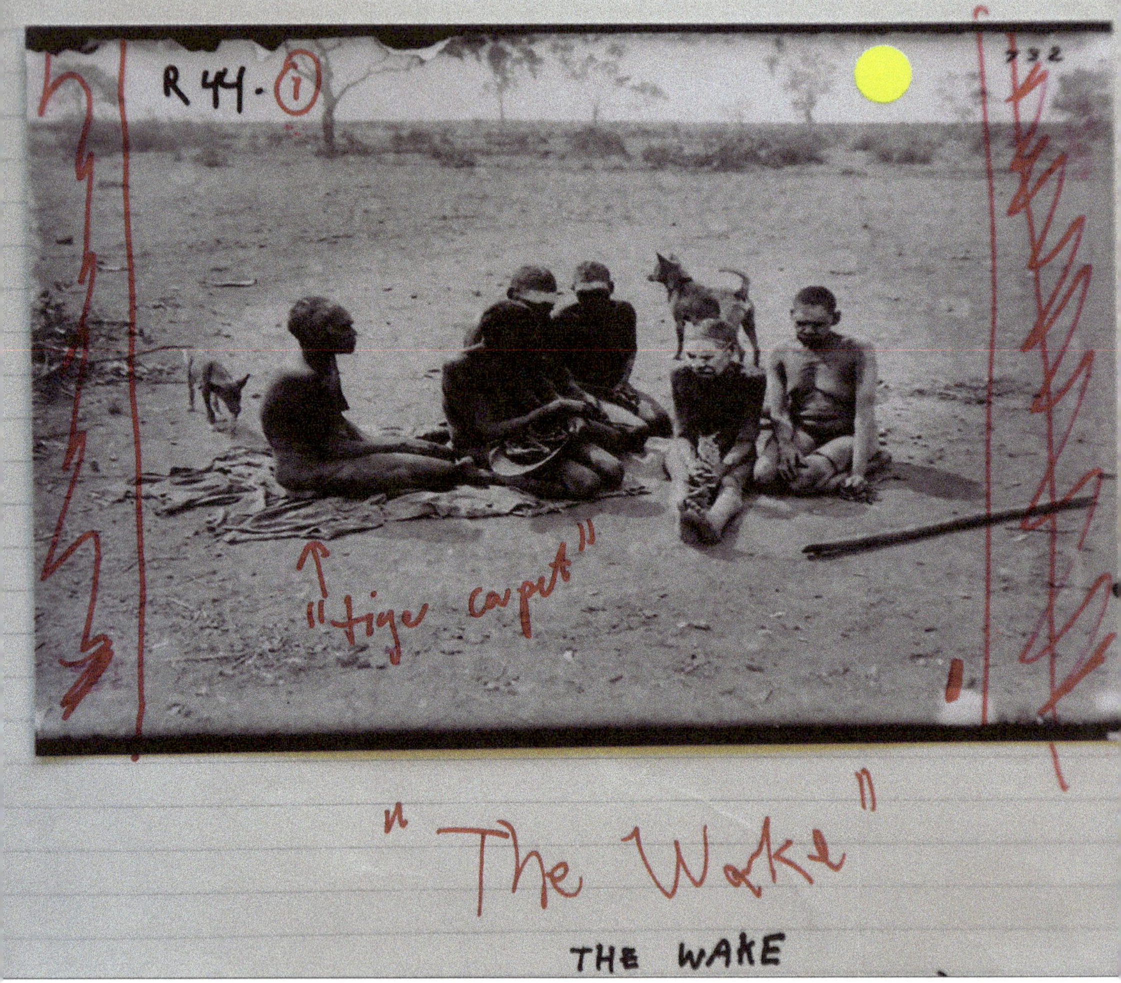
R44.
"tiger carpet"
"The Wake"
THE WAKE

10

Visual note-making

Photo-elicitation and photographic re-interpretations as collaborative anthropological techniques

Christian Vium

Introduction

> This could be... uhm ... healing ... a healing ceremony happening here. Or just women going through ... this older lady, she is educating these two or maybe just healing. Probably passing on their knowledge.

Marie, a forty-something Aboriginal woman of mixed Arrernte and Warlpiri descent, and one of my main interlocutors during fieldwork in Central Australia in 2014, was analysing a set of images as she flicked through one of the notebook albums containing a selection of Sir Baldwin Spencer and Frank J. Gillen's photographs, which have long held a canonical position in Australian anthropology (Morphy 1995; Mulvaney et al. 1997), and which I had brought along for the purpose of conducting in-depth photo-elicitation (cf. Buckley 2014; Richard and Lahman 2015). She pointed to a photograph of a group of naked women sitting in the sand.

Figure 10.1 (opposite) Detail from one of the author's notebook albums, in which the original photograph ('Death & Burial. War', B.W. Spencer and F.J. Gillen, Tenant Creek, Northern Territory, between July 1901 and September 1901, Museum Victoria XP9532, glass plate; silver gelatin emulsion, quarter plate) was repurposed, cropped and overwritten by the author in 2014.

> This is sorry business ... this is a mourning ceremony, where the women are all huddled up. They paint their bodies and faces with white clay.

'So, when somebody is dead, they are mourning?' I probed, as I continued jotting in my notebook, hoping to register details that could not be heard on the audio recording I was also making of our conversation. Marie continued her analysis:

> Yeah, they come together and uhm ... sometimes, this mourning is very close because, if you lose somebody that close, you know, you embrace that person's life, and help them. Sorry business also signifies that when they mourn, and they cry, and they scream out, it is like they are helping the spirit in the body to travel back home.

'So, they take the bad things, and hold it in them so the spirit can go free, or?' I asked. Marie pointed to another image (Figure 10.1) from the same series, and nodded:

> Yes, and this, it is the same. Similar. Women are gathered after the sorry business. The ladies they, you know, sit around and talk amongst themselves very quietly [...] It is like a funeral – a wake, you know...

I nodded, and scribbled down the words 'THE WAKE' in capital letters underneath the photograph, as I savoured the feeling of having realized something that I was certain would provide a new direction in my research. Later that evening, I extended the notes, as I listened to the conversation, making further annotations to the photographs in the notebook album. These were supplemented later by Marie in follow-up interviews.

In my research project, 'Temporal Dialogues', the collection, production, analysis and dissemination of (visual) notes occupied a central and instrumental role. Through an archive-based, collaborative method that combined anthropology and visual-art practice, the project focused on the collective trauma of colonization, and the anthropological representation of 'the Other'. This was done through a series of experimental interventions that interrogated and deconstructed the stereotypical white categorizations inherent in the colonial or imperial gaze. By redirecting this gaze, inviting 'the Others' themselves to articulate their analysis and perform themselves in direct dialogue with the archive, the aim was to reframe the practice of colonial 'Othering' inherent in the original archival material, and to produce a critical body of work that is open to interpretation.

In the project, I mine three significant archive collections of photographs and other material produced in the period between 1860 and 1920. I select and arrange the archive images in theme-based notebook albums, with the purpose of repatriating this material, using it for in-depth photo-elicitation with people in the areas where the original photographs were produced (Central Australia, the Brazilian Amazon and Siberia). Subsequently, selected photographs from the initial archive serve as a templates for photographic re-interpretations, made in close collaboration with local people – who are descendants of the people in the archive. These re-interpretations, which dramatize, mime, mock, reframe and re-contextualize the originals, are then juxtaposed with the originals in visual montages, along with sketches and texts of various kinds (my own notes, my interlocutors' notes and comments made during photo-elicitation sessions, academic quotes, and excerpts from interviews, newspapers and other sources) and videos. This material, and the specific method I developed to produce it, forms the basis for the production of scientific-journal articles, exhibitions and a book publication (see Vium 2017a, b and 2018).

In this chapter I discuss some parts of this complex comparative project, by homing in on my practical and analytical approach to note-making with reference to fieldwork in Central Australia. I emphasize the notion of making notes as opposed to the more widely used notion of taking notes, drawing attention to the creative, experimental and, in the context of this particular project, collaborative aspects of the process of making notes. To acknowledge the overflow of ideas, perspectives and concepts that characterize my experimental and exploratory research process (and note-making), I have chosen to include them here, rather than leaving them out, thus pointing to their integral role. Following Michael Taussig (2011), among others, I consider anthropological notes to be inherently ambiguous and in constant transformation. Visual notes, such as photographs, are particularly open to interpretation, and this may be used as a productive aspect in scientific knowledge-making that attends to the 'epistemic murk' (Taussig 1987:127) of 'the hermeneutic swamp' (ibid.:131) that we call the field. From the outset, the ambition of this project was to make room for associations in research design: to establish a dialogical space in which we could transgress more conventional dialectical forms of past-present comparisons. Together with my interlocutors, I was looking for other positions from which to interrogate, criticize and hopefully understand new aspects of the nature of the cultural encounters embedded in the archive photographs, and then reframe them, potentially subverting their meaning. As such, the project was fundamentally about cultural critique (Marcus and Fischer 1999), in that experiments with defamiliarization and juxtaposition were central to our collaborative engagement with the 'colonial' material.

With an empirical point of departure in my fieldwork in Central Australia in 2014, this chapter outlines the elements in the project that were particularly relevant with regard to the collaborative aspects of note-making. In so doing, I address how the conversations we had and the notes we made together, on the basis of the photo-elicitation, served as flexible scripts in our subsequent photographic re-interpretations and in later analysis and dissemination. I demonstrate and elaborate on how these scripts change throughout the various stages of the research process as a consequence of, among other things, the ongoing conversations and collaborations with interlocutors in the field. I propose the argument that our process of visual note-making may be understood as a form of anthropological *Durcharbeitung* (Lyotard 1988) for both anthropologist and interlocutors. In my use of the term *Durcharbeitung*, I follow Jean-Francois Lyotard's notion of working through, in which history 'acts' in the present, through what might be termed 'free' association, and by drawing attention to what may at first sight seem to be irrelevant details. In line with Lyotard's approach, which is derived in part from Sigmund Freud's seminal writings (Freud 1914), a central concern was to establish a practical space for dialogue that would allow my interlocutors and I to transcend conventional verbal, textual and visual forms of articulation (cf. Thompson 1994). As our collaboration unfolded, our conversations and photographic re-interpretations often assumed allegorical forms (Clifford 1986:98–121). Quoting James Clifford, I subscribe to the following definition of the term allegory: 'Allegory (Gr. *allos*, "other," and *agoreuein*, "to speak") usually denotes a practice in which a narrative fiction continuously refers to another pattern of ideas or events. It is a representation that 'interprets' itself... Allegory draws special attention to the *narrative* character of cultural representations, to the stories built into the representational process itself.' (Clifford 1986:99–100; added emphasis). During my fieldwork in Central Australia, my interlocutors would often use the original photographs as points of departure for complex reflections on relationships between past, present and future, in a way that integrated references to themes and questions beyond those immediately apparent in the material. In addition, the way in which different photographs were juxtaposed analytically with reference to emotional registers embedded in our conversations, opened it up to more abstract moral controversies common to many indigenous contexts. In this sense, our collaboration became a way to address and process deep emotional traumas rooted in past encounters with settlers, in ways that were more than mere verbal dialogues and lamentations. My interlocutors re-contextualized the photographs and composed new narrative montages by assembling a variety of photographs and notes during our collaboration. This process of 'working through' and collaborative scripting subsequently evolved into a series of dramatic choreographies, as we began to engage practically with the material through the specific technique of experimental photographic re-interpretations.

Notes on the Spencer and Gillen collection

Upon commencing my research project, I acquired three large notebooks that were to serve as the spine of my research throughout the entire process. I devoted each book to an overall theme, then divided them into four sections: one containing general notes that were applicable to all three field sites, and one section for each specific field site. In addition to my camera equipment and these 'master' notebooks, I carried a small pocket-sized notebook, in which I could jot down ideas, questions and references whenever and wherever I needed to do so. I used an audio-recording app on my smartphone to capture sound from conversations, interviews and spoken reflections along the way.

I began filling the notebooks with ideas, references to literature (academic and fictional), inspiration from the visual arts, photography and film. These notes were not extensive, but in the form of sketches, extended bullet points, specific quotes and ideas I imagined I would try out in the field. Each entry was dated, enabling me to trace the evolution of ideas and analytical points throughout the project. Alongside these notebooks, I established a system of folders on my laptop, progressively adding the material I produced during fieldwork in each location (photographs, video files, audio files and interviews, edited field notes, GPS data and so forth).

Before embarking on the first fieldwork in Central Australia, I had contacted Philip Batty of Museum Victoria in Melbourne. Batty was responsible for the comprehensive digitization of the renowned collection of Sir Baldwin Spencer and Frank J. Gillen, who, over nearly four decades between 1876 and 1912, produced one of the most influential records of Aboriginal Australian life, markedly influencing some of the canonical works of early social-scientific work by Émile Durkheim, Sir James Frazer, Sigmund Freud and others. This collection made up the basis of my work in Central Australia.

Over a period of several months in the early spring of 2014, which extended into the first part of my fieldwork in Central Australia, I went through the digitized collection of Spencer and Gillen's work (www.spencerandgillen.net). Before beginning the customary anthropological work of contextual analysis, I wanted to register how I, subjectively and intuitively, reacted to the images. What touched me, and which thoughts and emotions arose from this assemblage of vanished gazes? To answer this question, I initially began sifting through the images without reading any background literature, applying an open approach, attempting not to let myself be guided by pre-established

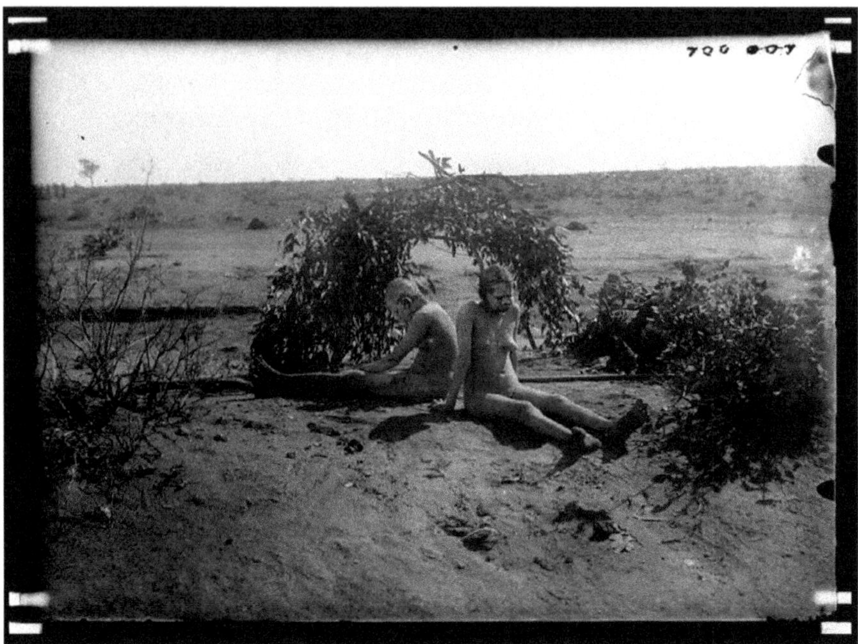

Figure 10.2 Two widows with cropped hair and covered with white pipe-clay sitting under a shelter they built themselves, Tennant Creek, Central Australia, 16–17 August 1901. 'Death & Burial. Widows. Warr.' (handwritten annotation), B.W. Spencer and F.J. Gillen, Museum Victoria XP9500, glass plate, silver gelatin emulsion, quarter plate, original glass-plate sleeve and print.

categories and master discourses. This was a deliberate strategy to enable me to partially bypass my intellectual analytical apparatus.

A photograph of two women sitting back-to-back in the sand in an open landscape (Figure 10.2) is representative of the kind of ambiguous images that attracted my attention in particular. These were photographs that had a particular strangeness to them; a kind of desolate tension, but also an atmosphere of intimacy. Who were these women? What were they doing? Why were they sitting back to back? Why were they naked? What is the white substance they were covered in? Did the plant structures surrounding them perform any function? These were some of the immediate questions I asked myself. Then, upon closer inspection, I noticed what appears to be a group of people in a circle, performing what I took to be some sort of ceremonial activity, in the distance in the upper left part of the image. Was this related to the two women in the foreground? My initial reaction was one of productive bewilderment and curiosity.

Another similar example is the photograph, commented on by Marie Ellis in the opening vignette, of four women in profile, facing each other, two

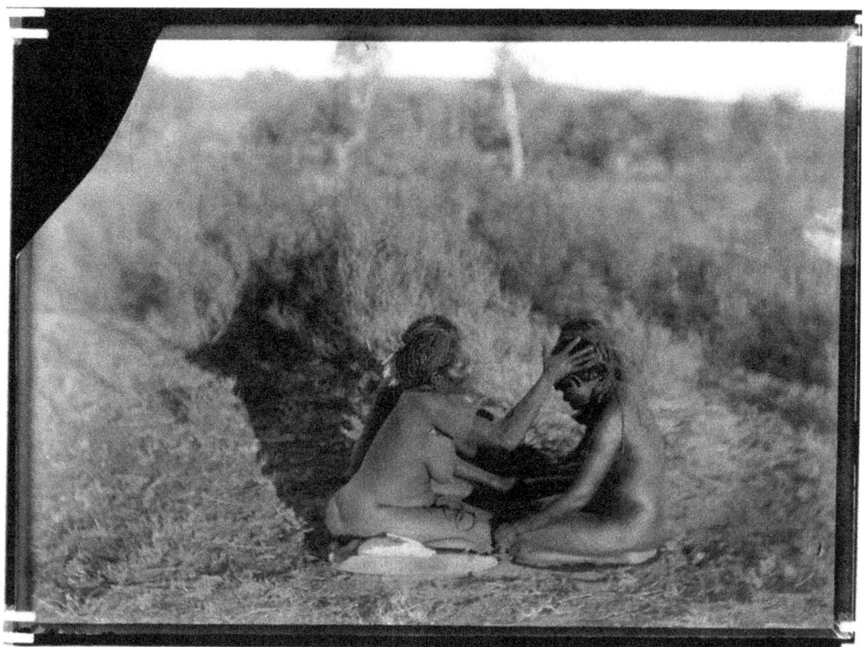

Figure 10.3 Museum Victoria XP15032, photograph, half plate, no glass plate exists.

by two (Figure 10.3). The woman on the left in front is touching the head of the woman to the front on the right, and behind them one can sense that the woman on the left is holding the wrists of the woman on the right. The women seem immersed in what appears to be a very intimate moment. Again, I was left with a feeling of not knowing what was taking place and why. My initial guess was that some sort of ritual or ceremonial practice was being carried out. As in the case of the photograph of the two women sitting back-to-back, I was affected by the intimacy and sadness that seemed to emanate from this century-old emulsion-coated glass plate.

Following this initial, 'subjective', reading of the archive, I progressively applied more specific parameters to the research. I investigated aspects such as composition, exposure, depth of field, typologies and patterns, themes or topics in the images, along with recurrent visual conventions, choice of vantage points, as well as technical aspects of the recording and development of the actual photographs. I contextualized the analysis of the images through historical and cultural research, as well as the literature on Spencer and Gillen, not to speak of their own letters, notes, diaries, books and scientific articles. I made duplicate prints of a selection of the images, which I then began arranging physically. Throughout this process, I kept notes. These were a mixture of immediate impressions of the images, the identification of

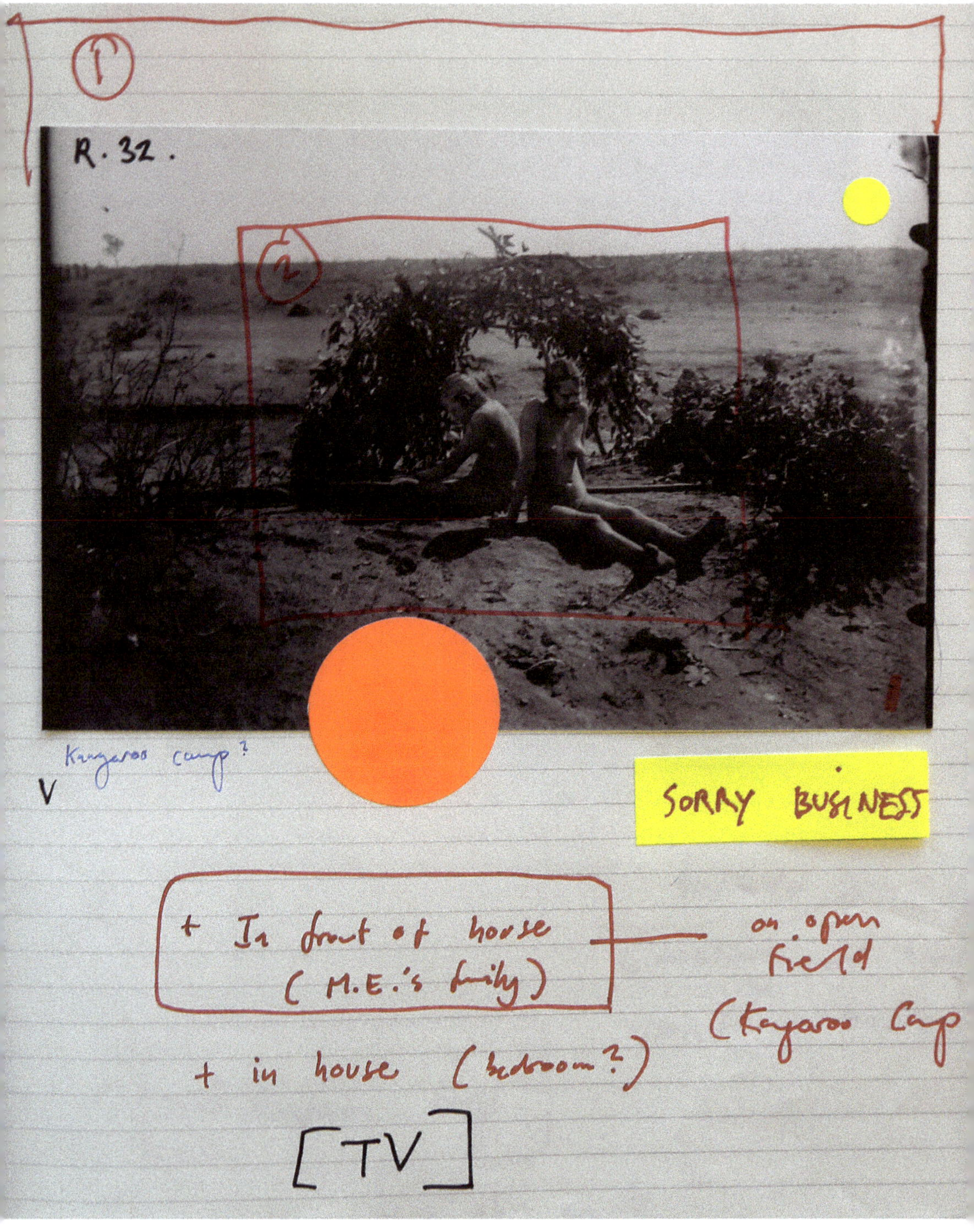
R. 32.
SORRY BUSINESS
+ In front of house (M.E.'s family)
on open field (Kangaroo Camp
+ in house (bedroom?)
[TV]

themes, comparative references across the regional literature, and systematic descriptions of individual images as well as of series. Once I had arrived at a selection of images, about 120 individual photographs, which I regarded as representative of the archive material, I assembled the photographs in three new albums, identical to those I used for notes, apart from the fact that they were red as opposed to black. These visual notebooks were, quite literally, to serve as fieldwork templates, as I describe in the following section.

Allegorical dialogues: from photo-elicitation to co-scripting

The process of introducing the archive images to my interlocutors in the field was delicate, given the sensitive content of the photographs, and the ambiguous ontological status of the photographic medium for Aboriginal Australians (Deger 2006 and 2008; Smith 2008; Smith and Vokes 2008; Vium forthcoming). Through a number of academic colleagues, I had set up some initial meetings with local people in and around Alice Springs. At these meetings, I presented my ideas and approach, showed a few of the photographs, and was advised to speak to yet other people. Hence, through a snowballing of connections, I managed to meet quite a substantial number of people. About a dozen of them became central collaborators, and a few members of this group served as actual gatekeepers throughout the fieldwork. I ended up focusing on two sites in particular: the so-called Aboriginal 'town camp' of Amoonguna, some 15 kilometres south-east of Alice Springs along the Ross Highway, and the indigenous women's centre called Akeyulerre, in the city centre.

I started by speaking to people informally, and only introduced the actual photographs at a later point. Sometimes I spoke to people in small groups, sometimes individually. Some people I would speak to on several occasions and for hours, others I only met briefly. Some knew the photographs in advance, some had seen them, and some had never heard of them before. Some had relatives who were portrayed in these original photographs. Most of the people I spoke to were women, and most of them were adults over thirty years of age, although these were not specific criteria set up by me in advance. My approach to the conversations was simple: I wanted my interlocutors to engage with and analyse the photographs, and I wanted them to lead the discussion. Throughout the initial research process, I had identified themes and images that I was interested in, and formulated a number of questions related to these. I would introduce these questions along the way, directing the

Figure 10.4 (opposite) Detail from one of the author's notebook albums, in which the original photograph (see Figure 10.2) was repurposed, cropped and over-written by the author in 2014.

conversation to a certain degree. But their interpretations and analyses were the main agenda. An example of the collaborative nature of our research into the original photographs occurred on the first day I showed the albums to a group of women in Akeyulerre. One woman gently pulled me aside and told me that I might want to consider re-organizing the material I had brought for them to see: 'These images are not for all to see. Too powerful.' This topic became central to our conversations that day, as the women and a few men offered their advice on how to go about re-organizing the material so that I could present it to people. I literally cut up the albums; and based on the detailed advice I was given, I was able to compose a new set of albums in which men and women were separated, with material that was not suitable for uninitiated individuals being set aside. Although I was working with material that had been cleared by the archive in consultation with indigenous communities, it turned out that there were specific ways of structuring the material in a sensitive manner so as not to create unwanted controversies. This was but one of many examples of how my initial notes and modes of organizing and understanding the archive were transformed through dialogue in the field.

As Elisabeth Edwards argues: 'photographs suggest meaning through the way in which they are structured, for representational form makes an image accessible and comprehensible to the mind, informing and informed by a whole hidden corpus of knowledge that is called on through the signifiers in the image' (1992:8). Hence, the interpretation of photographs largely hinges on the subjective; and often during the photo-elicitation conversations I registered that my analysis of a photograph differed significantly from that of my interlocutors. For most of my interlocutors, the experience of dispossession was very present in their lives, and the images I brought along formed part of this history in various ways. When they saw the photographs of their ancestors, many of my interlocutors were affected emotionally. A great number of them caressed the photographs, while speaking to them as much as about them. Burdened by the weight of centuries of dispossession, coupled with a cosmological frame of reference entirely different from mine, what they saw in these photographs was of a profound nature that I could only hope to intuit. The following excerpt from a photo-elicitation conversation I had with Marie Ellis, who was presented in the opening vignette of this chapter, provides an idea of how our conversations evolved from the photographs.

We had already been talking for a good three quarters of an hour in the afternoon sun outside Marie's house in Amoonguna. We were drinking tea and smoking cigarettes on plastic chairs in the shade. Her dogs were running around everywhere, and once in a while neighbours would wander by and greet us. Marie had agreed to spend some time looking through the notebook albums I had compiled with the original Spencer and Gillen photographs, to help me understand them. Our conversation oscillated between contextual interpretations of the events in the original photographs and the current situation facing Aboriginal Australians in Central Australia. On several occasions, our dialogue led us beyond the geographical context of Australia and into more allegorical landscapes inspired by details in the original photographs, taking us into areas beyond historical, political and societal topics. At this particular point in time, we were discussing a set of images that were related to the notion of 'sorry business', that is, rituals and practices related to mourning and sadness (see Glaskin *et al.* 2008). These particular photographs were among the ones that had intrigued me the most during my archive mining, and I soon discovered that my interlocutors also reacted strongly to this type of photograph. They told me there were several reasons for this. The high mortality rate among Aboriginal Australians nationally, not only in the Northern Territory and Central Australia, is an alarming indication of the continued marginalization of the indigenous population. The average life expectancy of an Aboriginal Australian is 20 years less than that of white Australians (Glaskin *et al.* 2008). In fact, death is so present in everyday life that rituals associated with sorry business, for example funerals, are among the most frequently practised, and thus also among the most familiar (Musharbash 2008:21–36). Paradoxically, the cultural traditions that characterize and sustain the Aboriginal cosmologies and life-worlds are also directly linked to the elevated mortality rate, which, in turn, is a result of their continued marginalization and dispossession. Hence, the notion of a wake, which I described briefly in the opening pages of this chapter, seemed an apt metaphor to use in exploring this profound theme.

Christian: So ... this one [Figure 2], I think, is really interesting.

Marie: Yes. Sorry business. Two women sitting down. Made a shelter so they can sleep and stay there for a long time. They may be widows, because they are all covered in white clay. So, they stay in a place away from the other group.

Christian: Is this still common here?

Marie: Yes, for example if Scott [her boyfriend] passes away, I move house. My children, my daughters, and niece, they come and clean and pack away and whatever. They sort out everything ... they would do all that: clean up. Arrange everything. My daughters and niece will be doing the cooking and stuff. So, me and my sisters and cousins would be out in the bush, probably for a month. Wait until there is a house come available. Then my daughters and sons and nephews are responsible to move all my stuff.

I flicked through a series of photographs depicting women in similar isolated situations.

Christian:	And all these images are also part of that [sorry business]?
Marie:	Yes, and they will stay isolated for a certain number of weeks or months.
Christian:	But they can't go back to the same house?
Marie:	No.
Christian:	Never?
Marie:	No.
Christian:	That sounds complicated.
Marie:	It is, and the government is talking about home ownership so... It is not really that complicated for us because we can sort of plan around that.
Christian:	So you move houses? And the cleaning is to ensure that nothing is left.
Marie:	Yeah, when Scott and I moved into this house. You should have seen it. [...] It took us nearly two weeks to clean this house before we moved here.
Christian:	That is not nice. But well it is a house.

Marie laughed and picked up the small microphone I used to record our conversation, and began to whisper into it, as if talking to an audience beyond us:

> We are talking about a house, corner of Waddle Street and Gum Tree. And Kumantye, Christian, is going all over the board now – he is drifting from the conversation and we were supposed to be talking about these pictures...

Christian:	Yeah, but this came out of the pictures...

We laughed, and the conversation continued well into the evening. While we were discussing, I would jot down notes in a notebook, commenting on Marie's body language, her tone of voice and other non-audible aspects. Simultaneously, I would make notes and sketches directly in the notebook albums containing the photographs. On several occasions, Marie spoke

Figure 10.5 (opposite) Montage by the author. Left image, see Figure 2; right image, Roseanne and Lynette, photographed by the author in Amoonguna, Northern Territory, June 2014.

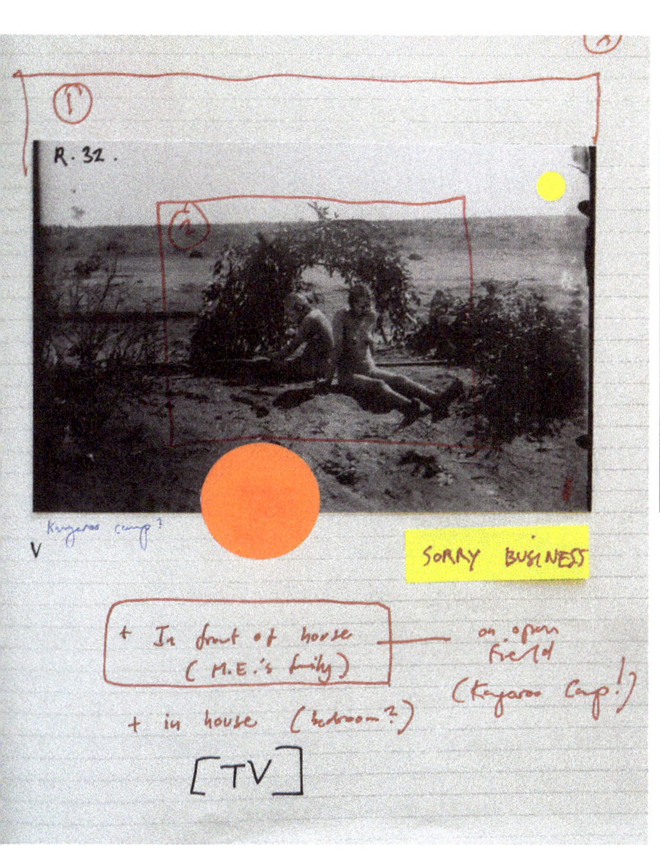
R. 32.
SORRY BUSINESS
+ In front of house
(M.E.'s family)
on open field
(Kangaroo Camp!)
+ in house (bedroom?)
[TV]

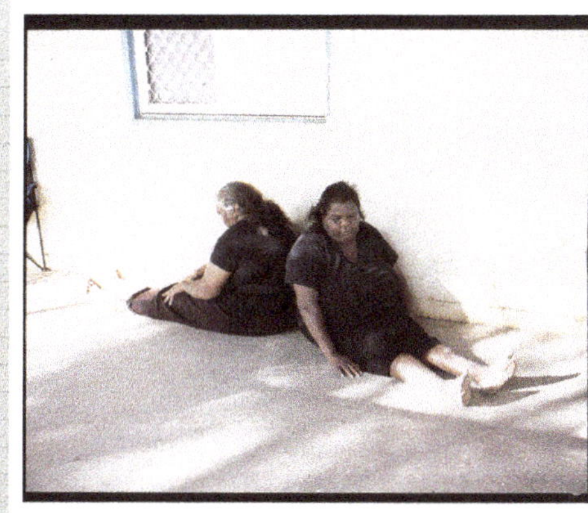

messages in her native language into the audio recorder and added her own words and illustrations in my notebook.

As I continued these elicitation sessions with a host of different people, alone and in (focus) groups, the notebooks were progressively altered, and notes and markings from previous conversations started to inform the new conversations. In the case of the photograph discussed above (Figure 2), we made two sets of frames (see Figure 4) to guide our forthcoming photographs based on this image. In addition, we identified the possible site the original photograph was taken, a place called 'Kangaroo Camp', not far from where we were sitting when we discussed the photographs. The yellow label under the photograph is part of a colour-code system to remind me that this image depicts 'Sorry Business'. Along with Marie Ellis, we planned to re-enact this photograph with two of her sisters, Lynette and Roseanne, either in the bedroom inside a house, or outside in an open field. In addition, as the letters 'TV' suggest, we pondered whether to include a television set in the scenario for the photographic re-interpretation. What we were engaged in was a particular form of poetical or allegorical fictionalization, hinging on on-site improvisation. The photographs I brought along not only evoked the past but also enacted the present, as my interlocutors reflected on their current situation through the prism of the past layered in the photographs. The subtlest details in a photograph could lead to unexpected discussions of existential, and in many respects traumatizing, questions related to cultural encounters. Hence, our dialogues assumed the form of what I understand as cross-temporal dialectical allegories that brought disparate time frames together in the present. Together, we were inventing new worlds through our dialogues and subsequent photographic collaborations.

Co-creative re-interpretations: performing cultural critique

We began to select the photographs that we wished to re-enact together. By cross-referencing our conversations with the archive material and re-editing the notebooks containing the archive photographs, along with our notes, I managed to produce a list of images to engage with. This was accompanied by my own notes about what I hoped to achieve in combination with the aspirations of my interlocutors, based on our conversations. From this collaborative script, I could then begin preparing the actual re-interpretations with my Aboriginal interlocutors. I invited them into a performative space in which they could present themselves in a direct dialogue with the original photographs of their ancestors. Although I imagined that my interlocutors would engage in a qualitatively different kind of reflexive analysis and knowledge-production when they were invited to embody their ancestors, they did so in a manner I did not predict. I understand this as a kind of 'allegorical improvisation' embedded within the particular processes of *Durcharbeitung* that grew out of our collaboration. The following example provides some clarification.

The afternoon was saturated with a strange atmosphere. Throughout the day, Marie Ellis, her sisters Roseanne, Lynette and Nola, and I had been engaged in a practical dialogue with a set of Spencer and Gillen's original photographs in Amoonguna. The women had identified a small batch of images focusing on the theme of mourning and healing rituals, as they found these spoke to central Aboriginal Australian issues in the past, present and potentially also the future. More specifically, they were inspired and touched by the intersection of grief and pride, as well as the intimacy and tenderness they registered between the women in the original photographs. In a combination of individual and group photographs, we had been attempting to dramatize the original Spencer and Gillen motifs. The women had all insisted on wearing black clothes for the duration of the day, and were very solemn and concentrated. We had already been photographing for a couple of hours and, as I showed them the photograph (Figure 10.4), I asked the women if we could attempt to engage with this image. Marie proposed that we could do it at a relative's house in Amoonguna, close to where we were. As we arrived at the house, an elderly woman with grey hair appeared in the door, pushing a walking-frame. She greeted us and exchanged a few words with Marie, after which she asked us inside with a smile. Inside, two teenage girls were lying on a carpet on the floor, watching some sort of reality programme on the television set. Apart from two strangely large and tremendously dirty blue chairs, the television was the only piece of furniture in the room. The walls were covered with dirty marks, and against the back wall the kitchenette was barely visible under piles of stained dishes and glasses. Two other teenagers, a boy and a girl, came out of an adjoining room, and a woman in her mid-thirties joined us from her seat in a dilapidated plastic chair on the porch. Marie presented the elderly woman, Kathleen, as a knowledgeable traditional healer. I briefly introduced myself and explained what I was trying to achieve, while showing her the Spencer and Gillen images of the women performing 'sorry business'. She smiled, and looked through the album. The woman from the porch and the teenagers gathered around the album, and began talking about the images amongst themselves. Together with Roseanne and Lynette, I proceeded to make a series of photographs on the porch, with them replicating the positions of the two women sitting back-to-back in the original photograph. An example of one of these photographs is shown in Figure 10.5. In my view, this image contains some of the same enigmatic qualities as the original. It is an image which does not explain itself, and there is an odd mixture of melancholy and isolation in the situation. The plastic chair discernible on the left side of the image contributes to this feeling of being somehow out of place. But more importantly, the melancholy that in my view emanates from the image of Roseanne and Lynette was a result of their dedication and concentration. They really did embed themselves in the situation, and performed the grief which they felt was contained in the original photo. The session, which took no more than fifteen minutes, was an intense moment, in which I believe Roseanne and Lynette effectively approached their ancestors through an act of embodied mimesis. Afterwards, they were both exhausted and excused themselves.

Meanwhile, the woman who had been sitting in the plastic chair on the porch signalled to me that we should go inside. Kathleen had placed herself in one of the oversized blue soft chairs, the walking-frame parked on her right-hand side, next to what appeared to be some children's books strewn on the floor. Kathleen pointed to the image of the women engaged in what Marie, along with several other interlocutors, had identified as a healing session (Figure 10.3), proposing that we make a new interpretation of that same photograph. She stretched out her hands as the other woman, whose name I cannot find in my notes, sat down in front of her. In complete silence and concentration, they now 'mimed' the original (Figure 10.6), while the teenagers, who had regained their position in front of the television set, observed this quiet spectacle unfold before them. And so, we shared a speechless moment, somehow inviting the past into this small living room, re-enacting a moment that had transpired more than a century earlier. Later, Kathleen explained that it was important for her to show that these healing traditions were still practised in the community. There was something profoundly intimate about this moment even though – or perhaps because – it was performed entirely for the camera. In that space, the women taught me a valuable lesson about the importance of intimacy and togetherness in a time of sorrow and oppression.

This example from one afternoon in Amoonguna illustrates how the dialogues we had when looking at the original photographs were extended and became embodied and performative. These re-interpretation sessions, as I call them for lack of a better word, were never overtly dramatic in terms of pace or volume. They were quiet and intimate moments we shared between us, and with the groups of people who were nearby and who would take part as spectators in this *Durcharbeitung* of themes which were central to their lives, past and present.

Overall, our collaborative re-interpretations are best understood as manifestations of a practical form of cultural critique based on experimenting

Figure 10.6 (opposite) Montage by the author. Left image, see Figure 10.4; right image, healing session, photographed by the author in Amoonguna, Northern Territory, June 2014.

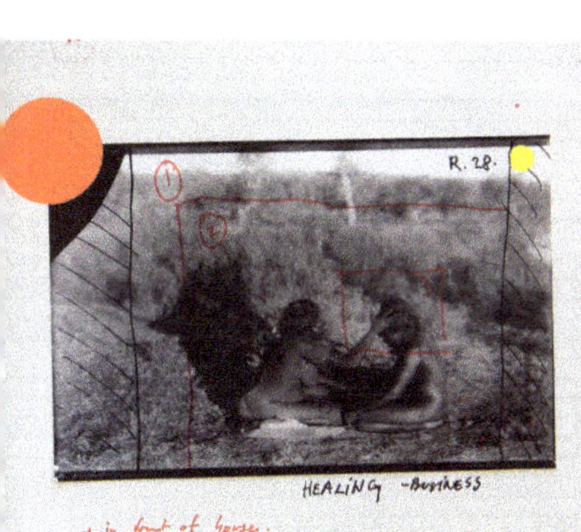
R. 28.
HEALING -BUSINESS
+ in front of house.

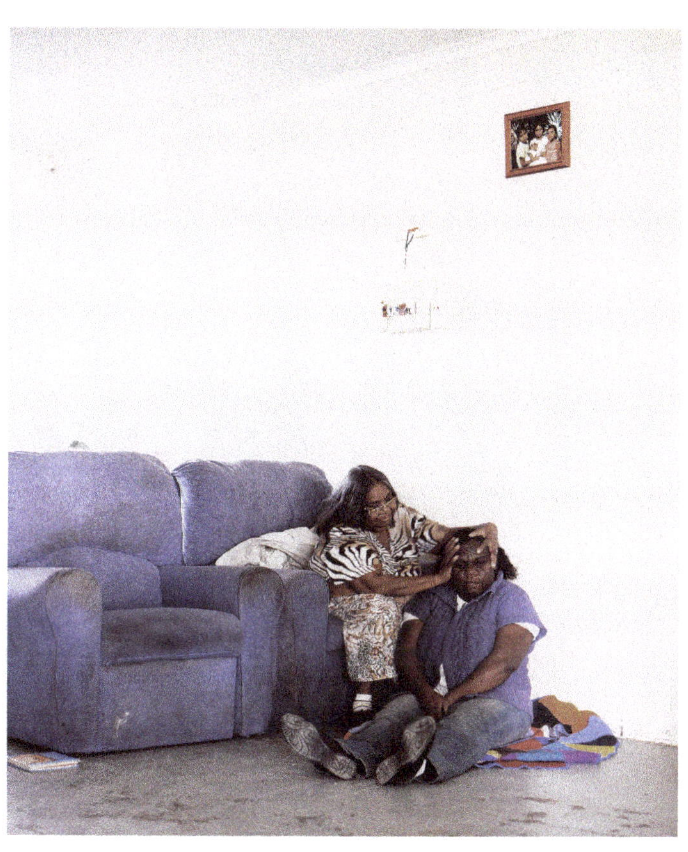

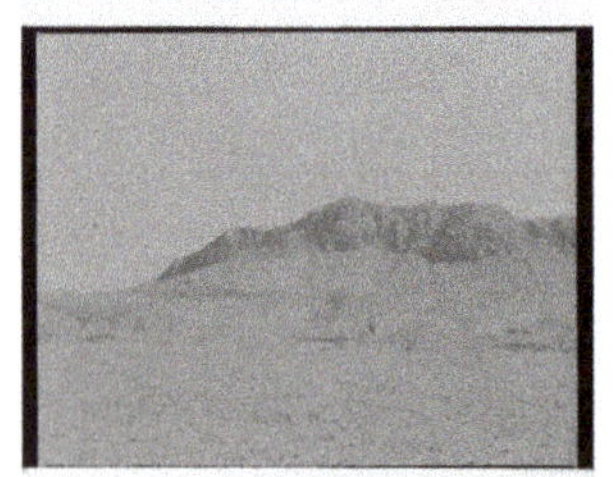
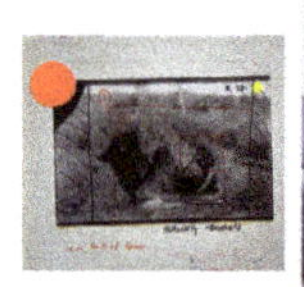
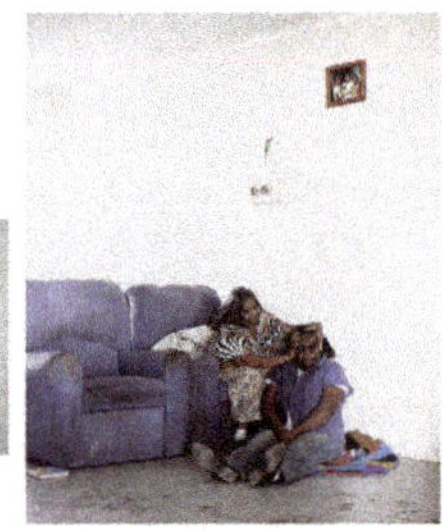
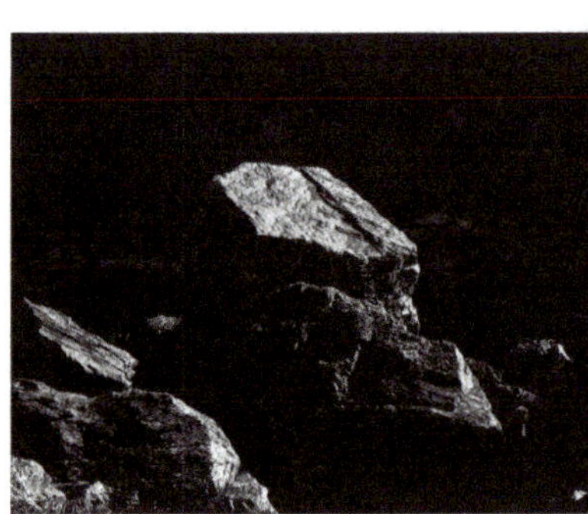

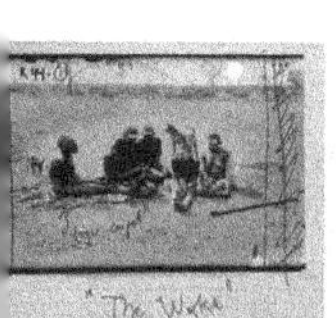
THE WAKE

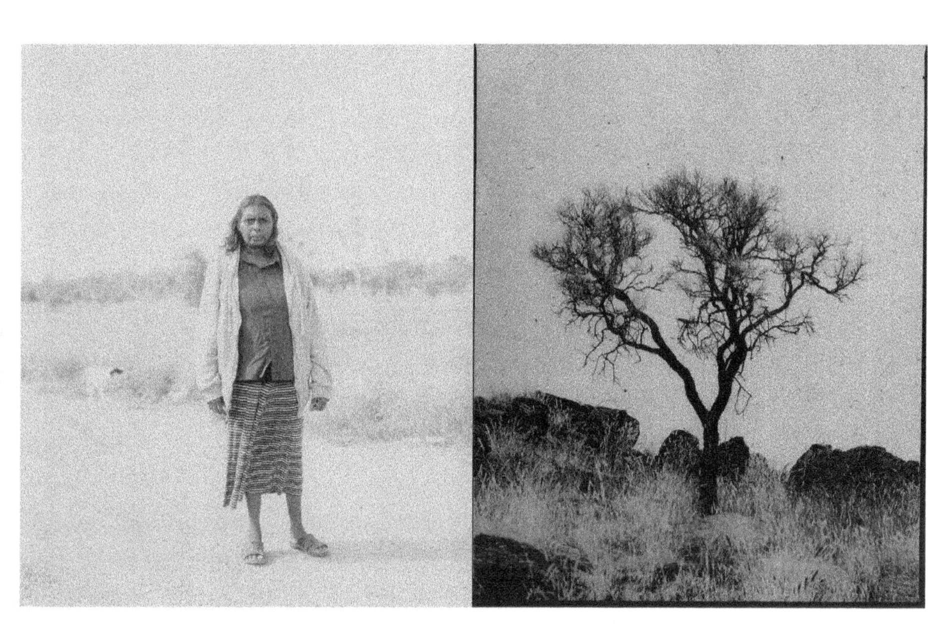

with note-making, (allegorical) scripting, juxtaposition and defamiliarization techniques. I think of it as cultural critique, because in working with these photographs we turned the colonial gaze around, interrogating the colonial encounter through the prism of our contemporary dialogues, which were crystallized in the photographic re-interpretations that we made. More specifically, the juxtaposition of materials (images and texts) in conversations and photographic *mises-en-scène* enabled us to enter into dialogue about Aboriginal Australian everyday life, cosmology, and the encounter with the other through time. Though I have not space to write in detail about it here, this approach continued when I returned from the field and started organizing and analysing the empirical material. As mentioned above, the project also integrates material produced during fieldwork in the Brazilian Amazon and Eastern Siberia, using the same overall methodological framework developed specifically for the research project.

Conclusion

Working with images demands particular registers for dialogue that are different from strictly textual and verbal ones. Photographs are fundamentally ambiguous in nature and are open to interpretation. Analysing them – understanding them – is a subjective endeavour that is highly contingent on the context in which they are viewed. I have thought about the work I did with my interlocutors in Central Australia as a form of *Durcharbeitung*, a form of praxis that acknowledges the necessity to explore the individual associations and impressions – feelings, moods and sentiments – of the people who are engaged in the process of doing 'memory work' (Kuhn 2007). By combining photo-elicitation conversations with practical, collaborative photographic enactments based on the original material and prior conversations, we opened up a space for dialogue that moves beyond conventional forms, often giving rise to what I term allegorical improvisations.

By juxtaposing and employing the concepts of *Durcharbeitung* and allegorical improvisation, this chapter has demonstrated the iterative potential of a collaborative, experimental approach that constitutes a series of analytical moves. As I have described above, these moves were hinged on a practical, empirical 'working through', progressively propelling the research into new and often unforeseen domains. The result, I argue, is a palimpsest of fragments assembled across temporal and spatial contexts and held together by 'poly-vocal' and 'poly-material' collaborative notes: 'allegorical scripts'. These

Figure 10.7 (previous page) Layout of montage for installation of works, FOAM Talent 2015 exhibitions, June 2015.

extend throughout the project, from its earliest inception to the completion of physical installations, and beyond.

As part of my research, I produced installations and exhibitions that served as analytical vehicles in the knowledge-making process. In an interactive move between image work, i.e. editing and re-touching (that is, the manipulation of the image content through image-processing software such as Adobe Photoshop) and writing, the analysis began to take shape. As I went along, the physical arrangements of juxtapositions of old and new images grew and mutated into montages on walls, tables, floors and in editing programs on the computer (Figure 10.7). The first exhibition was installed and opened in August 2015, and since this time the material from Central Australia has been exhibited in 14 venues in 12 countries, and published in a number of newspapers and magazines, reaching a diverse audience beyond academia. Hence, what began as an idea and a collection of ethnographic photographs from the nineteenth and twentieth centuries has become a series of palimpsest installations that collapse time and space, as well as scientific and narrative registers.

Finally, I want to emphasize the fact that my work with indigenous peoples in different settings, involving the analysis of historical archives and the subsequent production of new forms of representation, is part of a collective endeavour to produce new archives that can be used by our descendants – be they academic or not – in the future. The curation of material in various formats is part of this strategy, and one example is that our notes and conversations, as well as each photograph we make, can be traced geographically using GPS coordinates, enabling future generations to revisit our work and perform the same (or entirely different) dialogues and reinterpretations of it, as we have done with the work of Spencer and Gillen in this case.

Acknowledgements

This project was part of the Camera as Cultural Critique research project at the School of Culture and Society, Aarhus University, funded by the Independent Research Fund Denmark (grant number DFF-1319-00111). In addition to the many people I have met and worked with in Central Australia, I am particularly grateful for the ongoing discussions with members of this unit: Ton Otto, Christian Suhr, Peter Crawford, Arine Kirstein Høgel and Karen Waltorp.

References

Buckley, L. 2014. 'Photography and photo-elicitation after colonialism', *Cultural Anthropology* 29(4):720–43.

Clifford, J. 1986. *Writing Culture: The Poetics and Politics of Ethnography*. Berkeley: University of California Press.

Deger, J. 2006. *Shimmering Screens: Making Media in an Aboriginal Community*. Minneapolis: University of Minnesota Press.

——— 2008. 'Imprinting on the heart: photography and contemporary Yolngu mournings', *Journal of Visual Anthropology* 21(4):292–309.

Edwards, E. (ed.) 1992. *Anthropology and Photography*. New Haven: Yale University.

Freud, S. 1914. 'Remembering, repeating and working-through (further recommendations in the technique of psychoanalysis II)', *The Standard Edition of the Complete Psychological Works of Sigmund Freud*, Volume 12 (1911–13):145-56.

Glaskin, K., Tonkinson, M., Musharbash, Y. and Burbank, V. (eds.) 2008. *Mortality, Mourning and Mortuary Practices in Indigenous Australia*. Farnham: Ashgate.

Kuhn, A. 2007. 'Photography and cultural memory: a methodological exploration', *Visual Studies* 22(3):283–92.

Lyotard, J.-F. 1988. *L'Inhumain Causeries sur le Temps*. Paris: Galilée.

Marcus, G.E. and Fischer, M.M.J. 1999. *Anthropology as Cultural Critique: An Experimental Moment in the Human Sciences*. Chicago: University of Chicago Press.

Morphy, H. 1995. 'More than mere facts: repositioning Spencer and Gillen in the history of anthropology'. In S.R. Morton and D.J. Mulvaney (eds.), *Exploring Central Australia*, pp. 135–49. Sydney: Surrey Beatty.

Mulvaney, J., Morphy, H. and Petch, A. 1997. *My Dear Spencer: The Letters of F. J. Gillen to Baldwin Spencer*. Melbourne: Hylland House.

Musharbash, Y. 2008. '"Sorry business is Yapa way": Warlpiri mortuary rituals as embodied practice'. In K. Glaskin, M. Tonkinson, Y. Musharbash and V. Burbank (eds.), *Mortality, Mourning and Mortuary Practices in Indigenous Australia*, pp. 21–36. Farnham: Ashgate.

Richard, V.M. and Lahman, M.K.E. 2015. 'Photo-elicitation: reflexivity on method, analysis, and graphic portraits', *International Journal of Research & Method in Education*. 38(1):3–22.

Smith, B.R. 2008. 'Ties that bind: photographs, personhood, and image relations in northeastern Australia', *Journal of Visual Anthropology* 21(4):327–44.

Smith, B.R. and Vokes, R. 2008. 'Introduction: haunting images', *Journal of Visual Anthropology* 21(4):283–91.

Taussig, M. 1987. *Shamanism, Colonialism, and the Wild Man*. Chicago: Chicago Press.

——— 2011. *I Swear I Saw This. Drawings in Fieldwork Notebooks, Namely my Own*. Chicago: University of Chicago Press.

Thompson, G.M. 1994. *The Truth about Freud's Technique. The Encounter with the Real.* New York: New York University Press.

Vium, C. 2017a. 'Interventionistiske Skabeloner: Fotografisk iscenesættelse som dialogisk metode i antropologien', *Tidsskriftet Antropologi* 76:109–28.

——— 2017b. 'Experimental re-enactment as anthropological device', *Visuel Arkivering* 10:39-45.

——— 2018. 'Temporal dialogues: collaborative photographic re-enactments as a form of cultural critique', *Journal of Visual Anthropology* 31(4–5):355–75.

11

Stimulating presence

On the materiality of field notes and a few Brazilian flip-flops

Anne Line Dalsgård

In a cardboard box on the top shelf in a corner of my office, next to other boxes with similarly otherwise unplaceable objects, lie eight pairs of rubber flip-flops and two green ones that have lost their partners. They are all of the Havaianas brand. In other respects, they are quite different from each other. The differences are many. Beginning with the green and unpaired ones: one is brand new, still unmarked by human movement and weight, and with a neat, regularly patterned sole that remains unspoiled by stones or mud. It is vividly green, yellow, blue and white, in layers, and on each of the green straps sits a small Brazilian flag. The other green and solitary flip-flop has been used. You can tell this from the worn pattern on the sole, the stiffness of the straps, and the crumbled rubber around the holes in which the straps are attached to the footbed. If you turn it over, you can also tell from the sole that it has walked a lot with its owner. The pressure of the foot on the rubber has made some parts of it more crumbled than others. This flip-flop has no flag on its straps and it is of one colour only: faded green.

In addition to the two green flip-flops, there is a pair of used blue ones with a wave-like design of different blue colours on the footbed of the sole, which is stiff and crumbled; three monochrome pairs, in red, pink and brown, all three used and darkened by dirt and sweat; an unused pink pair decorated with plastic pearls on the straps by an inventive woman; and another pair of green ones, quite large for Brazilian feet, and used so much that the inner side of the heel of the right flip-flop has become very thin. A black pair still looks useable, though the front part is worn thin on both feet. One last pair distinguishes itself from all the others, as it is of the traditional model, with the upper side being white and the bottom and straps being blue. I bought it only a few years ago, so it is not from the 60s or 70s, when this was the only Havaianas model one could buy. It has become fashionable again, 'retro', and sells incredibly well according to the producing company, Alpargatas. But that is another story. The relevant question here is what are they all doing in that cardboard box on my shelf? How did they get there, and why don't I throw them away?

The answer is simple: I just can't do it. I feel a certain awkwardness whenever I try to decide to get rid of them. Not that they give any meaning lying there. They do not represent, so much as present something to me, tokens of an interest, of something not yet comprehended. In this chapter I will argue that they are like field notes for me – and that, as field notes, they demonstrate the odd and not at all linear progression of ethnographic research. I will begin though, with a description of the Havaianas brand and the way I became interested in it.

From *chinelo* to *sandalia*

The Havaianas brand has a remarkable history. In the 1960s, when Havaianas was launched, salesmen drove round the whole country to remote villages. Anyone who was used to walking barefoot or with homemade leather shoes bought these rubber flip-flops of allegedly good and modern quality. There were other similar products on the market, but Havaianas was promoted as the only proper rubber flip-flop under the slogan: '*Havaianas. As legítimas. Não deformam, não soltam as tiras e não têm cheiro*' ('Havaianas. The authentic. They do not deform, do not lose the straps and do not smell'). The latter characteristic, the absence of smell, apparently had to do with other products' smell of rubber. Poor people's dignity rests significantly on cleanliness, in Brazil as probably elsewhere, and you want your body to smell nice. It is interesting, though, how a sensuous quality is tied to the product from the very beginning.

During the military dictatorship, well into the 1980s, Havaianas were sold in grocery shops as part of the *cesta basica* (basket of basics), the staples that were subject to price control. However, over the years that I have known Brazil, that is, since 1997, Havaianas have become more and more fashionable and expensive. They are not at all a poor man's shoe any more. So what happened?

According to Alpargatas, the producing company, the turning point occurred at the beginning of the 1990s, when sales had dropped from around 80 million pairs per year in the late 80s to 65 million per year in 1993. Until then, the warm climate of the north and north-east regions, and the low price and the durability of Havaianas, had made them a preferred choice among poor people. But as the economy improved and people could afford more, durability and low price were no longer attractive parameters. People wanted real shoes, with heels and preferably made of leather, and they wanted the fashion of the year, not a product branding itself as traditional and never changing. In an interview I did with the Alpargatas director Carla Schmitzberger in September 2013, she explained how the company achieved the change in the fortunes of the brand by paying attention to consumers' ingenuity. Some people, for instance surfers who used Havaianas even though they could afford more, pulled out the straps and turned the sole upside down, which made the footbed and the straps the same colour. The company began to produce similar monochrome sandals in attractive colours and they became hugely successful. Since then, designs in many colours and fancy patterns have been added. In 2012, when the company celebrated its fiftieth anniversary, over 200 million pairs of Havaianas were sold. Today around 450 different styles and colours exist, some still relatively cheap, many quite expensive.

Havaianas have changed from being a *chinelo* (a traditional slipper) into being a consumer product of high standard, a *sandalia*. They are fashionable on a global scale. Well-off people may use them in the streets, not only at home or at the beach, and Havaianas are today an integral part of a proper wedding party among those Brazilians who can afford them: a pair of Havaianas is given to each of the female guests who want to get out of their high-heeled shoes late in the evening and dance. This has happened even though cheaper models are still on the market for less affluent consumers. The Alpargatas director Carla Schmitzberger explained that for the well-off it is part of the charm that poor people still use Havaianas. They represent a simple life, the Brazilian spirit, optimism, summer, leisure. Recently, the 2017 collection was even promoted with the opportune slogan 'Slow down with Havaianas', inspired by 'the notion of unplugging, slowing down, and enjoying every single moment of your day'.[1] This is indeed a clever slogan, although it is certainly not aimed at people who struggle with unemployment and have too much time on their hands. But as the brand has succeeded in creating an image of Havaianas as truly Brazilian, and of Brazil as truly Havaianas (Ribeiro 2013:366), poor people can also feel included in this celebration of simplicity. At least according to the branding.

Havaianas have been branded effectively as 'happy objects', in the sense of objects 'towards which good feelings are directed, that provide a shared horizon of experience, and that shape an affective community with which all are assumed to be aligned' (Da Costa 2014:1; see also Ahmed 2010). A relatively recent video advertisement for Havaianas shows the most

---

1 www.trapholt.dk/presseside-funk/122-stjerner-paa-den-internationale-designhimmel-til-trapholt (accessed 29 June 2019).

captivating, colourful pictures of happy people enjoying life at the beach, football, music and in love, while the voice-over (I reproduce here the English subtitles) goes as follows:

> Feet say a lot about people.
> But they say everything about Brazilians.
> Brazilians have the most famous feet in the world.
> The happiest feet in the world.
> The ones with the most graceful moves.
> The foot understands what goes on in Brazilian minds.
> And since it has discovered Havaianas,
> it discovered its perfect mate.
> More than a partner,
> Havaianas is the perfect companion
> for the easy-going and fun-loving Brazilian way of being.
> That is why the world fell in love with Havaianas.
> Because it discovered that it could be that way too:
> Simple, uncomplicated and happy.
> Havaianas made the planet kick off their shoes
> and dive into this universe of colours and fun.
> When a foot slips into Havaianas,
> it's entering Brazilian territory.
> But since everyone's welcome,
> there is no need for a passport.
> Because complications don't match with Havaianas.
> In fact, what goes with it?
> Comfort, is a perfect match.
> Happiness, it never looked so good.
> And freedom, that goes perfectly well with it.
> Because freedom, ladies and gentlemen,
> mesdames et messieurs,
> is represented here in the most simple
> and spontaneous form for everyone's feet.
> If you're Brazilian, enjoy your Havaianas.
> If you're not, try slipping them on.

Nowhere in this video, however, do you see any visibly poor people. Nor does anything in the video correspond with the conversation I had with a taxi driver in São Paulo in November 2013, probably the same year as the video was released. He was from the north-east, and had arrived in São Paulo in the 1980s as a young man, when many migrated to the metropolis. Since then he had worked hard and made himself an honest life. But many people still ignored him, he told me, passing by him as if he did not exist, because – this is what he thought – he was a *nordestino*, i.e. from the north-east. They treated him as a *Zé Ninguem*, an insignificant nobody. As I had asked others, I asked him if he used Havaianas. He answered that he would never leave his home in *chinelos*. Their father taught them this back home – *chinelos* are for the poor. They had to take turns going to school, he and his brother, as they had only one pair of proper shoes. To be respectably dressed is important, and this applies in the metropolis even more than in the north-east. He concluded by stating that he only used Havaianas for taking showers, to avoid getting a shock from the electrical heater. In other words, the branding strategy has not completely wiped out Havaianas' *chinelo* image, even though today young people of low-income status wear their Havaianas with pride. The underbelly of the cherished consumer product is a social inequality that is deeply engrained in people.

Brazilian inequality exhibited

I grew interested in the social status of Havaianas when I interviewed Sonia, a woman in her forties, back in 1997. At that time Sonia still lived in the low-income neighbourhood where I was doing fieldwork, located on the outskirts of the city of Recife in north-east Brazil. I asked her what it meant to be a *pé de chinelo*, an expression I had heard several people use about themselves. *Chinelo* is the Brazilian word for slipper, I knew that, and *pé* means foot. But Sonia informed me that *pé de chinelo* also means a poor person who is generally ignored by Brazilian society. She told me about entering shops in which salesmen keep an eye on you, suspecting that you will steal; and about entering a public hospital where no one attends to you despite the fact that you are quite visibly in pain. Sonia formulated it like this: 'The "*pé de chinelo*" is the poor, society is the heels, and when the heels arrive everybody is running, they are all treated well, received well, it is only nice talk. But with the "*pé de chinelo*" they say, 'When I have time, I'll go there!"' (Dalsgaard 2014:142).

By using the *chinelo* as the metaphor for poverty, Sonia turned my attention towards the ubiquity of flip-flops in the neighbourhood. More often than *chinelos* they were, however, called Havaianas, as a generic term resulting from the brand's dominance in the market. By using footwear more generally as a metaphor for social status, Sonia also aroused my interest in the way bodies are physically marked by economic power, or the lack of it. For instance, if you can afford a pair of closed shoes your feet will look different than feet exposed to weather, stones and various other factors. This was relevant to me at that time, as I was researching female sterilization and the motivations of low-income women for pursuing this option. Sterilization meant taking responsibility, making sure you would not give birth to children you could not bring up, and who would later become criminals or street children. Uncontrolled fertility was one stigma of the poor; feet marked by the use of flip-flops were another, I discovered; and together with other markers of poverty they formed a complex of shame that the women wished to escape.

However, having returned frequently to the neighbourhood since then, I have observed that the status of Havaianas has changed. They have become smarter and smarter, more and more expensive, and recently friends and family back in Denmark have enjoyed receiving the new models as presents. I remember taking a photograph of a colourful collection of Havaianas in a shop window in Aarhus, where I live, at prices way beyond any of my informants' purchasing power. I also remember presenting a paper in 2003 based on Arjun Appadurai's *The Social Life of Things* (1986), in which I discussed the movement of Havaianas from context to context on a global scale.[2]

Knowing about my interest in Havaianas, Karen Grøn, the director of the Danish design museum Trapholt, asked if I would contribute to an exhibition on Brazilian design opening in March 2014. The main attraction was an exhibition of the internationally renowned Brazilian designers Fernando and Humberto Campana's furniture made of waste products, such as cardboard, rope, pieces of cloth and wood scraps, plastic tubes and aluminium wires. In the press release it said:

> The primary starting point in the work of the Campana brothers is 'the material' […] The material determines the form and function. They [the brothers] often include Brazilian culture and craft traditions. They themselves have the following to say about their work: 'Our work flirts with the materials, as if they were asking us: What can we be transformed into?'[3]
>
> (my translation)

On the opening day of the exhibition the Campana brothers made explicit references to poor people's design practices, formed by necessity and available resources. Their designs were intended to be a celebration of the creativity of the poor.

The Havaianas exhibition that we envisioned would have been exhibited parallel to the Campana exhibition. But it never came to pass, as will become

2 This paper was mainly theoretical, revolving around questions of value and consumption, and as I lost it in a change of computers. It has no further relevance to this chapter.

3 www.trapholt.dk/presseside-funk/122-stjerner-paa-den-internationale-designhimmel-til-trapholt (accessed 10 July 2019).

clear below. We would have told the story of Havaianas: how the product was developed first as cheap footwear and then turned into a fashion product; and we would have talked about the invention of Brazilian culture that this process displayed and also formed part of (Ribeiro 2013:366). When we planned the exhibition, I was not aware of the potential criticism of the Campana approach the exhibition might be seen to imply. My take on Havaianas was not an innocent contribution to the museum's fascination with Brazilian culture. Instead, I was interested in the social aspects of what was otherwise defined as 'design'. Much more strongly than I would have presented the issue, but still relevant here, political scientist Janice Perlman presents a fervent critique of both Havaianas and the Campana brothers in her book *Favela*:

> Havaianas, the colored rubber flip-flops that are popular in favelas and cost about US$ 3.50, are selling in fashionable London boutiques for US$ 170. If that weren't absurd enough, a 'favela chair' created by Italian designers Fernando and Humberto Campana in 2003 seems to cross over the line from homage to insult. [...] a highbrow cultural phenomenon of simultaneously imitating, mocking, and exalting the poor has taken hold.
>
> (Perlman 2010:330)

Perlman goes on to ask how people who live in the favelas of Rio de Janeiro are to react to the existence of 'favela chic' fashion shows in Paris, when their sons and brothers are being killed for a pair of Nike shoes; and how they should feel about an expensive 'favela chair', which may not even be comfortable (my comment), when their everyday is full of impossible choices between buying this or that necessity (ibid.:333). Apart from her mistake about the nationality of the two brothers (they are Brazilian), I think Perlman is right. By telling the story about Havaianas we would also be telling the story of persistent and disturbing social inequalities in Brazil, and the irony of celebrating the simplicity that poverty necessitates.

Still unaware of this potential, I travelled to Brazil to collect material for the exhibition with the photographer Hans Christian Jacobsen. Hans Christian took a series of tripartite photos such as in Figures 11.1–3.

I also had a Brazilian friend, Josenita Duda, collect a number of used Havaianas, which we intended to display along with an installation of perhaps one hundred brand-new and colourful Havaianas hanging from the ceiling in the middle of a wonderful square, light room. Josenita collected the used Havaianas in the neighbourhood where she lives by exchanging new flip-flops for old ones. She later told me that one elderly woman hesitated about doing this because she was afraid of black magic. The idea of exhibiting her old worn *chinelos* was deeply suspicious to her. However, along with other pairs

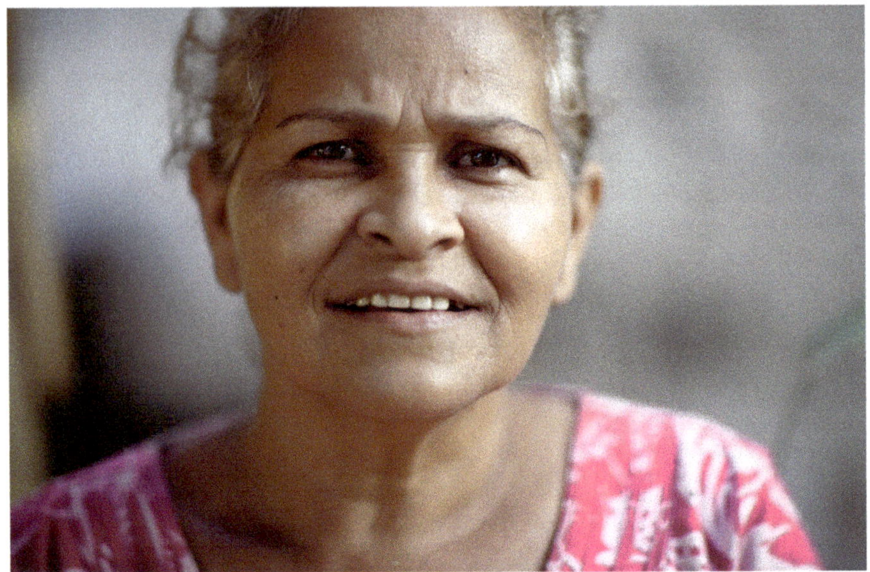

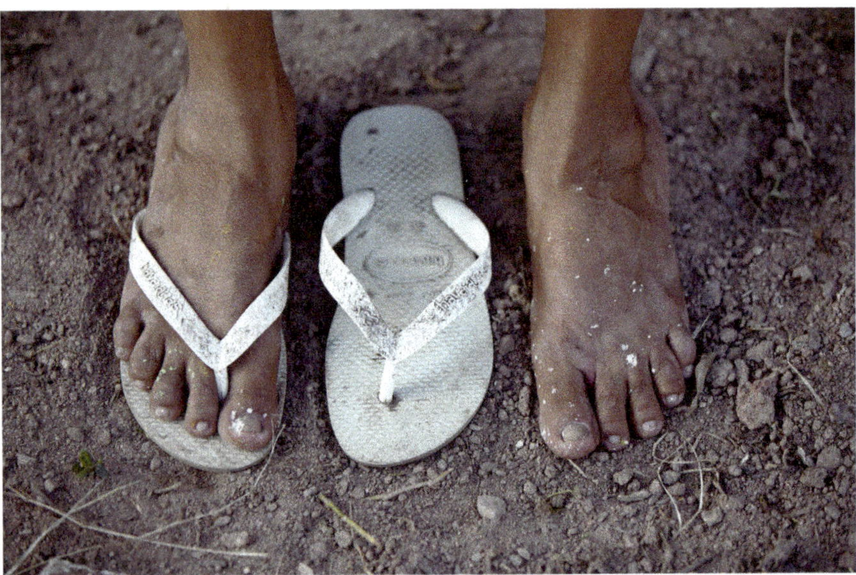

Figures 11.1–3 Inez Ferreira in her Havaianas (photographs, Hans Christian Jacobsen).

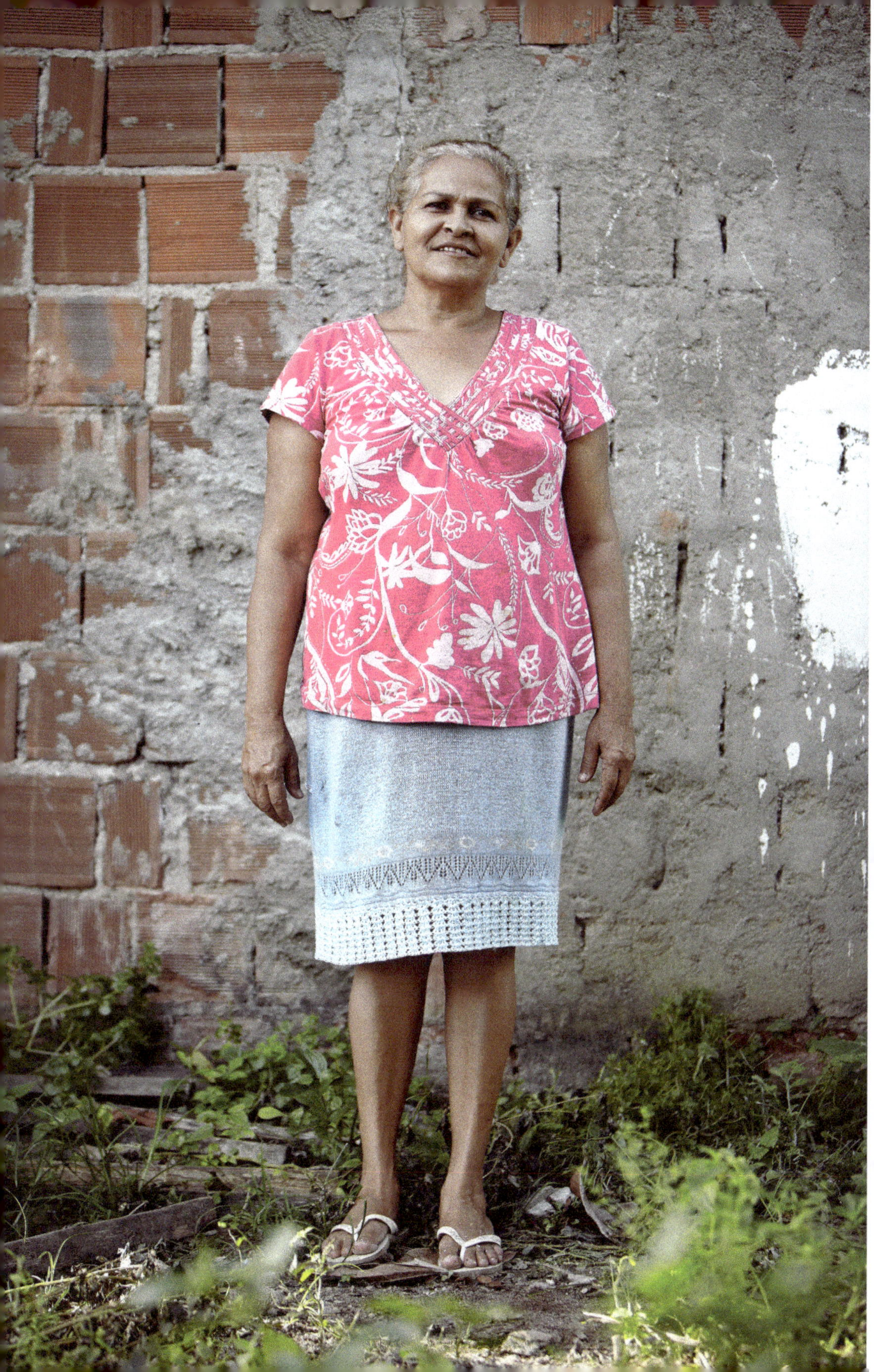

of used Havaianas, her flip-flops arrived at my office one day in a well-taped cardboard box sent by Josenita.

But it was all in vain. We did not manage to get the new flip-flops and the permission we needed from Alpargatas in time, so our plans for the exhibition were abandoned and the material we had collected no longer had a destination.

The haptic experience of flip-flopping

Hans Christian's photographs, the used Havaianas and the material that I did receive from Alpargatas (a marvellous selection of old and new branding material including many TV advertisements) call out for some kind of use. Particularly the Havaianas, as they take up space on my shelf. No longer items for a museum display in their own right, as samples of an existing describable social reality, I have kept them as reminders. Sitting with them in my hand, observing their different marks of use (or lack thereof), I am reminded of life in the neighbourhood that has been my research location for many years now. But what shall I do with them? Can I use them as a source of inspiration for further research, and if so, which project are they part of? The change of framework from 'exhibition' to 'research' is a change from illustration to question and potential answer, a process in which the flip-flops have begun to challenge me as they lie there in their mute tangibility.

The idea of exhibiting the flip-flops sprang from my original interest in the concept of *pé de chinelo* and in the somatic sensation of poverty implied in this concept. Now, sitting with the concrete Havaianas in my hands, it is manifest that they are part of lived lives, which themselves are embedded in larger societal structures: the worn-down material speaks of inequality and daily toil. But were their users aware of this when the flip-flops were still in use? Did they sense their own walking with flip-flops as a marker of social status? Philosopher Edward Casey tells us that social institutions and cultural practices permeate our sensing bodies – they become 'infusions into the infrastructure of perception itself' (1996:19). But is this 'infrastructure' of perception discernible for the perceiver? And if it is, how can I explore if Casey is right in this particular case of flip-flops? Philosophical claims call for ethnographic substantiation, because in themselves they are no more than qualified propositions. However, asking 'how does it feel to walk with Havaianas?' has not taken me very far:

> Rosa: I am in love with Havaianas. They are comfortable, you can use them anytime. They are fashion, the trend.
>
> (Rosa, 18 years old, living in a low-income neighbourhood, September 2013)

Silvia: I have a cousin who only walks in heels all day, she arrives home with swollen legs. Another walks in Havaianas all day, wherever she goes, and she arrives home with no swollen legs, much more comfortable. But some wish to be more *arrumada* [neat].

Anne Line: Did you try other brands? Is [another brand] also good?

Silvia: It is good, but it gets dry after some time. I have one in the house, and I get a bit tired when I walk with it. I do not like that one so much.

(Silvia, mid 30s, living in a low-income neighbourhood, September 2013)

Felipe: I have tried [to repair Havaianas with a nail]. My father liked to use up a thing. But my foot was too thick. When you put a nail into the strap it gets tighter, so we had to make a hole in the sole [for the nail to sink into it].

(Felipe, late 30s, living in a lower-middle-class neighbourhood, September 2013)

Josalia: My father used a *chinelo* of leather. It was heavier, made another sound. Havaianas is also a *chinelo*, but the one of leather made a sound more like lapto-lapto-lapto…

(Josalia, mid 50s, living in a low-income neighbourhood, September 2013)

At first, at least, I did not really get beyond this kind of statement in my interviews. But slowly some insights began to appear. Here is an excerpt from an interview with Carla, September 2013. Carla lives in a favela and works as a nanny in a rich family, who also provide her with a white uniform and white Havaianas for the job:

> Everyone comes home, takes off their shoes, puts on Havaianas, that is a tradition, a comfort. You feel relief. I don't walk barefoot, the material embraces the feet, I like that.

It embraces the feet! I know that experience. Floors can be cool in Brazil, welcoming cool on hot days, but chilly on colder days, especially in the morning. The rubber is warm. It is soft, but not too soft. It is also clean and protects you from whatever dirt the floor may be perceived to carry. In his article 'Haptic geographies', Mark Paterson observes that the studying of others' haptic experiences is inescapably mediated by the researcher's own haptic experience (2009:776). Paterson's insight draws on the work of Paul Stoller, who noticed that: 'To accept sensuousness is […] to lend one's body to the world and accept its complexities, tastes, structures, and smells' (Stoller 1997:xvii). And indeed, over the years that I have done fieldwork in north-east Brazil, I have lent my body to that world and walked extensively with flip-flops. The experience of the 'embrace' is woven into my experience of the field and my interest in Havaianas. An embrace both in the sense of a feeling of warm rubber touching your foot, and in the sense of a sentiment in the whole body, almost as if you give in to something and let your body loosen up. Walking with flip-flops is a particular sensuous experience due to their design. If you are inexperienced, when the weather is wet you get mud up along your legs and back (as the rain pours down, covering the street with water, mud and rubbish in a confusion that whirls towards the gutter, which is always blocked or not properly designed for the conditions). But even on such days your flip-flops make you move your hips differently, your spine, your shoulders. Your whole organism is affected by the casual flip-flopping of the rubber sole and the way your toes hold on to it by the small strap between them. As you grow used to walking around in flip-flops, you no longer have to focus upon the adjustments of your body. The movements when you slip them off in front of the entrance of a house – or if they are your indoor flip-flops, when you pull your legs up into the sofa or bed – are full of grace. The best way to put it, is that they are 'easy'.

The direction of my own haptic experience towards the Havaianas in the box has changed them for me. They are no longer only representatives of social inequality and consumption in Brazil, they are also linked directly to my body.

Everyday aesthetics observed

My own experience is complemented by observations of the way other people use Havaianas. One day in February 2014, Josenita and I had just had lunch in a small local restaurant, where you can buy a simple meal on workdays and pay by weight. Josenita went home, and I sat down on a bench outside to write some notes on our talk. Sitting there, watching the movement in the local shopping street Avenida Elisa Cabral, I began to take notes of the Havaianas passing by. Who wears them and how? Havaianas are easy to identify and can be distinguished from other flip-flops by their design and the conspicuous brand name on the straps. I remember writing these notes on a casual piece of folded paper, first in one corner, then turning it and writing somewhere else, and then on the back, slowly filling the piece with a rather decorative jumble of jottings. When I returned to my computer, I organized them like this:

> A tiny lady with silver hair
> blue dress

seemly sleeves
parasol and bottle green Havaianas
in doll size.
Elderly white-haired
scurfy almost black toes
well-worn black Havaianas
the sole is paper-thin.

Mobile phone by the ear
blue blouse
the thighs are too bulky for the shorts
the chinelos are white and turned in towards each other
as she's sitting there on the bench.

Fair skinny girl
perfectly clean toes
very slim straps on the chinelos.

A red bicycle
he's crossing the street in a large curve
stopping by the guy on the other side of the road.
In passing, a pair of worn-out white chinelos.

Two girls on a bench
lazy
one pair of knees leaning against each other
the other one spreading to the sides
both in blue chinelos.

Belly first
white chinelos, brown toes
walking on the outside
the backpack carelessly thrown over one shoulder.

He's sitting with a tired slouch
white shirt, still sparkling clean
one foot out of the chinelo, resting on the instep of the second
black Havaianas.

Grey curls
short and compact

the dress in a brightly coloured pattern, most likely home sewn
orange, green, black
gentle smile
probably a grandmother
golden straps on her chinelos.

Nimble walk
rasta hair, long yellow shirt, green shorts
casual
black, always black.

Elderly man
no more than 1.30 tall
soft black hat
the shirt neatly placed behind the belt
in the brown, once dapper, pants
worn-out child-sized chinelos.

At least 1.90 tall
plump masculine curves
white Havaianas that generously allow the hips to sway.

Golden chinelos
golden parasol
proud walk with the grocery bag.

Tired on a stool
One foot halfway out of the chinelo.

The process of organizing of these notes gave rise to a certain feeling while I did it – and also now when I look at them again – the different attitudes with which the Havaianas were used radiate from the short descriptions of their users. The choices of clothing and footwear, the forms of bodies and movements, the speeds and rhythms and sounds, and in all this, the Havaianas. The freshness and fragmentation of these quickly scribbled notes convey an aesthetics of everyday life, as it displayed itself with all its charm and humour that midday on Avenida Elisa Cabral.

I use the term 'aesthetic experience' here to denote an experience of pleasure and meaning, which on an everyday level may have everything to do with 'the agreeable' and the familiar (Leddy 2005:7). According to Jonathan Smith, 'Most people live their lives surrounded by familiar things persons and activities, whose beauty is to be found not by treating them as if they were endlessly novel, but by delighting in their easy familiarity' (2005:xi). And this is what I saw: walking in Havaianas along Avenida Elisa Cabral meant showing oneself in public in a familiar and agreeable way; meeting people you know and perhaps contemplating your relationship to it all, while you sit on a bench watching the world go by. But what is familiar needs to be thematized and expressed in words if I wish to go on with this analysis. I did not ask the people sitting on the benches any questions, and I did not stop any passers-by to ask them any questions either. I just enjoyed the aesthetics. Left with a wish to write poetry (if only I could) instead of anthropology, I sometimes ask myself why 'evidence', 'triangulation' and 'conclusion' are the standards we hold on to. Why dissect life's beauty?

Rubber cut-up, August 2015

'Why?' was also how I ended that August at Helenekilde in 2015. Twenty anthropologists were gathered around the question: 'Can comedy be used as a method for exploring how anthropological knowledge is made?'[4] None of us really knew what to do, except follow the organizers' instructions and try to be inventive. We had each brought two items along to the experiment – one that belonged to the field and one that belonged to what we considered 'home': mine were two green Havaianas, a brand-new one with a flag on the straps, of the expensive kind that people gladly pay for in Denmark, and a used one, faded and crumbled here and there.

At a certain point in the playful atmosphere that arose, we decided to relate to our things as materials, nothing else. We wanted to smash and cut everything into pieces in order to bring the material itself into focus. In one sense we were doing the opposite of the Campana brothers (though this was not on my mind at that point), who flirted with materials that asked them 'what can we be transformed into?' We wanted the materials to become materials, nothing else, no context, no meaning, just glass, rubber, textiles or plastic, and we were not flirting. We laughed a lot, but as in any good game we were also utterly serious. I began to cut the brand-new Havaianas into small coloured cubes. As the sole was green, yellow, blue and white, in layers, the cubes were coloured in the same way; the colours of the Brazilian flag. I made a neat pile. But the straps were difficult. They did not lose their identity as Havaianas straps, with their particular tire-like pattern and the name. I remembered straps, like the ones I was struggling with, lying in the mud in the neighbourhood. Owing to wear and tear, they get pulled out of the sole, and, annoyed with the situation, people often leave them lying wherever they

4 comedyofthings.com (accessed 10 July 2019).

fell off. The soles are kept though, because they can be reused by buying new straps (copies, of course) at the market. But if the hole in the sole has become too wide, and the straps pull out when you walk, a nail through the strap beneath the sole can also fix it. I thought of nails and mud, while I continued. I had cut up one green flip-flop now. But I had brought two.

The other one was different. I began to cut it, but the situation was uncomfortable, like when humour suddenly turns wrong and you get a bad taste in your mouth. It was as if someone was looking at me disapprovingly. The sense of the rubber resisting the scissors became mixed with this uncanny awareness of transgressing a border. In a way it should not have surprised me that I was affected by destroying something that was so expensive that some of the people I know in my fieldwork neighbourhood would never allow themselves to buy one, let alone spoil one. This was certainly true of the brand-new flip-flop that I had cut up. However, there was more to my experience of discomfort than knowing this financial reality and feeling guilty for being careless. It was the used flip-flop that stirred me, not the new one. It carried the marks of long use, the sole being much flatter and more rounded around the edges after walking everywhere with its owner, an elderly woman. She had mistrusted our explanation when we wanted to buy it, or rather exchange it for a new one – literally taking it from her foot while she was sitting there at the market selling vegetables – as she feared that we would use it for black magic. It was her flip-flop, to the degree that it was almost part of her.

In her book *Flip-flop* Caroline Knowles notes that the material of the flip-flops she studied 'vibrates with the vitality of the social lives with which it is enmeshed' (2014:4). And yes, the *chinelo* I held in my hand vibrated with vitality – in the resilience of the rubber, dirt from the street, the sweat and probably the regular cleaning with chlorine, as people do out of a concern for hygiene, but also owing to the stigma of poverty that obliges you to stay as clean as possible. This vibrating vitality pulled me out of the moment, back to the field. I felt a sense of estrangement. Who was I to cut up that sandal? An exhibition, a study of the haptic, poetry and, now, destruction? My role as an anthropologist in search of insight and meaning was being scrutinised from a point of view that I could not identify, and I felt awkward. Awkward about accepting the invitation to comedy, when the item I had in my hands told stories about poverty and social inequality. Awkward because the flip-flop reminded me of a world which had not yet been subjected to the dissection and analysis of anthropology. And awkward because I kept the unspoiled strap, as if it was still of some value without the rest of the sandal. It was a comedy, perhaps, but one exhibiting my commitment to a concrete life in an urban neighbourhood in north-east Brazil.

The note-worthiness of flip-flops

So why keep the Havaianas? I have been flip-flopping on my flip-flops, but I have not yet found out what to do with them. They switch between being stepping-stones towards an argument about something else (inequality, everyday aesthetics), and being an object of analysis in their own right (the material, the style and familiarity). There are several promising analytical directions, but as described here they all need more fieldwork. Meanwhile, the box stays on my shelf. I have portrayed my attempts as if they were chronologically ordered, and it is true that certain things have happened in a chronological sequence. But looking back upon them now, as if they lie in the past, is mostly for the sake of narrative structure. In practice, the temporal order is not one of linear progression. For instance, I did not realize back then that the jottings from Avenida Elisa Cabral would have the described effect. I just liked them and kept them, and only when I began to write this chapter, encouraged by my co-editors, did I try to be explicit about why I liked them. As Sjørslev (2013) writes, to a large extent the significance of fieldwork is only grasped in retrospect, and, additionally, in this case the significance was realized through collaboration with others. But not only did the retrospection and collaboration disappear in my narrative. The awkwardness of cutting the rubber related to a general sense of estrangement that I frequently associate with fieldwork, and also this 'multi-temporality of the relationship between fieldworker and the field' (Dalsgaard and Nielsen 2013:1) was not represented in the narrative above.

If my flip-flops can be said to be notes from a field – and I think they can – the temporality of the note-field relationship is more muddled than words generally suggest. 'Taking a note' does not mean taking something with you from an existing field site, as in 'collecting data'. It is much more like making a mark in a landscape, where something particular happened, in the hope of being able to return to the same spot at a later date and relate it to other events. The landscape may be imagined, and the event was perhaps 'nothing other than the almost imperceptible sensation that something significant was taking place' (Dalsgaard and Nielsen 2013:6), but you may wish to return to it again and again in order to explore its vivifying quality. The fact that the mark I have returned to in this chapter is a cardboard box full of Havaianas is not as metaphorical as it may sound. It works as a mark exactly because it takes up space on my shelf, and I frequently have to consider whether I should get rid of it (and if so how this should be done). Matter and practical dilemmas force me to ponder.

This is probably not specific to my flip-flops. Many field notes may have this flip-flop quality to them. Not only are field notes 'a reinterpretable and contradictory patchwork of perspectives' (Lederman 1990:90), they are also often more active in what they 'are' than in what they represent or reflect. By their presence, their form, the speed of the handwriting, the smell of the paper or cloth, or the weight or deterioration of the material, or other factors, they touch the ethnographer. And some are more insistent in this than others. I wrote about 'mute tangibility' above. I took that expression from Esther Fiehl, who used it in her reflection upon the organizing of items in a museum collection (Fiehl 2003). Artefacts from long-forgotten contexts raise questions, Fiehl writes, through their mute tangibility. In my comparison between the art project of the Campana brothers and a research process, I have here written about flirting versus serious play, insinuating a lack of social responsibility in the Campana project. By doing so, I probably differentiated research from (the Campana brothers') art too rigidly. It is therefore appropriate here, close to the end of the chapter, to acknowledge that the art piece, the museum artefact and the material field note share at least one important characteristic: their presence. In being present they are always more than thought can capture. This is probably why they are so stimulating.

References

Ahmed, S. 2010. *The Promise of Happiness.* Durham, NC: Duke University Press.

Appadurai, A. (ed.) 1986. *The Social Life of Things: Commodities in Cultural Perspective.* Cambridge: Cambridge University Press.

Casey, E.S. 1996. 'How to get from space to place in a fairly short stretch of time: phenomenological prolegomena'. In S. Feld and K. H. Basso (eds.), *Senses of Place*, pp. 13–52. Santa Fe, NM: School of American Research Press.

Da Costa, A.E. 2014. 'The (un)happy objects of affective community', *Cultural Studies* 30(1):24–46.

Dalsgaard, A.L. 2004. *Matters of Life and Longing. Female Sterilisation in Northeast Brazil.* Copenhagen: Museum Tusculanum Press.

Dalsgaard, S. and Nielsen, M. 2013. 'Introduction: time and the field', *Social Analysis* 57(1):1–19.

Fiehl, E. 2003. 'Samlingen: at forfølge tingenes biografi'. In K. Hastrup (ed.), *Ind i Verden: En Grundbog i Antropologisk Metode*, pp. 184–205. Copenhagen: Hans Reitzel.

Knowles, C. 2014. *Flip-flop: A Journey Through Globalisation's Backroads.* London: Pluto Press.

Leddy, T. 2005. 'The nature of everyday aesthetics'. In A. Light and J. Smith (eds), *The Aesthetics of Everyday Life*, pp. 3–22. New York City: Columbia University Press

Lederman, R. 1990. 'Pretexts for ethnography: on reading fieldnotes'. In Paterson, M. 2009. 'Haptic geographies: ethnography, haptic knowledges and sensuous dispositions', *Progress in Human Geography* 33(6):766–88.

Perlman, J. 2010 *Favela: Four decades of Living on the Edge in Rio de Janeiro.* Oxford: Oxford University Press.

Ribeiro, M. dos S. 2013. 'Por uma biografia das coisas: a vida social da marca *Havaianas* e a invenção da brasilidade', *Etnográfica* 17(2): etnografica.revues.org/3148

Sjørslev, I. 2013. 'Boredom, rhythm, and the temporality of ritual: recurring fieldwork in the Brazilian Candomblé', *Social Analysis* 57(1):95–109.

Smith, J.M. 2005. 'Introduction'. In A. Light and J. Smith (eds.), *The Aesthetics of Everyday Life*, pp. ix–xv. New York City: Columbia University Press.

Stoller, P. 1997. *Sensuous Scholarship.* Philadelphia: University of Pennsylvania Press.

12
Fourteen endnotes

Michael Taussig

1. Ethnographic notebooks evoke an interesting world, a world without edges, frontiers or order. It is an indeterminate world, seething with possibilities. Real life, you say. Maybe. But not one that finds its way into books on 'method', which are more commonly meant to shore up order.

2. Chaos as method? Is that what stands out in notebooks? Something like that; the luck of the draw, the odd moment, the odd encounter that changes everything. Only (and here's the catch), you have to be ready, you have to be observant while at the same time allow space and time for dreaming and day-dreaming. All this goes into the field notes and notebooks, which like sandcastles are revised, and revised some more, and which can become unbearably baroque with layerings and marginalia and afterthoughts chasing afterthoughts.

3. How strange that notebooks start to take on a life of their own. As with a fetish, the thing made comes to assume power over its maker. The ethnographic notebook is a fetish, and the anthropologist, knowing something of the history of the discipline, should be in a good position to understand that and accommodate – if not going even further and exploring – this relationship. But to recognize this is one thing. More exciting still is to enjoy the fetish. This requires a thorough-going sensitivity to something unnamed – another continent, or is it an island? – situated between psychoanalysis and history, experience and memory. It is to inhabit that crossroads where the trickster lives, the same crossroads

conjured by Adorno with his castigation of what he saw as the mistaken method in Benjamin's Arcades Project, that crossroads where positivism and magic converge.

4. Why restrict such a book to writing, when all manner of doodling, drawing, sketching, colouring and reformulation of pages (divided vertically or horizontally) cry out for inclusion? Think of the scrapbook with its cuttings from magazines and newspapers, and its photographs of family and friends, ancestors and times long forgotten. The scrapbook presents a eureka moment when we try to figure out the hidden potentials of the ethnographic notebook.

5. There are drawings so relevant to the ethnographic enterprise. John Berger and others remind us that when you draw something you see it with a sharpness not present at other times, and, what is more, there is a strongly mystical process set in motion whereby the drawer becomes one with the thing drawn. Imagine that!

6. Surely all this deserves a place alongside writing? Quotation is part of this, as with Walter Benjamin's notebooks, his *Origin of the German Trauerspiel*, and especially *The Arcades Project*. Most of the latter's 1,000 pages consist of quotations, such that the work can be considered a gigantic ethnographic notebook involving fieldwork in the memory and history of the nineteenth century, as the past reveals the flash-points constituting the 'now' of the present.

7. Both stranger and friend, confidant and taskmaster, the notebook is likely to become both an artwork and a logbook. This possibility is inherent to the form and should be allowed to flourish, because ethnography is as much about the inner experience of the ethnographer as it is about the field. Not only can the ethnographic notebook combine these realities, is not this combination more truly scientific than so-called objectivity, because it observes the observer as well as the observed? And not only more scientific, in that sense, but richer also in terms of its intertwining of the psychic life – emotions, anxieties, fantasies, memories – with the life of one's surroundings. The palette is wide. Now the 'field' is constituted by Self as much as by Other and, furthermore, each set of understandings, each 'echo' and reciprocation, breeds more of the same. Sometimes we spiral upwards. Sometimes downwards into gloom and despair. Whatever the direction, whatever the affect, it is lively and subject to change.

8. One move I am making here is to more or less equate the ethnographer's notebook with the diary. Strictly speaking, this is not always the case. Malinowski, for instance, had his personal diary apart from the notebooks reserved for ethnographic observations. But my point is that these two forms interconnect, that the ethnographic notebook is but an extension or metamorphosis of a constantly disassembling Self in a field of strangeness. Imagine if Malinowski's diary was combined with his ethnography as the one published volume! This would be Brechtian in its 'showing showing'. And it would be revelatory in its displaying the weaknesses of the white observer in the colony, his techniques of bodily and emotional control, his regulation of the relationships with the islanders, his trickery – see George Stocking's (1988) biographical study – and the terrifying collapse of the stiff-upper-lip patriarchal exterior of the writer: a bodily, emotional, and philosophical collapse of Being that inflames the diary as much as his very body in its interactions with the environment, both colonial and physical.

9. The question arises as to how such a composite diary/monograph might be written? At least two approaches come to mind. One is avant-garde literature, as in Virginia Woolf, James Joyce, Beckett, or William Burroughs, and therewith speed up the overdue demolition job of your standard anthrospeak, with its hefty dose of what Clifford (1983) called 'ethnographic authority'. The other is to learn from the diary or ethnographic notebook form itself, and to use that as the model for the composite. By this I mean the hesitant, sporadic, foray nature of the diary form, with its tentativeness and its blurting, paragraphic mixing of inner and outer worlds like the segments of a caterpillar. Instead of chapters. Instead of narrative. Instead even of an argument (heaven forbid!), truth is struck and revealed through a multitude of disparate observations, contradictions, and changes of tone in short passages varying from paragraphs of, say, ten lines to three or four pages, perhaps enlivened by another epistemic plane of immanence provided by drawings, diagrams and photographs.

10. I take the 'paragraphic form' to follow on from Nietzsche's aphoristic writing, as in The Gay Science and later attempts by Benjamin in *One Way Street* and *The Arcades Project*, as well as Adorno's *Minima Moralia*. Such writing has been given the name of *Denkbilder* – thought-figures or -images. It is a writing that does not reduce or dissolve contradiction, but instead maintains the tension in constellations. It is a writing that eschews the search for structure, depth, the code, and similar spin-offs from monotheistic religions and Plato's forms. To whom does one write when

writing in one's notebook? To oneself? That seems naïve. What self? Is not this self (or selves) itself being constructed as the pen moves across the page? What of Barthes' idea of the death of the author; that a force outside of the writer guides the pen, as the song is sung through the shaman by the spirits? Can one's ethnographic diary and notebook be thought of in this way, thereby opening out onto a whole theory of (postmodern) writing in which, with the death of the author, two overlapping possibilities concur: namely, that the writing writes itself; and/or, to the extent that there is an author, the intended readers are firstly spirits, and only afterwards actual flesh and blood persons (as occurs with a shamanic seance)?

11. What I am saying here, what I am trying to do, is to alienate the act of writing itself and see it as a highly unnatural and complicated activity. Even if we adhere to the simplistic theory of Saussure that language is but a system of signs communicating information, this is true. And how much more true if we see language as performing something far more than communication, as actually forming reality itself such that there is no outside of language?

12. Ethnographic-notebook writing alienates writing. It is writing degree zero, a leap from experience to unmediated or barely mediated writing – first thoughts, first stabs, unadorned writing, 'basic writing' – that for all of that, and because of all of that, comes closest to the magic of writing.

13. How strange that ethnographic notebooks are relegated to invisibility, to being mere means to what is generally considered a far nobler end, that of a real book or a real article. Well, maybe not so strange! Nevertheless, is it not a little sad to see such a lost opportunity; a betrayal, really, of one's tools and one's practice, including the occlusion of one's being and of the tumult of creating oneself anew within strangeness?

14. Ethnographic notebooks undermine attempts to identify ethnography and anthropology as a science, instead of the art of writing stories or memoirs, or the compiling of a scrapbook, which when all is said and done is another form of science, meaning knowing. If considered as an end in itself, the humble notebook challenges the authority of texts no less than the institutionalization of knowledge, which today, geared to bureaucracy and professionalization, threatens to destroy thought itself.

References

Stocking Jr, G.W. 1988. *Malinowski, Rivers, Benedict, and Others*. Madison: University of Wisconsin Press.

Clifford, J. 1983. 'On ethnographic authority', *Representations* 2(Spring):118–46.

Contributors

Sofie Isager Ahl is a PhD fellow at the Department of Anthropology at the University of Copenhagen, Denmark. Her research is focused on regenerative agriculture in Scandinavia. She is the author of *Naboplanter* (2018), co-editor of *Ny Jord – Tidsskrift for naturkritik* 1 (2015) as well as translator of Eduardo Kohn's *Soul Blindness* (2016) and Mei-mei Berssenbrugge's *Hello, the Roses* (2019).

Astrid Oberborbeck Andersen is Associate Professor at the Department of Culture and Learning, Aalborg University. Her research centres on human-environment relations. She has carried out fieldwork in Peru and Greenland, and published on issues related to water politics and urban ecology, the societal aspects of climatic changes, knowledge infrastructures, and mapping of ecosystems uses. Her current research project is 'Musk Ox Pathways: Ecologies and Resources in Greenland'.

Anne Line Dalsgård is Associate Professor in the Department of Anthropology at Aarhus University, Denmark. She is the author of *Matters of Life and Longing: Female Sterilisation in Northern Brazil* (2004) and co-editor of several edited volumes. She has carried out extensive fieldwork in Brazil since 1997, and has published on issues related to motherhood, youth, poverty and temporality. Presently, she is involved in research on the reading of literature in Denmark and Brazil.

Martin Demant Frederiksen is Associate Professor in the Department of Anthropology at Aarhus University, Denmark. He is the author of *Young Men, Time, and Boredom in the Republic of Georgia* (2013) and *An Anthropology of Nothing in Particular* (2018). He has carried out fieldwork in Georgia, Bulgaria and Croatia, and has published on issues related to subcultures, marginality, urban reconstruction, temporality and meaninglessness. His current research revolves around surfaces, emptiness and decay in relation to tourism infrastructure.

Ester Fritsch is a PhD Fellow at the IT University of Copenhagen, Denmark. She has carried out fieldwork in different European sites since 2010, mainly exploring questions of ethics, technological intervention and environmental change. Presently, she is conducting research among creators of Internet of Things (IoT) technologies across Europe in the wake of GDPR (General

Data Protection Regulation). Ester is a board member of the Anthropology Association Denmark.

Marianne Viftrup Hedegaard is a PhD fellow at the Department of Cross-Cultural and Regional Studies at the University of Copenhagen, Denmark. She holds an MA in anthropology from the Department of Anthropology at the University of Copenhagen. Her PhD research investigates the influx of Buddhist-derived mindfulness practices in Danish workplaces. She has carried out fieldwork in India and Copenhagen, and has published on issues related to contemplative body-mind practices, affective labour and ethnographic methods.

Mette Lind Kusk is Assistant Professor at the School of Social Work at VIA University College Aarhus, Denmark. She has carried out extensive fieldwork in the northern regions of Uganda, where she has explored questions related to various post-war challenges such as reconciliation, land rights, and intimate, everyday conflicts. She is currently pursuing research on marginalized youth in a Danish context.

Maria Nielsen holds a master degree in anthropology from Aarhus University. She is enrolled as a PhD student at the department of Anthropology at Aarhus University. She has conducted long-term fieldwork in the suburban part of Recife in north-east Brazil, and is currently working on her PhD project, which focuses on temporality and infrastructure in the region.

Marianne Holm Pedersen is Senior Researcher and Head of Section in the Special Collections Department at the Royal Danish Library. She is the author of *Iraqi Women in Denmark: Ritual Performance and Belonging in Everyday Life* (2014). While her current research focuses on cultural perceptions and practices of voluntariness in the grass-roots movement Friendly Neighbours, she has previously published on topics such as belonging, family and generational relations, ritual performance, religious socialization and everyday life among refugees and immigrants in Denmark.

Lars Christian Kofoed Rømer is CEO and co-owner of the storytelling company Sansâga and business manager at the People's Meeting in Denmark. He defended his PhD thesis 'Tales in an Underground Landscape – Anthropological Excursions in the Danish Island Bornholm' at the University of Copenhagen and The Royal Danish Library in 2018. He combines folklore and contemporary anthropology to study issues related to nature beings, (dis) enchantment, landscapes, archaeology, ancestry and ghosts in Denmark.

Cecilie Rubow is Associate Professor in the Department of Anthropology at the University of Copenhagen. Since the 1990s, she has published extensively on religion in Denmark, and ethnographic design. From 2007 she took up studies in diverse intersections between environmental change, ethics and cultural metaphysics, first in the Cook Islands and currently in relation the research project 'Enchanted Ecologies in Scandinavia'.

Mikkel Rytter is professor MSO in the Department of Anthropology, Aarhus University. He is currently the Principal Investigator on the projects 'ARTlife – Articulating life among Afghans in Denmark' (2017–21) and 'AISHA – Ageing immigrants and self-appointed helper arrangement' (2017–20). Rytter is author of the monograph: *Family Upheaval: Generation, Mobility and Relatedness among Pakistani Migrants in Denmark* (2013) and has co-edited the special issue 'Rituals of Migration', *Journal of Ethnic and Migration Studies* (2018) with Marianne Holm Pedersen.

Morten Schütt is an independent teacher of qigong, t'ai chi and Russian. He participates and facilitates in men's therapeutic circles and is an advocate for masculinity in general. A devoted husband and father of three, he lives with his family on an old farmstead in rural Denmark, where he cultivates his still mediocre skills at tending animals, growing organic vegetables and building and repairing things. He is also an anthropologist, currently working on his PhD thesis with the tentative title 'Kto ya? Opening your soul in Siberia and elsewhere'.

Michael Taussig is Class of 1933 Professor of Anthropology at Columbia University and author of several books, which range from a critique of agribusiness to the study of shamanism and colonialism, as well as gold mining, beauty, and the arts of ficto-criticism. He is currently working on 'corpse magic'.

Mille Kjærgaard Thorsen defended her PhD thesis at the Department of Anthropology, Aarhus University, Denmark in 2019. It was entitled 'Sweetness Under Pressure: Living with Diabetes and Uncertainty in Cairo'. She has carried out fieldwork in both Egypt and Denmark on issues related to chronic illness.

Christian Vium is Associate Professor in the Department of Anthropology at Aarhus University, Denmark. Over the past several years, he has undertaken a large-scale comparative research project, creatively reframing colonial photographic archives together with descendants of the people in the original photographs. Parts of the project have been exhibited in more than 15 international venues and are being edited into a monograph to be published in 2020. He is currently undertaking a three-year research project on Danish colonial history, financed by the Carlsberg Foundation.

Index

Page numbers in *italic* refer to figure captions.

www.ingramcontent.com/pod-product-compliance
Lightning Source LLC
LaVergne TN
LVHW052351100826
845147LV00013B/815

* 9 7 8 1 9 1 2 3 8 5 2 1 8 *